Northern California cheap sleeps

Northern California cheap sleeps

Eats, Sleeps,

Affordable

Adventure

Rebecca Poole Forée
Matthew Richard Poole

SASQUATCH BOOKS
SEATTLE

Printed in the United States
Distributed in Canada by Raincoast Books Ltd.

Second edition.

04 03 02 01 00   6 5 4 3 2 1

ISSN: 1-528-9389
ISBN: 1-57061-185-8

Copy editor: Kris Fulsaas
Interior design & composition: Kate Basart
Cover design: Karen Schober
San Francisco map: GreenEye Design
Regional maps: Karen Schober
Cover photographs:
    top: Peter Dokus/Stone
    bottom: Jean-Francois Gate/Stone

Special Sales
Best Places® guidebooks are available at special discounts on bulk purchases
for corporate, club, or organization sales promotions, premiums, and gifts. Special
editions, including personalized covers, excerpts of existing guides, and corporate
imprints, can be created in large quantities for specific needs. For more information, contact your local bookseller or Special Sales, Best Places Guidebooks, 615
Second Avenue, Suite 260, Seattle, Washington 98104, (800)775-0817.

SASQUATCH BOOKS
615 Second Avenue
Seattle, WA 98104
(206)467-4300
books@SasquatchBooks.com
www.SasquatchBooks.com

Contents

About Best Places® Guidebooks

Northern California Cheap Sleeps is part of the Best Places® guidebook series, which means it's written by and for locals who enjoy getting out and exploring the region. It's written for smart, adventurous people of all ages—people who know it's not necessary to pay top dollar to revel in a four-star experience. When we're traveling on the cheap, we look for independently owned establishments of good value, touched with local history, run by lively individuals, and graced with natural beauty. Every place listed is not only inexpensive but recommended.

Best Places® guidebooks, which have been published continuously since 1975, represent one of the most respected regional travel series in the country. Each guide is written completely independently: no advertisers, no sponsors, no favors. Our reviewers know their territory, work incognito, and seek out the very best a region has to offer. Because we accept no free meals, accommodations, or other complimentary services, we are able to provide tough, candid reports and describe the true strengths, foibles, and unique characteristics of each establishment listed.

Note: Readers are advised that the reviews in this edition are based on information available at press time and are subject to change. The editors welcome information conveyed by users of this book, as long as they have no financial connection with the establishment concerned. A report form is provided at the end of the book, and feedback is also welcome via email: books@SasquatchBooks.com.

Introduction

If there's one thing we overworked and underpaid travel writers have mastered, it's how to make the most of a limited travel budget. Sure, we'd rather be sucking Ritz Carlton mints during a grapeseed-oil massage, but if you've got *that* kind of cash you ain't reading *this* book.

Which brings us back to the underpaid part: as perennially budget-challenged travel writers, we have become experts on sniffing out the best cheap lodgings, restaurants, and attractions in Northern California. You should have seen some of the greasepits and roach motels we had to slog through to find the jewels-in-the-rough. But in the end it was all worth it because we're absolutely convinced that we've created the best damn guidebook to touring Northern California on a limited budget.

And, truth be told, it's actually far more fun to explore—and write about—a hokey old pub in Mount Shasta than review a four-star restaurant, simply because that pub's bound to have a lot more regional character and down-home appeal. That's the real difference between traveling cheap and touring in luxury: the latter's a form of escapism, while the former is a means to learning about the people and places that surround you. Stay and eat at the establishments we recommend in this book and you'll be hanging with the locals while getting a true sense of what it's like to live in these towns and cities.

This doesn't mean you have to endure substandard conditions, however, because we wouldn't include anything in *Northern California Cheap Sleeps* that we wouldn't visit ourselves (and trust us, we're picky). Fortunately, California abounds with inexpensive adventures, particularly those into the great outdoors (nature doesn't care if you're rich or poor). And because this brother-and-sister writing team was born and raised in Northern California, we know *all* the great places to go for next to nothing (mostly because our father is cheap, but that's another book).

Okay, okay—we hate long-winded intros to travel guides too, so we'll end this with just one piece of advice: don't ever let something as trivial as money prevent you from exploring one of the most beautiful regions on this planet, because our most memorable adventures have always been the ones that money couldn't buy.

—*Matthew Richard Poole and Rebecca Poole Forée*

Contributors

Rebecca Poole Forée and *Matthew Richard Poole,* a sister-and-brother writing team, have together written and edited more than 50 travel books on California and many of the world's great cities. Both are native Northern Californians who have made San Francisco their home for many years. More than half a million of their travel tomes are currently available in major bookstores around the world. Forée and Poole also share their travel news and reviews online and on various radio and television shows throughout California.

Mary Anne Moore and *Maurice Read* are freelance writers and editors, and contributors to several other travel guides, including *Northern California Best Places.* Moore is also a legislative consultant at the California state capital and she spends her free time traveling the globe in search of great getaways, first-class restaurants, idyllic jogging trails, and the world's best bookstores. Read is a Sacramento-based lobbyist and a gourmet cook who often tours California with his Australian shepherd looking for dog-friendly lodgings, great fly-fishing streams, and memorable meals.

Kristen Wright put her career helping the homeless in Sacramento on hold to spend more time with her daughter, Shelby, and stepson, Ace. When she is not busy changing diapers and baking cookies, she works as a freelance writer and editor.

What's Cheap?

Northern California Cheap Sleeps provides honest recommendations on great, inexpensive restaurants and lodgings throughout the region, from Big Sur and Yosemite north to the Oregon border. It also shares hundreds of money-saving tips for savvy travelers who want to explore the region's varied and fabulous destinations.

But there's one overriding principal that all cash-conscious visitors and day-trippers should remember: **You need to ask for a deal to get it.** Below are some general tips for budget travelers to keep in mind while planning a trip and making choices on the road.

Access

State and city **visitors bureaus** are an exceptional source of information, including details on travel packages and discounts—many of which include airfare, car rental, and transfers. They may also be able to tell you about rail or ferry travel packages, as well as provide you with maps. Call the bureaus or visit their Web sites; a few key offices are noted below:

California Tourism
801 K Street, Suite 1600
Sacramento, CA 95814
800/862-2543
916/322-2881
gocalif.ca.gov

San Francisco Visitor Information Center
900 Market Street
Lower Level Hallidie Plaza
San Francisco, CA 94102
415/391-2000
www.sfvisitor.org

Napa Valley Conference & Visitors Bureau
1310 Napa Town Center
Napa, CA 94559
707/226-7459
www.napavalley.com

Car rental companies usually have discounts for AAA members, as well as for airline mileage program members. Parking garages sometimes offer a discount for AAA cardholders, and, of course, AAA itself has free travel **maps** for all its members.

Exploring

As noted above, check with state and city **visitors bureaus** before you go, for extensive information on your destination. They'll send you free packets filled with brochures, coupons, and lots of ideas on what and where to explore once you arrive.

Many museums and other **major attractions** frequently have one day or evening each week when they're open for free or at a reduced rate; and most have standard discounts for students and seniors. (For museums, zoos, and aquariums, check to see if they have reciprocal arrangements for members of their counterpart in your home city.)

Discounts for theater and concert **tickets** are prevalent when you're exploring the region during off-season, especially in major cities. You can also find a multitude of dining and attraction discounts and hotel packages tied to cultural entertainment. Again, check with the visitors bureaus.

For interesting and less expensive gifts for the kids or co-workers, shop at **open markets** rather than at standard tourist outlets.

Cheap Eats

Our **cost guideline** for choosing inexpensive restaurants was based on dinner for two for $30 or less (including tax, tip, and dessert—and sometimes even alcohol). Most cheap eats fall in the $10–$20-for-two range; many spots are even less.

Other budget eating tips to remember: diners and cafes often feature daily or "blue plate" **specials** that usually include bread, salad, and dessert—all for one great, low price. At more upscale cafes and restaurants, pairing **appetizers** to make up a meal may be a better deal than ordering an entree. **Happy hours** in major cities can be a great source of filling, free (or inexpensive) munchies. At establishments that offer wine, consider bringing your own bottle and paying a **corkage fee,** which often costs less than even the cheapest vintage on their list.

Keep in mind that all prices are subject to change, places close, and owners change. Call ahead whenever possible.

Cheap Sleeps

All **prices** for lodgings are based on double-occupancy (two people, one night) during peak season, unless otherwise indicated. **Peak season** is typically Memorial Day to Labor Day, except in the case of ski resorts or other winter destinations. We did our best to include here only those budget lodgings that we could honestly recommend. On average, these places charge $35–$65; many listings, such as hostels, fire lookouts, or cabins, are even less expensive. Rates for a few places may go as high as $75 or so, but are such great deals for the area or for the facilities, that we felt compelled to recommend them anyway. And again, prices, along with ownership and management, may change; call ahead.

While **discounts** are more prevalent at upscale hotels and chains than at budget accommodations, it never hurts to ask about basic reduced-rate options: AAA, senior, and student discounts, credit card and mileage programs, corporate and group rates (the latter usually applicable for 4 or more adults), discounts for stays of three or more nights, and mid-week discounts. Carry your relevant cards with you; for corporate discounts, you don't need to look corporate, just drop the name of your company and you'll usually be rewarded.

During the **off-season** or shoulder seasons, lodgings are likely to have notable discounts—room rates sometimes drop by half. State and city visitors bureaus keep up-to-date information on seasonal discounts, as well as which establishments are participating in both off- and peak-season travel packages.

Some destinations have **reservation services** for the whole area, which can be a great source for finding a deal; we've included them whenever possible.

In general, most of the lodgings listed welcome **kids.** We make note of those that do not, but to be sure, call ahead.

Most establishments these days designate all rooms as **nonsmoking.** If you smoke and don't want to be relegated to puffing in the rain, call ahead.

Many of the listings here are smaller bed and breakfasts, older motels, and remote cabins. Not all of them are easily accessible to those with **disabilities.** If you have special needs, please make sure to call ahead.

A surprising number of the lodgings listed here do allow **pets,** though there are often many "okay, buts" involved: small pets but not large, only well-mannered ones, dogs but not cats. Whenever possible, we've specified those establishments that generally welcome pets. In cases where the owners were lukewarm, charged a steep fee, or attached too many qualifications, we did not mention a pet policy.

San Francisco Bay Area

san francisco

marin county

berkeley

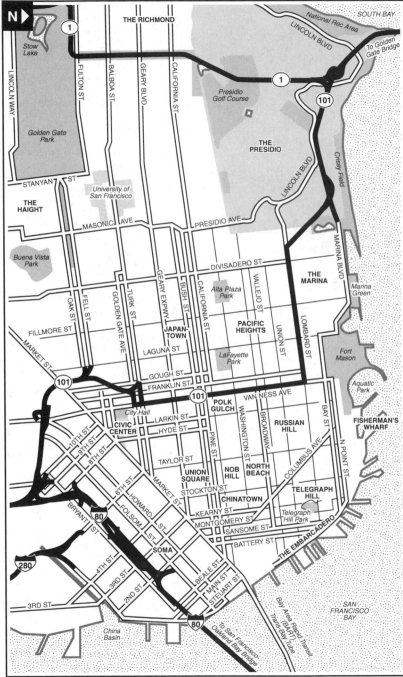

San Francisco

San Franciscans know they are uniquely blessed. In no other city in the country is the meeting of land and sea so spectacular. The late-afternoon sun flashes off the dark-blue bay, lighting up the orange towers of the Golden Gate Bridge, and the magnificent sails of boats and windsurfers add color in brilliant flashes. Almost every evening the fog pours in from the Pacific, spilling over the towers of downtown like a white wave. Lovers of all persuasions kiss on street corners. Poets still scribble in coffee shops. No wonder this is one of the world's favorite cities.

Over the years, however, San Franciscans have begun to view this magnetism as something of a liability. Drawn by the city's fabled beauty, cuisine, art, and culture, newcomers from around the globe have poured into this hilly, 46-square-mile oasis. Housing prices have soared, forcing many middle-class families to move to distant suburbs. On bad days, it seems the city is populated entirely by frazzled workaholic singles, weary long-distance commuters, and legions of the homeless. But even on those days, most people are still smiling.

Access

Parking in San Francisco can be an ordeal. Many neighborhoods limit nonresidents to only two hours of parking, and most downtown meters have a maddening maximum time limit of 30 minutes—about the time it takes to get change for the meter. To make matters even more frustrating, traffic cops are quick, ruthless, and abundant. Whenever you see a tow-away warning, take it very seriously. Public parking garages

Dressed to Chill

Years of propaganda about sunny California have left millions of tourists freezing in the City by the Bay. Although San Francisco's weather is usually mild and temperatures don't change drastically throughout the year (they rarely rise above 70°F or fall below 40°F), it's seldom warm enough to go without a coat or sweater. Spring and fall are the warmest, and summer is usually foggy, except at midday. Locals beat the summer-morning chills by dressing in layers.

abound, however, and if you look hard enough (or ask a local), you'll find a garage or park-and-pay lot that doesn't charge Manhattan rates. San Francisco taxis usually cruise only the most populated streets, so if you need a cab, call one.

Public transportation serves every neighborhood, but grows sparse after midnight. **San Francisco Municipal Railway (Muni)**—aptly nicknamed "Muniserable Railway" by *San Francisco Chronicle* columnist Herb Caen—comprises buses, above- and underground streetcars, and cable cars. Exact change is required, and free transfers (except for cable cars) grant two more rides within the next 1½ to 2 hours. One-, three-, and seven-day Muni passes are available at the San Francisco Visitor Information Center (900 Market Street at Powell Street, near the Union Square cable car turntable, 415/391-2000) and in the lobby of the War Memorial Veteran's Building (401 Van Ness Avenue at McAllister Street). For route, ticket, and bus-pass information, call 415/673-MUNI (and expect to be put on hold for a long time). **Bay Area Rapid Transit (BART)** is a clean, reliable underground commuter train that runs through the southeastern side of the city, with routes to Daly City and the East Bay; for schedule and ticket information, call 415/771-6000.

The **San Francisco International Airport** (SFO) 650/876-7809, is about 15 miles south of San Francisco on Highway 101 (the Bayshore Freeway); allow 30 to 40 minutes to drive there from the city and at least an hour during commute times. If you need transportation to or from SFO, reserve a seat with one of the fast, reliable shuttle services, such as Super Shuttle, 415/558-8500, or catch a ride on one of the two Sam Trans buses (800/660-4BUS) that travel between SFO and San Francisco's Transbay Transit Terminal at Mission and First Streets (one Sam Trans bus permits passengers to bring luggage, but the other allows only one carry-on bag per person). The **Oakland International Airport** (OAK), located about 5 miles south of downtown Oakland, often offers less expensive flights (and parking) than SFO, and it doesn't take much more time to drive there from San Francisco if you avoid the rush hours (off Hegenberger Road via Highway 880 S, Oakland, 510/577-4015 or 510/577-4000).

Exploring

San Francisco, like Paris, is a great walking town, and one of the city's most spectacular and scenic walks is along the **Golden Gate Promenade,** a 4-mile stretch from **Aquatic Park** in front of the Cannery, through the beautiful **Marina Green** and **Crissy Field,** to the historic Fort Point, a four-level fortification built in 1861 that's nestled under the south end of the Golden Gate Bridge. (If you're not too winded at this point, continue your tour with a walk across the blustery, and usually chilly, Bridge

A City with a View

San Francisco is famous for its beautiful, sweeping views, and you'll find some of the city's best at the following locations:

Alamo Square: *On the square's south side, on Hayes Street between Pierce and Steiner Streets*

Alcatraz Island: *Ferry access from Pier 41, at the east end of Fisherman's Wharf*

Angel Island: *Ferry access from Pier 39, at the north end of the Embarcadero*

Baker Beach: *On Gibson Road, off Lincoln Boulevard via 25th Avenue*

Coit Tower: *On Telegraph Hill, at the east end of Lombard Street*

Fort Point: *Under the southern end of the Golden Gate Bridge, at the end of Long Avenue, off Lincoln Boulevard*

Golden Gate Bridge: *On Highway 1/101 between San Francisco and Marin County*

Mission Dolores Park: *On the park's south side, on 20th Street, between Dolores and Church Streets*

Pier 39: *At the north end of the Embarcadero*

Point Lobos: *The westernmost tip of San Francisco; follow the trails from the parking lot at El Camino del Mar and Point Lobos Avenue*

Twin Peaks: *On Twin Peaks Boulevard, in the center of the city*

for a breathtaking view of the Bay Area.) Another gorgeous waterfront stroll follows the **Embarcadero** north from Market Street, past the landmark **Ferry Building** to the handsome pier just south of Broadway, where you'll get a good look at **Treasure Island** and the yachts and freighters sailing beneath the Bay Bridge. Heartier souls should continue up the Embarcadero to touristy **Pier 39** to see the hundreds of silly sea lions playing, barking, and basking in the sun on the pier's west side. The third-most-visited amusement attraction in the nation, Pier 39 is packed with kitschy shops and bad restaurants, but it boasts beautiful views of Angel Island, **Alcatraz,** and the bay, and has great entertainment for kids with its Venetian Carousel, jugglers, mimes, the "motion theater" Turbo Ride, and an arcade stocked with every gizmo and quarter-sucking machine the young-at-heart could dream of.

Once you've had enough of the pier, hop aboard a **ferry** for the surprisingly interesting audiocassette tour of Alcatraz, a San Francisco Bay cruise, or a scenic trip to the pretty little rich towns across the bay, Sausalito and Tiburon (highlights of these sister cities are outlined in the Marin County section of this chapter); for tour information and ferry schedules, call the Blue & Gold Fleet at Pier 39 (415/705-5444, recording, or 415/705-5555), or the Red & White Fleet at Piers 41 and 43½ (800/229-2784, California only, or 415/447-7340).

Just a short jaunt west of Pier 39 are the world-famous **Fisherman's Wharf, The Cannery,** and **Ghirardelli Square.** They're always mobbed with tourists, but they offer some interesting shops and are riddled with witty, wisecracking, watch-me-pull-a-rabbit-out-of-my-shoe street entertainers. From mid-November through June, this is also where you'll see the city's highly touted (and delicious) Dungeness crabs boiling in large metal pots on the sidewalks. All three attractions are located side by side on the waterfront at the north end of the Embarcadero and next to Aquatic Park.

What's Pink and Black and Read All Over?

The San Francisco Chronicle*'s "*Datebook,*" which is more commonly known as the "pink section" because part of it is printed on pink paper, appears in the Sunday newspaper and is the best Bay Area guide to current art events and other entertainment.*

Golden Gate Park Pass

Now you can see five top attractions at San Francisco's famed Golden Gate Park at a highly discounted rate with an Explorer Pass. Just flash your pass at the entrances to the California Academy of Sciences (home of the Steinhart Aquarium), Japanese Tea Garden, Asian Art Museum, M.H. de Young Memorial Museum, and the Conservatory of Flowers and walk on in. You'll save 25–30 percent off the cost of regular adult admissions. The pass allows a one-time entry to each venue and is valid for up to a year. Purchase your Explorer Pass at the Visitor Information Center at 900 Market Street at Powell (near the Union Square cable car turntable) or at any of the five participating attractions. Call 415/750-7145 for more details.

While tourists flock to Fisherman's Wharf and Pier 39, locals often head to Golden Gate Park to visit the extraordinary **California Academy of Sciences** (in Golden Gate Park off Middle Drive E, between John F. Kennedy and Martin Luther King Jr. Drives, 415/750-7145). Under one roof you'll find the **Natural History Museum, Morrison Planetarium, the Laserium,** and the superb **Steinhart Aquarium,** offering one of the most diverse collections of aquatic life in the world, including the popular seals, dolphins, and alligators. Another San Francisco favorite is the **Exploratorium,** 415/561-0360 or 415/563-7337, a unique interactive museum that brings scientific concepts to vivid life—it's a blast for those of any age. The marvelous **Tactile Dome,** 415/561-0362, where visitors must feel their way through a maze of hurdles in total darkness, requires reservations and a certain amount of nerve. The Exploratorium is housed within the magnificent **Palace of Fine Arts** (3601 Lyon Street, between Jefferson and Bay, near the on-ramp to the Golden Gate Bridge), designed by the renowned Bernard Maybeck for the 1915 Panama-Pacific International Exposition. The palace is surrounded by a natural lagoon—an ideal spot for a picnic and for tossing your leftovers to the grateful swans, pigeons, and seagulls.

Golden Gate Park, 1,017 acres of beautiful, lush grounds dotted with magnificent museums, lakes, and ponds, is a masterpiece of design. For a good introduction, join one of the free guided walking tours held every weekend from May through October; call the Friends of Recreation and Parks for more information, 415/750-5105. Park highlights include the **Strybing Arboretum** (near 9th Avenue and Lincoln Way, 415/661-1316), which boasts more than 6,000 species of

Presidio Pointers

After years of congressional debates and other political squabbles, the U.S. Army finally handed over the beautiful 1,480-acre San Francisco Presidio, one of the nation's oldest military installations, to the National Park Service in 1995. Established by Spanish colonists in 1776, the Presidio offers 14 miles of biking trails, 11 miles of hiking routes (including the spectacular Coastal Trail and Lover's Lane/Ecology Trail), picnic areas, lookout points, historic buildings, and even the last free-flowing stream in San Francisco. For a free guide about the Presidio's history and a detailed map, call or stop by the Presidio Visitor Information Center (on Montgomery Street in the Presidio, 415/561-4323) or the Presidio Museum (on the corner of Lincoln Boulevard and Funston Avenue). Or send your request to Golden Gate National Recreation Area (Presidio, Fort Mason, Building 201, San Francisco, CA 94123).

trees and plants. Right next door is the lovely but often crowded **Japanese Tea Garden** (to avoid the hordes, visit when it's raining). And nearby is the spectacular **Conservatory,** a Victorian fairyland hothouse of tropical flora, which was erected in 1879 and was the oldest operating conservatory in the country until high winds heavily damaged its structure in 1996. It is currently under reconstruction; on John F. Kennedy Drive near Conservatory Drive, 415/641-7978. The **Children's Playground** features a dazzling, restored Golden Age carousel that's guaranteed to make every child's heart go pitter-patter (at the intersection of Martin Luther King Jr. and Kezar Drives). Every Sunday, Golden Gate Park's main drag is closed to auto traffic, so skaters and joggers can let loose on the tree-lined street; skate rentals are available at **Skates on Haight** (1818 Haight Street, 415/752-8375).

The city's northwest corner is part of the **Golden Gate National Recreation Area** (GGNRA), the largest urban park in the world. Take a hike along its glorious wildflower-laced **Coastal Trail,** which hugs the headlands for more than 10 miles and offers fantastic views of the bay; start at Point Lobos (at the end of Point Lobos Avenue, near the Sutro Baths) and wind your way to the Golden Gate Bridge. **The Presidio,** formerly a 1,480-acre parklike military base, is now part of GGNRA and offers superb views to hikers and bicyclists. Nearby are **Crissy Field,** a fabulous windsurfing spot (and a great place to hang out and watch the surfing dudes and dudettes), and the **Marina Green,** prime kite-flying and jogging territory (both are located off Marina Boulevard, near the

8

Golden Gate Bridge on-ramp). Riptide-ridden **Ocean Beach** doesn't offer any water sports, but the long, sandy shore is a popular place for blustery walks and picnics (off the Great Highway). On warm days, sun worshipers bask at **Baker Beach** while gazing at the view of the Golden Gate (as at most of the city's beaches, unfortunately, swimming is unsafe here). The east side of the beach is a popular gay hangout, where sunbathers bare all (take 25th Avenue to the end, bear right, then look for signs to Baker Beach). Other scenic spots include **Glen Canyon Park,** which has a playground (on Bosworth Street at O'Shaughnessy Boulevard); the lush **Stern Grove** (on Sloat Boulevard at 19th Avenue); and **Lake Merced** (off Harding Road, between Highway 35 and Sloat Boulevard, near the zoo).

On the other side of the city, near the ocean, is the **San Francisco Zoo** (45th Avenue and Sloat Boulevard, 415/753-7080), a delight for animal lovers of all ages. Don't miss the famed Primate Discovery Center, where several species of apes and monkeys live in glass-walled condos. The zoo also boasts one of the world's largest gorilla habitats and a children's petting zoo, and it's one of the few in the nation that houses koalas.

City dwellers and their habitats are as fascinating to observe as the critters in zoo cages. For an up-close-and-personal look at San Francisco's multi-ethnic neighborhoods and architectural masterpieces, strap on your heavy-duty walking shoes and—starting in the **Russian Hill** neighborhood, at the top of the crookedest street in the world, **Lombard Street** (at Hyde)—wind your way down those multiple, red-brick, flower-lined curves, continuing east until Lombard intersects with Columbus Avenue. Then turn right and stay on Columbus for a tour of charming **North Beach**—a predominantly Italian and Chinese neighborhood where residents practice tai chi in Washington Square or sip espresso as they peruse Proust or the *San Francisco Bay Guardian*'s really racy personal

Fact Finder

The friendly folks at San Francisco's Visitor Information Center are available every day to answer questions and help you find your way around the city streets. Stop by the office at 900 Market Street at Powell (near the Union Square cable car turntable), or call 415/391-2000. For an up-to-date listing of San Francisco's hottest activities and events (some are even free), check out their Web site at www.sfvisitor.org.

Everybody Poops

The question most frequently asked by visitors to San Francisco is, alas, "Where's the rest room?" Well, San Francisco's tourists and residents don't have to travel far to find a public potty. The city's first self-cleaning, French-designed Decaux toilet was installed at the corner of Market and Powell Streets in the summer of 1995—a celebrated event christened (literally) by the mayor himself. Since then a couple dozen of the forest-green commodes have been erected on select corners. The cost of admission is only 25 cents, which may be the best bargain seat in town. Caveat emptor: You must do your duty within 20 minutes or the door will open automatically—and stay open till you deposit another quarter.

ads (guaranteed to make you blush—or send you running for the nearest phone). You can extend this tour by turning right off Columbus onto Grant Avenue, which takes you through the heart of the ever-bustling and fascinating **Chinatown**—the only part of the city where vendors sell live, 3-foot-long slippery eels next to X-rated fortune cookies and herbs meant to cure whatever ails you.

For those in need of an aerobic workout, take this tour: instead of turning off Lombard onto Columbus, keep following Lombard east all the way up to **Coit Tower,** 415/362-0808, on the top of **Telegraph Hill**—then reward yourself for making the steep ascent with a trip (in an elevator, gasp, gasp) to the top of the tower for a panoramic view of the Bay Area. And for those who'd rather ride than walk the hills, an outside perch on one of the city's famed **cable cars** is always a kick. The three cable-car routes are named after the streets they run on (you can take them in either direction): the Powell-Mason line starts at Powell and Market Streets and terminates at Bay Street near Fisherman's Wharf; the Powell-Hyde line also begins at Powell and Market, but ends at Victorian Park near Aquatic Park and the bay; and the California line runs from California and Market Streets to Van Ness Avenue, the widest street in the city. For cable car information, call 415/391-2000.

A tour of the town wouldn't be complete without walking through one of San Francisco's main attractions: the shops. The famous and oh-so-trendy **Union Square** district and the nearby **San Francisco Shopping Centre,** at Market and 5th Streets, boast a half dozen major department stores (including Macy's, Nordstrom, and Neiman Marcus) and more specialty shops than Imelda Marcos has shoes. A short walk away is the chichi **Crocker Galleria** (bounded by Post, Kearny, Sutter, and Montgomery Streets, 415/393-1505), a 67-foot-high, glass-dome, tri-level shopping mall modeled after Milan's 1867 Galleria Vittoria Emmanuelle. The vast **Embarcadero Center** (bounded by Clay, Sacramento, Battery, and Drumm Streets, 415/772-0585) is a sophisticated triple-level, open-air neo-mall well worth a spree. Many big-name fashion firms have factory outlets south of Market Street, including Esprit (499 Illinois Street off 3rd Street, 415/957-2500) and Jessica McClintock/Gunne Sax (35 Stanford Street, between 2nd and 3rd Streets, 415/495-3326).

Stroll down Sacramento Street (between Lyon and Locust) for elegant clothing and furnishings. For vintage, cutting-edge, and folksy fashions and crafts, shop on Noe Valley's 24th Street (between Castro and Church), Castro Street (between Market and 19th), Fillmore Street (between Jackson and Sutter), Haight Street (between Masonic and Shrader), and Union Street (between Gough and Steiner). The 5-acre **Japan Center** (on Post Street, between Laguna and Fillmore, 415/922-6776) houses several shops selling Japanese crafts, housewares, and books, with numerous sushi bars sandwiched in between.

Cosmopolitan cooks can stock up on Asian foodstuffs in Chinatown along Stockton Street (between California and Broadway) or in New Chinatown on Clement Street (between Arguello and 10th Avenue, and 18th and 25th Avenues). North Beach sells Italian treats along Columbus Avenue (between Broadway and Bay), while the Mission offers Latin specialties on 24th Street (between Mission and Potrero). Good bookstores include **City Lights Bookstore** (261 Columbus Avenue at Broadway, 415/362-8193), still Beat after all these years; **A Clean Well-Lighted Place for Books** (601 Van Ness Avenue, in Opera Plaza, between Golden

Free Tours of the Town

There's no better way to discover the City by the Bay than by following the footsteps of a savvy guide. City Guides offers more than two dozen different guided walking tours for free. You'll see everything from San Francisco's old brothels and Chinatown shops to its rooftop gardens, art deco architecture, and Haight-Ashbury haunts. The two-hour tours are offered year-round (rain or shine) and reservations are not required. For a list of topics and schedules, call 415/557-4266 or send a business-size SASE to City Guides, Friends of the Library, Main Library— Civic Center, San Francisco, CA 94102.

Gate Avenue and Turk Street, 415/441-6670); the city's largest bookstore, **Borders Books and Music** (400 Post Street at Powell in Union Square, 415/399-1633); **Stacey's** (581 Market Street at 2nd, 415/421-4687); and **Green Apple** (506 Clement Street at 6th, 415/387-2272).

While San Francisco's visual art scene isn't New York's, it still holds its own and continues to get raves from critics around the nation. Some of the not-to-be-missed highlights include the **M. H. de Young Memorial Museum** (in Golden Gate Park, off John F. Kennedy Drive, 415/863-3330), which showcases American art from colonial times to the 20th century and hosts many traveling international exhibits. In the de Young's west wing is the **Asian Art Museum,** 415/668-8921, site of a world-famous collection of Far East art, including many masterpieces from the Avery Brundage collection. The **San Francisco Museum of Modern Art** (in Yerba Buena Gardens, 151 3rd Street, between Mission and Howard, 415/357-4000), or SFMOMA for short, is housed in an impressive contemporary red-brick building designed by internationally acclaimed Swiss architect Mario Botta and offers works by Picasso, Matisse, O'Keeffe, Pollock, Warhol, and Lichtenstein, to name just a few. The new Sony **Metreon** (4th and Mission Streets, 415/537-3400) mega-audiovisual complex is also worth a visit, particularly if you want to catch a cheap matinee of new-release films.

Vibrant murals decorate many public spaces in the city, particularly in the **Mission District;** for maps outlining self-guided walks ($1 fee) or for two-hour guided tours ($7 per adult), contact the Precita Eyes Mural Arts Center (348 Precita Avenue at Folsom Street, 415/285-2287). For free guided walking tours of the Mission's murals, call City Guides, 415/557-4266. Galleries for established artists are located primarily on Grant Avenue near Market and in the vicinity of Union Square; up-and-coming artists tend to exhibit in SoMa (the area south of Market Street). For current art listings, check the *San Francisco Chronicle*'s "Datebook" in the Sunday paper.

While Los Angeles still reigns as the nation's movie capital, the Bay Area's motion-picture industry has garnered an international reputation, and San Francisco offers several highly regarded events for film buffs, including the **San Francisco International Film Festival,** held for a fortnight every spring (various venues, 415/931-3456); the **San Francisco International Gay & Lesbian Film Festival,** which takes place in June, 415/703-8650; and **Spike and Mike's Festival of Animation,** held in April at the Palace of Fine Arts (3601 Lyon Street, between Jefferson

Cheap Tickets

For a sweet deal on opera, theater, dance, and concert tickets, stop by **TIX Bay Area,** *which sells half-price, day-of-performance tickets. Discount info is not available by phone, so get in line early at 251 Stockton Street, between Post and Geary, in Union Square. Half-price tickets are sold—for cash only—Tuesday through Thursday, from 11am to 6pm, and Friday and Saturday, from 11am to 7pm (Sunday and Monday tickets are sold on Saturdays).*

and Bay); call 619/459-8707 for more information. For rare revivals and premieres, check the palatial **Castro Theatre** (429 Castro Street off Market, 415/621-6120), a flamboyant Spanish baroque–style movie palace designed by Timothy Pflueger in 1923; the funky (but finely programmed) **Roxie Cinema** (3117 16th Street at Valencia, 415/863-1087); and the homey **Red Vic Movie House** (1727 Haight Street, between Cole and Shrader, 415/668-3994).

The world-class **San Francisco Opera,** led by Lotfi Mansouri, alternates warhorses with rarities in May and June and from September through December at the beautiful **War Memorial Opera House,** which was modeled on Garnier's Paris Opera and first opened in 1932. Subscribers grab up most seats, but fans with smaller bankrolls can line up early on performance mornings to buy standing-room tickets (415/864-3330, box office, or 415/861-4008, information). The **San Francisco Symphony** performs from September through July at the modern **Louise M. Davies Symphony Hall** (201 Van Ness Avenue at Grove, 415/864-6000), a gorgeous $38 million concert hall with a wraparound glass facade. Other classical groups include the **Lamplighters Music Theatre** (Lindland Theatre, at Archbishop Riordan High School, 175 Phelan Avenue, 415/227-0331), performing Gilbert and Sullivan's comic operas; the **Women's Philharmonic** (Herbst Theater, 401 Van Ness at McCallister, 415/437-0123); and the **San Francisco Early Music Society** (Meadowlands Assembly Hall, Dominican College in San Rafael, 510/528-1725).

For 10 successive Sundays starting in June, families tote blankets and picnic baskets to the oldest continuous free summer music festival in America. The outdoor performances—everything from jazz to opera—are held at 2pm at the pleasant **Stern Grove** (Sloat Boulevard and 19th Avenue, 415/252-6252). The **San Francisco Jazz Festival,** one of the largest in the country, toots its horn every fall.

American Conservatory Theater (ACT), the city's best-known theater company, presents solid productions of new works and classics from late September to mid-June in the Geary, Stage Door, and Marines Memorial Theaters; call 415/749-2ACT for program information. Broadway shows on tour are performed at the Golden Gate, Curran, and Orpheum Theaters; call 415/551-2000 for the current lineup and ticket information. For off-Broadway acts, contact the Theatre on the Square (TOTS), 415/433-9500, and Marines Memorial Theatre, 415/771-6900.

Summer and early fall bring free outdoor performances by America's oldest political musical-comedy theater group, the **San Francisco Mime Troupe** (call 415/285-1717 for performance locations) and by the more serious **Shakespeare in the Park** theater group (in Golden Gate Park at Liberty Tree Meadow, off John F. Kennedy Drive near Conservatory Drive, 415/422-2222). The long-running *Beach Blanket Babylon* (Club Fugazi, 678 Green Street near Powell, 415/421-4222), is a cabaret-style show full of silly jokes and famous for its wild costumes and humongous hats. It remains a favorite of residents and visitors alike, although tickets are pricey and you need to reserve weeks in advance.

San Francisco has launched many comedians' careers, including those of the nation's reigning king and queen of comedy, Robin Williams and Whoopi Goldberg. See the latest talents at the **Punchline** (444

San Francisco's Street Fairs

Every winter, the two-week-long Chinese New Year celebration culminates in an electrifying parade led by a 150-foot-long dragon that winds through downtown, Union Square, and Chinatown; call 415/982-3000 for more information. In summer and spring, street fairs that typify their neighborhoods pop up from upscale Union Street to the still-hairy Haight; a St. Patrick's Day parade marches through downtown in March, 415/587-1452; Japantown launches its Cherry Blossom Festival with a parade in April, 415/563-2313; the Mission District draws crowds with its Cinco de Mayo Parade in late April or early May, 415/826-1401, and the Carnaval Parade on Memorial Day weekend, 415/826-1401; the San Francisco Lesbian, Gay, Bisexual, Transgender Pride Parade and Celebration draws up to a half million revelers every June, 415/864-3733; and in October the Italian community in North Beach kicks off Columbus Day celebrations with a big parade, 415/434-1492.

Theme Park Thrills

If you've set aside a chunk of cash for a day of amusement-park rides, go to Paramount's Great America, Northern California's largest family entertainment center. Expect to pay at least $35 a head for general admission (which gives unlimited access to all the rides). Great America is located off Highway 101 in Santa Clara, 45 miles south of San Francisco; call 408/988-1776 for more details.

Battery Street, second floor, between Clay and Washington, 415/397-7573) and **Cobb's Comedy Club** (in the Cannery, 2801 Leavenworth Street, Building S, courtyard entrance at Beach Street, 415/928-4320).

The internationally renowned **San Francisco Ballet,** led by artistic director Helgi Tomasson, kicks off the season in mid-December with the classic *Nutcracker* and dances to more contemporary pieces beginning in February; call 415/865-2000 for tickets. Ethnic dance troupes abound in the Bay Area, and they come together in June for the **San Francisco Ethnic Dance Festival,** 415/474-3914. Fans of modern and contemporary dance shouldn't miss the high-flying acrobatics and extraordinary energy of **ODC/San Francisco** dance troupe, one of the premier modern dance troupes in the country; call 415/863-6606 for more information.

If your feet were made for dancing, San Francisco offers dozens of great nightclubs, all of which have little or no cover charge. For live blues, jazz, and rock, **Slim's** (333 11th Street, between Folsom and Harrison, 415/621-3330)—co-owned by Boz Scaggs—can't be beat. Those who prefer hip-hop, rock, purple hair, and nipple rings should venture into the **DNA Lounge** (375 11th Street at Harrison, 415/626-1409). You can dance among the masses at **1015 Folsom** (1015 Folsom Street at 6th, 415/431-1200). For a mix of live music, the trendy set kicks up its heels at **Cafe Du Nord** (2170 Market Street, between Church and Sanchez, 415/861-5016).

To hear the sounds of the city's new bands, stroll **Haight Street.** Numerous venues line both sides of this famous strip, still populated by drugged youth, the homeless, and various eccentrics. Be sure to stop in at **Kan Zaman** (1793 Haight Street, 415/751-9656) to smoke from a hookah—trust us, it's a blast—and watch the belly dancers. Over in the Tenderloin area, the ornate **Great American Music Hall** (859 O'Farrell Street, between Polk and Larkin, 415/885-0750) attracts the over-30 crowd with its mix of Motown, rock, and jazz bands. For some live rhythm and blues (and possibly an appearance by the man himself), take a taxi to **John Lee Hooker's Boom Boom Room** (1601 Fillmore Street, 415/673-8000). **Biscuits & Blues** (401 Mason Street, 415/292-2583) is also a great venue for live blues bands.

San Franciscans need to have something to cut the chill of those long foggy nights, so many head to North Beach, which has more than its share of popular watering holes, including **Little City** (673 Union Street, near Washington Square, 415/434-2900), a great spot for flirting over drinks and plates of antipasto; the pleasant (and semisecret) **Specs' Twelve Adler Museum Cafe** (on tiny Saroyan Place off Columbus, south of Broadway, 415/421-4112), an old Beat-generation hangout; the charming but rough-around-the-edges **Savoy Tivoli** (1434 Grant Avenue, between Union and Green, 415/362-7023); and **Tosca Cafe** (242 Columbus Avenue, near Pacific, 415/391-1244), where locals and celebs hang out and sip the house specialty: coffeeless cappuccino made with brandy, milk, and chocolate.

When the fog burns off and the weather heats up, grab a chair on the patio of **Cafe Flore** (2298 Market Street at Noe, 415/621-8579) and order a latte or a glass of wine, or get the full array of spirits on the outdoor decks of such funky local favorites as **The Ramp** (855 China

Sports Roundup

*Fans of the **San Francisco 49ers** are justly proud of their championship football team, but many are less enthusiastic about their windswept, bone-chilling home stadium, Candlestick Park (nicknamed "The Stick"). Bring your jacket if you're going to watch the players strut their stuff. Individual 49er tickets cost the same no matter where you sit; call 415/468-2249 for prices and ticket availability. The **San Francisco Giants** took over the new Pacific Bell ballpark for the 2000 baseball season, and you can buy bleacher-seat tickets (on the day of the game only) for less than the price of a movie; call 415/467-8000.*

*If your idea of fun is to race against two-legged Brillo boxes, centipedes, Snow White and the Seven Dwarfs, and a Whitney Houston clone in drag, sign up for the wild and wacky 7.5-mile **Bay to Breakers** race (and walk), held in mid-May—it's the largest footrace in the world; call 415/808-5000, ext. 2222. In the South Bay you'll find the **San Jose Sharks** duking it out with their ice-hockey sticks in the San Jose Arena from October through April; call 510/762-BASS for ticket information. If you're a fan of the Oakland As, Oakland Raiders, or Golden State Warriors, see the "Oakland" box in the Berkeley section of this chapter.*

The Driver's Guide to San Francisco

Introduce yourself to all sides of San Francisco by cruising in your automobile along the 49-Mile Scenic Drive—a four-hour journey along the city's prettiest streets and past its most scenic sights. The route is marked by blue-and-white signs with pictures of seagulls—but don't follow the birdie during the rush hours unless you also enjoy staring at lots of license plates. Free detailed maps outlining the course are available at the San Francisco Visitor Information Center (900 Market Street at Powell, near the Union Square cable car turntable, 415/391-2000).

Basin Street off 3rd, 415/621-2378) and **Pier 23** (on the Embarcadero near the end of Lombard, 415/362-5125). For a more romantic retreat, splurge on a cocktail at the gorgeous **Redwood Room** in the Clift Hotel (495 Geary Street at Taylor, 415/775-4700); the lounge of the **Carnelian Room** which, perched at the top of the 52-story Bank of America skyscraper, offers a spectacular panoramic city view when the sky is clear (555 California Street at Kearny, 415/433-7500); or the **Equinox** (5 Embarcadero Center, 415/788-1234), the unique revolving rooftop lounge and restaurant at the Hyatt Regency in Embarcadero Center that gives patrons a 360-degree view of San Francisco and the bay. Union Square's best bustling bar is at **Kuleto's** restaurant (221 Powell Street, between Geary and O'Farrell, 415/397-7720), and for the best Irish coffee in town, the **Buena Vista** takes top honors (2765 Hyde Street at Beach, 415/474-5044).

Cheap Eats

Caffe Freddy's
901 Columbus Avenue, San Francisco ☎ 415/922-0151

Caffe Freddy's consistently reaffirms our belief that good Italian food shouldn't cost a fortune. Pastas, pizzas, sandwiches, salads, soups, and a large assortment of appetizers are available, as well as a few chalkboard surprises such as a thick cut of Atlantic salmon with all the trimmings for under $14. Start with the fresh warm cabbage salad with goat cheese, currants, walnuts, rosemary, and spinach, or

the antipasto plate of bruschetta, fresh melon, ham, sun-dried tomatoes, and pesto. Then on to the seafood dishes, such as the fresh fish
soup, a steaming bowl of fat mussels, or fresh Idaho trout. The open-
faced sandwiches topped with melted mozzarella are excellent as
well. On a typically cold and blustery day, the house-made stew and
a cup of real Italian coffee is just the ticket to warm your budget-
minded bones. *AE, MC, V; no checks; lunch Wed–Sun, dinner Tue–Sun;
beer and wine.*

Cha Cha Cha

1801 Haight Street, San Francisco ☎ 415/386-5758
2327 Mission St, San Francisco ☎ 415/648-0504

When we're asked which San Francisco restaurants are our favorites
(and we're asked all the time), one of the first we mention is Cha Cha
Cha. It's fun, it's festive, the Caribbean food is fantastic, the prices
are totally reasonable, the sangria is addictive, and every meal ends
with a free Tootsie Roll. What's not to like? The cafe is wildly decorated with Santeria altars and such, which blends in perfectly with
the varied mix of pumped-up patrons quaffing pitchers of sangria
while waiting for a table (often for up to an hour on weekends, but
nobody seems to mind). The tapas-style dishes we always start with
are the sautéed mushrooms, fried calamari, fried new potatoes (dig
the spicy sauce), Cajun shrimp, mussels in saffron (order more bread
for the sauce), and plantains with black-bean sauce. Check the specials board for outstanding seafood dishes as well, but skip the so-so
steak. A second branch recently opened in the Mission, which serves
exactly the same food in a much larger space (and also has a full bar).
MC, V; no checks; lunch, dinner every day; beer and wine.

Dottie's True Blue Café

522 Jones Street, San Francisco ☎ 415/885-2767

Don't let the sketchy neighborhood deter you from venturing to one
of the best breakfast cafes in the city, sequestered within the Pacific
Bay Inn downtown. The staff at this small, simply decorated, and
family-owned restaurant is always in an addictively jovial mood, and
everyone's made to feel welcome (many customers are on a first-name
basis). Though Dottie's serves lunch, it's the all-American morning
fare served all day that everyone lines up for. Hefty portions of French
toast, cornmeal pancakes, bacon and eggs, and omelets look especially

appealing on the blue-and-white checkered tablecloths. The clincher, though, is the fantastic fresh-baked breads, muffins, or scones that accompany your order. *DIS, MC, V; no checks; breakfast, lunch Wed–Mon; beer and wine.*

Eliza's

2877 California Street, San Francisco ☎ 415/621-4819

1457 18th Street, San Francisco ☎ 415/648-9999

Eliza's is not only one of our favorite Chinese restaurant in San Francisco, it's one of our favorite San Francisco restaurants, period. Where else can you get such fresh, high-quality cuisine in an artistic setting for under $7 a dish? You'll love the decor—oodles of gorgeous handblown glassware, orchids, and tasteful neon lighting create a soothing, sophisticated ambience despite the crowded dining room. The menu offers a large array of classic Hunan and Mandarin dishes, all served on beautiful Italian plates. Start with the assorted appetizer dish, which is practically a meal in itself. Regardless of what you order you're likely to be impressed, and the $5 lunch specials are a steal. The only drawback is the line out the door that often forms around 7pm, and they don't take reservations. FYI, the second Eliza's is located on Potrero Hill. *MC, V; no checks; lunch, dinner every day; beer and wine.*

Fog City Diner

1300 Battery Street, San Francisco ☎ 415/982-2000

If you get a déjà vu flashback when you enter the Fog City Diner, it's because you've seen it on a Visa commercial ("And they don't take American Express"). Which, of course, has made this upscale California-style diner a hit with the tourists, who arrive in droves on summer weekends. But even without the heavy-duty plug, it's still a fun place to meet with friends over a cheeseburger and a milk shake. The glimmering chrome, glass, polished woods, and neon decor is sleek and sophisticated, but it does a poor job of absorbing the decibels. Besides the usual diner fare (gourmet chili dogs, sandwiches, salads, and damn good onion rings), the kitchen also offers a medley of "small plates" such as crab cakes, Asian-style prawns, or quesadillas with chili peppers and almonds. If you're feeling gluttonous, feast on Fog City's fat banana split, which can easily feed a threesome. *CB, DC, DIS, MC, V; no checks; lunch, dinner every day; full bar.*

Hamburger Mary's

1582 Folsom Street, San Francisco ☎ 415/626-1985

If you want to take a safe peek at San Francisco fringe society (bull dykes, heroin addicts, bike messengers, transvestites, tattoo artists, and such), head to Hamburger Mary's at Folsom and 12th Streets. For years this SoMa greasy spoon has been a popular meeting spot for those with alternative outlooks, but even the normal, boring types like us drop in for a fat, juicy burger (served on great whole wheat bread with a side of spicy home fries) and to admire the wild decor, which looks like a flea market that imploded. Sandwiches, salads, and vegetarian dishes are available as well, all at low prices. Mary's also serves breakfast, and it's always interesting to see what stumbles in from an all-nighter. *DC, DIS, MC, V; no checks; lunch, dinner Tues–Sun; full bar.*

House of Nanking

919 Kearny Street, San Francisco ☎ 415/421-1429

The dinnertime waiting line outside this tiny, greasy, wildly popular hole-in-the-wall starts at 5:30pm; by 6pm, you may face a 90-minute wait for a cramped, crowded, itsy-bitsy table with a plastic menu that lists only half of the best dishes served here. When owner/chef/head-waiter Peter Fang can give you his full attention, he'll be glad to apprise you of the day's unlisted specials: succulent chicken or duck dumplings, an exotic shrimp-and-green-onion pancake with peanut sauce, or tempura-like sesame-battered Nanking scallops in a spicy garlic sauce. Or just take a look at what the diners sandwiched around you are eating and point to what looks good (it's hard to go

San Francisco's Farmers Market

*Even if you don't have a place to store any farm-fresh fruits and veggies, stroll through the fantastic **Ferry Plaza Farmers Market** and sample some of Northern California's finest bounty. From award-winning homemade salami and Berkeley's famous Acme bread to delicious organically grown produce and sheep's-milk cheese, you'll find the makings for a great meal right here. There's free live enter-tainment, too. Held year-round (rain or shine) on Saturdays from 8am to 1:30pm in front of the Ferry Building on San Francisco's Embarcadero and Tuesdays at Justin Herman Plaza; call 415/981-3004.*

wrong in this place). While Nanking's food is outstanding and the prices are some of the most reasonable in the city, the service is downright terrible. *Cash only; lunch Mon—Sat, dinner every day; beer and wine.*

La Taqueria

2889 Mission Street, San Francisco ☎ 415/285-7117

Among colorful fruit stands, thrift shops, and greasy panhandlers lining bustling Mission Street sits La Taqueria, the Bay Area's best burrito factory. Don't expect a wide variety of fare, for the folks behind the counter just churn out what they do best: burritos, tacos, and quesadillas. It's all fresh, delicious, and guaranteed to fill you up—for little more than pocket change. The moist, meaty fillings include grilled beef, pork, sausage, beef tongue, and chicken (you won't find any rice in these burritos), and the *bebidas* vary from beer and soda to cantaloupe juice and even *horchata* (a sweet rice drink). *No credit cards; local checks only; lunch, dinner every day; beer only.*

Marcello's Pizza

420 Castro Street, San Francisco ☎ 415/863-3900

Every neighborhood has to have one: a late-night pizza-by-the-slice old standby that's always there for you when you leave the party drunk, stoned, and starving. In the Castro that place is Marcello's, which must make a small fortune serving a wide array of slices to a *very* eclectic crowd until 1am Sunday through Thursday, and until 2am Friday and Saturday. Both thick- and thin-crust pizzas with a wide array of toppings are enticingly set behind the glass counter, and it usually takes only one big slice to do the trick. Chicken wings, calzone, salads, and sandwiches are also available, but most everyone sticks with the thick, gooey, God-this-tastes-good pizza. Beer and wine are available as well. There are only about a half dozen stools in the cramped and narrow pizzeria, but the crowd moves quickly. *Cash only; lunch, dinner every day; beer and wine.*

Mario's Bohemian Cigar Store

566 Columbus Avenue, San Francisco ☎ 415/362-0536
2209 Polk Street, San Francisco ☎ 415/776-8226

You can't consider yourself a San Franciscan unless you've had a focaccia-bread sandwich at this classic century-old North Beach Italian institution, which serves the city's best espresso. Tourists and locals alike squeeze themselves into this adorable little low-key cafe overlooking Washington Square. There are several kinds of sandwiches to choose from, but the best are the hot meatball and the eggplant, both topped with melted Swiss cheese and cut into triangles for easy pickings. The newer and larger Mario's, located on Polk between Green and Vallejo, offers live jazz Wednesday and Sunday nights, but it doesn't have the classic charm of the original. *Cash only; lunch, dinner every day; beer and wine.*

Mel's Diner

2165 Lombard Street, San Francisco ☎ 415/921-3039

When you're in the mood for a cheeseburger, greasy fries, and a chocolate shake, there's no place that does it better than Mel's Diner. Modeled after an *American Graffiti*–style '50s diner, Mel's is replete with glimmering stainless steel, large comfy booths, and even nickel jukeboxes at each table. Along with the diner standards—hot dogs, cheese sandwiches, hot fudge sundaes—are a half dozen "blue plate specials" such as a turkey dinner complete with stuffing and mashed potatoes, and meatloaf just like Mom used to make. A classic American breakfast is served each morning as well. Mel's best attribute, however, is that it's open late (till 3am Sunday through Thursday and 24 hours Friday and Saturday). *Cash only; breakfast, lunch, dinner every day; beer and wine.*

Park Chow

1240 9th Avenue, San Francisco ☎ 415/665-9912

There just aren't enough good things to say about Park Chow, one of our all-time favorite places to eat in the city. First of all, it's cheap (you get hefty servings of quality food for around $10–$13), it's consistently good, the service is fast and friendly, the atmosphere is lively and fun, and you always leave feeling imminently satisfied. The restaurant, which is fashioned after a rustic ski lodge, is located in the Inner Sunset District near Golden Gate Park and caters mostly to a local clientele who come for Park Chow's outstanding braised short ribs served with fresh greens and addictive mashed potatoes. Other popular dishes are the giant portobello mushroom cap served with creamy polenta, and the linguine with calamari, mussels, clams, and shrimp. Burgers, chicken, salads, and a reasonably good wine-by-the-glass list are on the menu as well. On sunny days, request a table in the roof garden. Brunch is served until 2:30pm on weekends. *MC, V; no checks; lunch, dinner every day, brunch Sat–Sun; beer and wine.*

Sears Fine Food

439 Powell Street, San Francisco ☎ 415/986-1160

Sears is your classic San Francisco–American coffee shop, where the decor and the staff haven't changed since the Nixon administration. Story has it that Sears first opened in 1938 when Ben the Clown decided to retire from the circus and open his own restaurant. His Swedish wife, Hilbur, chipped in her family's secret recipe (still a secret to this day) for Swedish pancakes (18 silver-dollar-size cakes to a serving), and there's been a line out the door every weekend morning ever since. If pancakes aren't your thing, try the crispy waffles or sourdough French toast. The fresh fruit cup marinated in orange juice is also quite popular. Lunch is served as well, offering just what you'd expect—club sandwiches, BLTs, homemade pies—but it's the only-in-SF breakfast experience that makes Sears worth the wait. *Cash only; breakfast, lunch Thur–Mon; no alcohol.*

Tu Lan

8 6th Street, San Francisco ☎ 415/626-0927

If you're a fan of hole-in-the-wall ethnic dives in seedy locations that serve top-notch food at bargain prices, have we got a gem for you. Located in one of the sketchiest and foulest-smelling parts of the city, Tu Lan is a greasy, grimy little Vietnamese diner that, unless you are hip to the secret, you would neither find nor frequent. This makes it all the more bewildering that a drawing of Julia Child's unmistakable face graces the cover of the greasy menus, but apparently she's one of Tu Lan's biggest fans. And once you try the light, fresh imperial rolls served on a bed of rice noodles, lettuce, peanuts, and mint, you'll become one too. Other recommended dishes include the lemon beef salad, the fried fish in ginger sauce, and the pork kebabs. *Cash only; lunch, dinner Mon–Sat; beer and wine.*

Cheap Sleeps

The average daily room rate of a San Francisco hotel is around $120, although a surprisingly large number of establishments offer rooms for much less. The following are some of the best. Prices range from $19 to $75 per night, and all are in relatively safe areas. If the budget-priced rooms are full, contact the Visitor Information Center (900 Market Street at Powell, near the Union Square cable car turntable, 415/391-2000) and ask for their free "San Francisco Lodging Guide," which lists hundreds of accommodations and their room rates. Beware: Several of the city's budget beds (including those listed in that lodging guide) are in questionable neighborhoods; ask the center to recommend a safe place to stay. In a pinch, try one of the many motels along Lombard Street between Van Ness and Lyon. Free parking in San Francisco is as rare as a royal flush in Las Vegas, so don't expect to find it at the following establishments unless otherwise noted.

The Adelaide Inn

5 Isadora Duncan (off Taylor Street, between Post and Geary),
San Francisco, CA 94102 ☎ 415/441-2261
District: Union Square

This European-style pension is hidden on a street so small it's rarely—if ever—shown on a San Francisco map. Once you arrive, however, you'll feel as if you've stumbled on a cluttered country inn that would be right at home in an old French village. The 18-room inn was originally an apartment building and has a lot of steep stairs (but no elevator). Unfortunately, the Adelaide has lost a lot of its former grace and style, and now its age is starting to show; the hodgepodge of photos and prints don't quite hide the rips and tears. The rooms are poorly lit and can be lackluster or garish, the queen-size or double bed sometimes sags a little, and the tiny black-and-white TV has poor reception. However, the bathrooms are clean (there's a 10-minute time limit in the shower), each room is equipped with a small basin, and guests have access to a large kitchen with a refrigerator, microwave, and several small tables. A breakfast of coffee and rolls is included in the low rates, and the amiable innkeeper will be happy to tell you how to get around the nearby theater district and Union Square. *AE, MC, V; no checks.*

The Amsterdam Hotel

749 Taylor Street (between Sutter and Bush), San Francisco, CA 94108
☎ 800/637-3444 or ☎ 415/673-3277

District: Union Square

Slightly more expensive and definitely more upscale than most budget lodgings in San Francisco, this 1909 Victorian offers 30 handsome rooms, each with a four-poster bed, matching armoire holding a cable TV, and a table with cushy chairs by a bay window. The private baths have tub showers and niceties such as blow-dryers and boxes of tissue that aren't usually offered in budget hotels. If you tire of sitting in your room gazing at Taylor Street, you can relax on the cream satin couches in the large lounge or take a short walk to the Union Square shops or the top of Nob Hill. A continental breakfast is included. *AE, MC, V; no checks; www.amsterdamhotel.com.*

Golden Gate Hotel

775 Bush Street (between Powell and Mason), San Francisco, CA 94108
☎ 800/835-1118 or ☎ 415/392-3702

District: Union Square

Quick! Book a room here before the owners realize what a bargain they're offering for their lovely little rooms bathed in Laura Ashley fabrics and wallpaper. This turn-of-the-century bed-and-breakfast inn couldn't be more pleasant: light, airy rooms are furnished with antique dressers, white wicker chairs, pedestal sinks, cable TV, phone, twin reading lights, and pots of beautiful, bright flowers in each room's sunlit window. Some of the "shared bath" units even have a private shower stall in the room. The Golden Gate is nowhere near its namesake bridge, but it is just a couple of blocks from Union Square and the top of Nob Hill. *AE, DC, MC, V; no checks; www.golden gatehotel.com.*

Grant Plaza Hotel

465 Grant Avenue (at Pine), San Francisco, CA 94108 ☎ 800/472-6899 or ☎ 415/434-3883

District: Chinatown

The word is out about this terrific hotel in the busy heart of San Francisco, so make your reservations early. The small, pleasant rooms were recently renovated and are available at great prices (particularly if you're traveling in a group of four and need only two beds). Many of them boast a terrific view of the Financial District skyscrapers, and if you peer down at the street below, you'll see vendors galore hawking their back-scratchers, calendars, and live chickens. It's a prime location for exploring the most fascinating parts of Chinatown (the Chinatown Gate is a few yards south), and Union Square and the cable cars are only a short jaunt away. In the glitzy lobby, crystal chandeliers hang over plum leather couches, and the large storefront windows are perfect for looking out at all the passersby. The hotel's 72 compact rooms are contemporary in decor, and each has a tiny bath with a gleaming white shower as well as a TV and phone. The rooms over Grant Avenue have the best views, but they're also the noisiest. Ask about the "Super Saver Package," which includes free parking and breakfast. *AE, MC, V; no checks; www.grantplaza.com.*

Herbert Hotel

161 Powell Street (at O'Farrell), San Francisco, CA 94102 ☎ 415/362-1600
District: Union Square

You can't get much closer to the square in the Union Square district without paying top dollar, but you'll be hard-pressed to find a duller room in the city than what you'll get at the Herbert. Still, the rates for a spacious room start at around $55 a night for a shared bath and somewhat higher for a private bath. The furniture in the bare-walled rooms looks like garage-sale specials, but at least the pieces match, and if you tape a couple of pictures to the bare walls, perhaps they won't look so grim. Smoking is permitted in all 90 units—and it smells like it, too. Ask for a room overlooking Powell Street, and expect to hear a lot of cable car bells ringing. The boarded-up interior of the elevator looks as if it suffered from a bomb blast, but don't let that scare you away. *MC, V; no checks; www.herberthotel.com.*

Hostel at Fort Mason

Fort Mason (enter via Franklin Street at Bay Street), Building 240
(at Funston and Pope), San Francisco, CA 94123 ☎ 415/771-7277
or ☎ 415/771-3645 (reservations)
District: The Marina

One can only imagine what the Hyatt Regency's top brass would pay to get their hands on this fantastic piece of real estate. The Hostel at Fort Mason has the best locale of any lodging—cheap or expensive—on the north side of San Francisco, if not in the entire city. Perched on a grassy bluff above the bay, this 150-bed hostel offers views of the Golden Gate Bridge and practically sits on the scenic Golden Gate Promenade—an ideal stretch of land for strolling, jogging, skating, and bicycling. And Ghirardelli Square and Fisherman's Wharf are an easy walk away. Combine that with its $20-per-night rate for members and $24-per-night rate for nonmembers, plus free parking, and it's almost too good to be true. There's one small catch: you have to pitch in with a simple chore such as sweeping, vacuuming, or emptying the trash (don't worry, toilet cleaning is not on the list). In exchange for the help and low rates, you get bedding and towels; clean bathrooms and hot showers; a massive, fully stocked kitchen; lockers for storing your gear; and 24-hour hostel access. Other pluses: a laundry room, jukebox, first-rate pool table, old piano, redwood deck with picnic tables, and lounge with couches, books, and fireplace. A free movie or live entertainment is offered nightly, and there are free city tours and organized events such as baseball games and museum trips. No smokes or booze allowed. *JCB, MC, V; no checks; www.norcalhostels.org.*

Hostel at Union Square

312 Mason Street (at O'Farrell), San Francisco, CA 94102 ☎ 415/788-5604
District: Union Square

Set on a prime lot next to fashionable Union Square, this terrific new hostel (formerly the Hotel Virginia) has 260 beds—40 of them in private rooms for couples. The rates are hard to beat ($19 a night for an American Youth Hostel member, $22 for a nonmember), and you don't have to worry about curfews, chores, or bringing sleeping bags or sheets. The rooms are equipped with either bunk beds (complete with little ladders), twins, or doubles. The couple's rooms are first-come, first-served;

Historic Open House

Architecture and history buffs should get their hands on the 31-page booklet Bay Area Historic House Museums. *A guide to 27 historic homes spread throughout the Bay Area, it features maps, photos, descriptions, hours, and admission fees (many allow visitors for free). For a copy, send a request and $3 to Bay Area Historic House Museums Association (22701 Main Street, Hayward, CA 94541). For more information, call 510/581-0223.*

if they're full, ask about the four- or five-person rooms for men or women. Bathrooms are shared, of course, but there are plenty of them, so lines shouldn't be a problem. The large furnished kitchen area is very pleasant and tidy and is equipped with the essentials, from microwaves to flatware. Coffee and tea are free, as is the movie shown in the TV room every night. Another plus: free guided city walking tours are offered regularly to all guests. *JCB, MC, V; no checks; www.norcalhostels.org.*

Hotel Astoria

510 Bush Street (at Grant), San Francisco, CA 94104 ☎ 800/666-6696 or ☎ 415/434-8889

District: Chinatown

If the Astoria were any closer to the ornate Chinatown Gate, it'd be sitting on top of it. Like its neighbor, the Grant Plaza Hotel, this seven-story hotel is smack-dab in the center of one of the city's best shopping districts. About half of the 75 rooms have private baths, and although they're larger than the Grant Plaza's, they're not as attractive. The quite ordinary furnishings are color-coordinated in shades of tan and cream and, perhaps in an effort to spruce things up, an angular high-tech light hangs incongruously over the queen-size bed. The TV is on a dresser alongside the bed, requiring you to either crane your neck or lie sideways to see the screen. The rates are very reasonable—particularly if you go for the shared bath. *AE, MC, V; no checks.*

Marina Motel

2576 Lombard Street (between Broderick and Divisadero), San Francisco, CA 92123 ☎ 800/346-6118 or ☎ 415/921-9406

District: The Marina

Tucked among the scores of characterless motels lining busy Lombard Street is the pretty Spanish-style Marina Motel. Pink fuchsias and bougainvillea and brilliant purple and red petunias grow along the stucco exterior, and behind each polished-wood door is a handsome room with a queen-size bed, twin brass reading lights, TV, phone, and a clean tile bathroom with a large shower. The rates vary with the seasons (summer weekend rates may be a bit too steep for you, so call ahead), but for only $5 extra you can get a fully equipped kitchen, which can really cut down on dining expenses. This family-run motel also offers a precious commodity: your own private parking garage, gratis, right on the premises. Such favored attractions as the Marina Yacht Harbor, trendy Union Street, the Palace of Fine Arts, and the Exploratorium are only a few blocks away, and the Golden Gate Bridge is a mile to the north. It's also quite easy to catch a bus on Lombard to other parts of town and even to Marin County. Ask for a room set far back from the street. *MC, V; no checks; www.marina motel.com.*

Pacific Tradewinds Guest House

680 Sacramento Street (between Kearny and Montgomery),
San Francisco, CA 94111 ☎ 415/433-7970
District: Chinatown/Financial District

Sleeping in a bunk at the Pacific Tradewinds is like sharing a small room in a college dorm—the atmosphere is relaxed, the rooms have recently been updated, and you can swap stories with your new roommates before falling asleep. This little guest house, tucked between the Financial District skyscrapers and the bustling Chinatown shops, caters to the overseas backpacking set, but Americans (especially students) are also welcome. For a few bucks less than the $22 a night you'd pay at the local AYH, you can stay in this more intimate 31-bed facility run by friendly folks eager to help you plan your city forays. Bedding is provided, and you won't have to do chores (but you will need to stand in line to use one of the two bathrooms). Other perks include a free safe-deposit box, a telephone, international fax service, luggage storage, kitchen use, laundry service (for only $2), and—something you certainly won't find in any other lodging in town—free sock washing. There's no curfew, but guests must check in between 8am and midnight (reservations are guaranteed only with a deposit in cash or traveler's check). And six nights' payment gets you the seventh night free—one of the best deals in San Francisco. *MC, V; no checks; www.hostels.com/pt.*

Pension San Francisco

1668 Market Street (between Gough and Franklin), San Francisco, CA
94102 ☎ 800/886-1271 or ☎ 415/864-1271
District: Civic Center

Nestled between several storefront windows on bustling Market Street is the handsome Pension San Francisco—just look for the forest-green awning emblazoned with the words "Tourist Hotel." This is the kind of budget lodging even your fastidious mother would appreciate. The 36 small, tidy rooms have bright white walls, carpeting that doesn't look too trampled, glossy pine dressers, small basins and closets, and phones. Most have double beds with a view of the Civic Center skyscrapers. The tiny but clean bathrooms are shared, and there's a small, comfortable sitting room on each of the four floors. Though some of the rooms are designated for nonsmokers, the scent of cigarettes often lingers in the air, but the windows usually provide plenty of ventilation. Zuni Cafe, 415/552-2522, one of San Francisco's best restaurants, is just steps away, and although a meal there would probably cost more than your room, the bar is a great place to get a nightcap and watch the locals in action. Be careful about roaming too far from the hotel at night, though—the Tenderloin and the Western Addition, two unsafe neighborhoods, are a few blocks away. Small pets are welcome. *AE, MC, V; checks OK for mail deposit; www.citysearch7.com.*

The Red Victorian Bed & Breakfast Inn

1665 Haight Street (at Cole), San Francisco, CA 94117 ☎ 415/864-1978
District: Haight-Ashbury

To say that the Red Vic is not a typical tourist hotel is putting it a tad mildly. About 20 years ago, owner Sami Sunchild (her real name) sort of accidentally acquired this sprawling 1904 Victorian hotel in the heart of the Haight, world capital of '60s hippiedom. The 18 upstairs guest rooms have sinks and telephones, but most share New Age bathrooms: one is lined with mirrors and strips of twinkling lights, and another has a fish tank suspended over the toilet plus a sunken tub. The rooms are equally intriguing, with fanciful decor ranging from feline-inspired artwork and tie-dyed canopies to bright ceiling and wall murals of rainbows, clouds, and the sun. Unfortunately, the Vic's immense popularity has prompted Sunchild to practically double her rates, and now there's only one bargain bed in the house: the small Butterfly Room, with a canopied double bed and soft-colored lights, rents for about $65 a night if you stay for at least seven nights. Four other rooms run about $10 more (some rates are reduced if you're sleeping alone). In the morning, you're encouraged to hang loose with other guests at breakfast in the Gallery of Meditative Art. *AE, DIS, MC, V; checks OK; www.redvic.com.*

San Remo Hotel

2237 Mason Street (between Francisco and Chestnut) San Francisco,
CA 94133 ☎ 800/352-7366 or ☎ 415/776-8688
District: North Beach

Hidden in a quiet section of North Beach between Fisherman's Wharf and bustling Washington Square, the San Remo is within easy walking distance of San Francisco's main attractions, including Chinatown, the Embarcadero, Pier 39, and one of the main cable car stations. Combine that with the inexpensive rates, and you have one of the best bargains in town. This charming, well-preserved, three-story Italianate Victorian originally served as a boardinghouse for dockworkers displaced by the great fire of 1906, so the 62 rooms are rather small, bathrooms are shared, and walls are thin. If you can live with these minor inconveniences, however, you're in for a treat. The rooms are reminiscent of a European pension, modestly decorated with brass or iron beds, porcelain sinks, and white wicker furniture; most have ceiling fans. Those on the second floor, particularly numbers 36, 43, and 45, which overlook Mason Street and have views of Coit Tower, are favorites. The old-fashioned bathrooms, spotlessly clean and restored to their original luster, have brass pull-chain toilets with oak tanks, claw-footed tubs, and showers. In the lobby and hallways, antiques and plants are bathed by sunlight filtering through leaded-glass skylights. There's even a laundry room with vending machines stocked with detergent, sodas, and snacks. And you can count on the friendly, city-savvy staff to help you plan your day on the town. *AE, DC, MC, V; no checks; www.sanremohotel.com.*

Temple Hotel

469 Pine Street (between Montgomery and Kearny), San Francisco, CA 94104 ☎ 415/781-2565
District: Chinatown/Financial District

The one feature that saves the Temple from being a basic bed-in-a-box is the pretty floor-to-ceiling print drapes that elegantly frame the windows. Ask for a room facing Pine Street so you'll have a view of the 52-story Bank of America world headquarters across the way, one of the best (and tallest) skyscrapers in San Francisco. And thanks to B of A's gardening team, your view includes the perfectly maintained trees and flower gardens on the high-rise's grounds. The rooms are furnished comfortably, with a double bed, an old white-marble pedestal table, and comfortable Naugahyde chairs, though the rabbit-ear antenna on top of the black-and-white TV doesn't do what it's supposed to. Still, the Temple is in a great part of town for shopping and sight-seeing, and literally a few steps from the front door is the popular Belden Square alley, where Financial District drones take their coffee and lunch breaks. Better yet, the room rates are dirt cheap, and if you share a bath and stay more than four nights, you'll pay only $45 a night; weekly rates are even lower. *Cash only; romsdahl@earthlink.net.*

Twin Peaks

2160 Market Street (between Church and Sanchez), San Francisco, CA 94114 ☎ 415/621-9467
District: The Castro

In an area where lodgings tend to be pretty pricey, you'll be relieved to find some great rates at the 60-room Twin Peaks, in the heart of San Francisco's gay and lesbian neighborhood. For about $50 you can get a comfortable room with shared bath, TV, and a bay window overlooking the hustle and bustle of Market Street; the price drops even lower if you're willing to travel during the off-season. Rent by the week and rates go down to less than $40 a night, but the weekly units are small and cramped, with battered furniture, tiny black-and-white TVs, shared bath, and no view (ask for a peek before you pay). The hip Cafe Du Nord bar and nightclub, 415/861-5016, is three doors up the street, and the heart of the Castro is only 2 blocks away. *MC, V; no checks.*

Van Ness Motel

2850 Van Ness Avenue (at Chestnut), San Francisco, CA 94019 ☎ 415/776-3220
District: The Marina/Russian Hill

Although this two-story 42-room motel faces the major artery of Van Ness Avenue, it's just steps from such popular attractions as Ghirardelli Square, the Cannery, Aquatic Park, and Fisherman's Wharf, attracting many German, French, and Japanese tourists. The rooms are nothing special, but they're tidy and include a comfortable queen-size bed and a small private bath with shower, TV, and phone. Be sure to ask for a unit located off the busy street. The loquacious manager has been working here for nearly 20 years and goes out of his way to provide travel tips. Nearby Polk Street and the west end of Chestnut Street are great shopping areas lined with several popular cafes, coffeehouses, boutiques, and some of the locals' favorite watering holes. The rooms get pricey on summer weekends, but they're reasonable the rest of the year, and free parking (practically unheard of in the city) is an added plus. *AE, DC, DIS, JCB, MC, V; no checks.*

Marin County

If you listened to all the ballyhoo, you'd believe everyone in Marin drives a BMW, soaks in a hot tub under the stars every night, and smokes two joints in the morning. Granted, these portrayals characterize some local residents, but certainly not all of them, as Marinites are quick to point out. Nonetheless, this North Bay community, the wealthiest county in California, does boast a Little League team coached by rock star Huey Lewis, and proud parents do sit in the bleachers munching designer popcorn and yelling, "We got money, we got stocks, don't need no credit cards to clean your clocks!"

What they've also got—much to the envy of the rest of Northern California—is a home surrounded by thousands of acres of public parkland, wilderness, redwood canyons, mountain meadows, and pristine beaches, not to mention sunny weather practically year-round. As a result, Marin is a mecca for hikers, bicyclists, bird-watchers, sunbathers, and beachcombers. Although the beautiful hillside and waterfront towns of Sausalito, Tiburon, and Mill Valley aren't exactly rich in inexpensive lodgings, they do have numerous attractions and recreational offerings for the budget traveler, and their incredible natural beauty alone is worth the trip over the Golden Gate Bridge.

Exploring

To get to those alluring rolling hills and seacoast towns on the north side of the bay, drive, walk, or bike across the 4,200-foot-long Golden

Friends of the Sea

----

*Since 1975, veterinarians and hundreds of volunteers at the nonprofit **Marine Mammal Center** have been rescuing distressed seals, sea lions, dolphins, porpoises, whales, and sea otters on the Northern and Central California coast. Every year, hundreds of marine mammals are taken to the center, nursed back to health, and then returned to the sea for a second chance at life. Public visiting hours are 10am to 4pm daily, and admission is free. The center is located in the Marin Headlands at Fort Cronkhite, between the Marin Headlands Visitor Center and Rodeo Beach, 415/289-SEAL.*

Gate Bridge, which at midspan hangs 249 feet above the water—an awesome height requested by the Navy so its big battleships could pass underneath. About three-quarters of the way over, you will have crossed the Marin County line. Before you descend into Marin, take a moment to admire the breathtaking view of San Francisco at **Vista Point,** the first exit off the bridge.

The bridge's next turnoff is Alexander Avenue, and if you head west up Conzelman Road (follow the signs), you'll reach the **Marin Headlands,** 12,000 acres of undeveloped, windswept land that served as a military camp in the late 19th and early 20th centuries. Several miles of trails wind along the rolling hills, and many are littered with old battlegun sites and bunkers. The vistas from the trails are mesmerizing. Hike down the steep, 3.25-mile-long road (not accessible by car) leading to Kirby Cove (park in the small lot at Battery Spencer) and you'll find a quiet little beach where you can gaze at the belly of the bridge.

The **Marin Headlands Visitor Center,** 415/331-1540, in the former post chapel, offers a wealth of information, including free trail maps outlining where you can take your dog, horse, and bike; handouts on free campsites in the area; free workshops and nature programs (see the quarterly "Park Events" newsletter); intriguing exhibits on the history of the region's Coast Miwok Indians and Portuguese dairies; and a large selection of guidebooks and maps. It's open daily. Take the Alexander Avenue exit off the Golden Gate Bridge, make an immediate left, follow the "Marin Headlands" signs leading up the hill—it turns into a one-way road at the top—and then down; keep bearing right, and you'll find the center at Fort Barry, at the intersection of Field and Bunker Roads.

Follow Alexander Avenue toward the east side of Marin and you'll reach the pretty little town of **Sausalito,** a former Portuguese fishing village that's now home to the well-heeled owners of many spectacular hillside mansions. Stay on Alexander, which eventually turns into Bridgeway, the main drag through the center of town. Pricey boutiques and waterfront restaurants line this street, and a paved promenade offers an unobstructed view of Angel Island, Alcatraz, and the San Francisco skyline. To best appreciate Sausalito, park your car (you may have to hit a municipal lot or a side street to find a spot) and walk along the promenade and through the tiny village. For the perfect perch on the bay, walk through the touristy—and pricey—**Horizons** (558 Bridgeway, Sausalito, 415/331-3232) restaurant and grab a seat on the wind-sheltered deck, where you can sip the spirit of your choice and wave at the yachters sailing just a few feet under your nose.

The **No Name Bar** (757 Bridgeway, Sausalito, 415/332-1392) is probably the only place on Bridgeway where you'll find a local resident. Don't try looking for the name, because it's marked only by a small, handsome wooden sign that says "Bar" in gold letters. The No Name's free jazz and R&B concerts (held Tuesday through Sunday nights) draw crowds. Stroll across the street and you'll see the pier, where you can catch a ferry to San Francisco. Nearby is the tiny **Plaza Viña del Mar,** graced by a pair of elephant statues and a fountain from the Panama-Pacific International Exposition of 1915. One of the highlights of Sausalito is its gorgeous yachts—walk down the wooden planks and try to guess how many greenbacks it takes to own (and maintain) one of these glistening beauties.

The four-story **Village Fair** (777 Bridgeway, Sausalito, 415/332-8106), on the west side of Bridgeway, is a quaint shopping mall honeycombed with shops and flowers and even a little waterfall. Don't expect to find any bargains here, but it's worth a quick look.

Armchair Travel

No matter where you plan to journey next, you'll undoubtedly find a book and a map on your upcoming destination at **Book Passage,** *Marin County's premier bookstore specializing in guidebooks and travel literature. When you tire of flipping through the hundreds of travel tomes, you can take a seat at Book Passage's small corner cafe, sip an espresso, and snack on a sweet until you're ready to plunge into the shelves again. The store is located about 10 miles north of the Golden Gate Bridge, at 51 Tamal Vista Boulevard, in the Market Place Shopping Center, Corte Madera, 800/999-7909 or 415/927-0960.*

Where the Wild Things Are

*You can get splashed by magnificent killer whales, feed the gentle giraffes, play tug-of-war with a 5-ton elephant, and watch Bengal tigers swim with their trainers at **Six Flags Marine World**, a one-of-a-kind wildlife park/oceanarium and now more recently a theme park with $25 million in new rides, shows, and attractions all on 160 acres. Open year-round, the park is located in Vallejo, a 30- to 40-minute drive from Marin and San Francisco, and 15 minutes from Napa. From Highway 101 north, take Highway 37 east to Marine World Parkway, 707/643-ORCA.*

Across the street and down the hill from the town barbershop with its red-white-and-blue spiral pole is the **Bay Model** (Marinship Way, off the east side of Bridgeway, Sausalito, 415/332-3871), a gigantic working hydraulic model of the San Francisco Bay and the Delta region used by the U.S. Army Corps of Engineers to study the tides and various bay problems. The Bay Model also offers interactive exhibits and a World War II shipyard display; admission is free. Just before Bridgeway merges with US Highway 101, you'll find Sausalito's community of houseboat dwellers. Take a gander at the **floating homes,** which vary from funky little wooden abodes covered with pots of bright flowers to swanky houseboats with helipads (park at the Waldo Point Harbor Houseboat Marina at the north end of Bridgeway).

Before you say so long to Sausalito, take a spin through the lush, landscaped hills, zigzagging your way from one end to the other to get a taste of how the rich really live. It's hard to get too lost—all of the streets eventually wind down to Bridgeway—just don't get distracted by the magnificent mansions as you navigate the twisting roads. For a tour of tiny Tiburon and Belvedere, the waterfront towns directly across the bay, head north on Bridgeway until it hooks up with Highway 101, then follow the signs to Tiburon Boulevard and downtown Tiburon (about a 15-minute drive).

Formerly a railroad town and until 1963 the terminus of the Northwestern Pacific Railroad, **Tiburon** (Spanish for "shark") is now a quaint New England–style coastal village. Its short Main Street is packed with expensive antique and specialty shops as well as restaurants with incredible bay views. You can leave your car on the outskirts and walk to the village, or park in the large pay-lot off Main Street. (An even better way to get here is by bicycle or by taking the ferry from San Francisco; it drops off passengers at the edge of town.) At the tip of the Tiburon

Best Bets for Bicyclists

The hilly, scenic bike trails of Marin are a haven for amateur and professional cyclists alike. A favorite not-too-strenuous route takes you north across the Golden Gate Bridge, then follows the bike trail under the bridge and down a steep hill to downtown Sausalito. The paved trail hugs Sausalito's waterfront, leading past houseboats and marshes to Bayfront Park in Mill Valley; the ride takes about two to three hours. To avoid riding (or pushing) your bike uphill to the bridge for the return trip, coast onto a ferry in Sausalito or Tiburon and sail back to San Francisco's Fisherman's Wharf (Red & White Fleet ferry, 800/229-2784).

The Marin Headlands and Mount Tamalpais are the bicycling hot spots for diehards, although you don't need Stallone-size thighs to make it up all the trails. Maps to the numerous bike paths are available at many Marin and Bay Area bike stores and bookstores; the Pan Toll Camp/Mount Tamalpais Ranger Station, 415/388-2070; and the Marin Headlands Visitor Center, 415/331-1540.

Recommended bicycle rental shops include American Bicycle Rental (2715 Hyde Street, in Fisherman's Wharf, San Francisco, 415/931-0234), Marina Cyclery (3330 Steiner Street, San Francisco, 415/929-7135), and Bike Sport (1735 Tiburon Boulevard, Tiburon, 415/435-5064).

peninsula is a small grassy park with benches, and on sunny days people flock here with picnics to admire the panoramic view of San Francisco and Angel Island.

Stroll west on Main Street and you'll bump into the intimate **Tiburon Deli** (110 Main Street, Tiburon, 415/435-4888), which offers Bud's ice cream, frozen yogurt, and $4 sandwiches. The deli is part of Tiburon's historic **Ark Row,** an assembly of charming 100-year-old restored arks that now house several shops. Follow Main beyond the shops to Beach Road for another amazing view of the bay, one that includes the prized yachts docked in front of the members-only San Francisco Yacht Club. This is where Tiburon blends into **Belvedere** (Italian for "beautiful view"), an ultra-exclusive community that makes Sausalito look like a poor cousin. The entire city comprises only one-half of a square mile of land—but this is one tony piece of real estate. Drive up Belvedere's steep, narrow roads for a glimpse of the highly protected, well-shielded multimillion-dollar homes where international celebs like Elton John have been known to hide out. After your hillside cruise, drive along San Rafael Avenue, which hugs Richardson Bay on the north side of Tiburon, for another great view of the water. You can't tell from the

Escape to Angel Island

Hikers, mountain bikers, and sun worshipers hop aboard the ferries to Angel Island every sunny weekend to escape the city crowds and admire panoramic views of the Bay Area. This heavily wooded 740-acre island, the San Francisco Bay's largest, is only a mile from the Tiburon peninsula, but it feels as if it's far from civilization, particularly if you hike to the top of 781-foot Mount Livermore. The island is known as the "Ellis Island of the West," having once served as an immigration station for millions entering the United States. Angel Island has also been a Native American settlement, a Civil War fort, a prisoner-of-war camp, and a Nike missile site. Now it's all been set aside as a state park and wildlife preserve, home to deer, raccoons, birds, and harbor seals.

Mountain-bike rentals and one-hour, open-air tram tours are available on the island; call 415/897-0715 for details. Free docent-led tours are offered on weekends from May through October; for more information call 415/435-3522. To pitch your tent at one of the island's nine environmental campsites, call California State Parks Reservations at 800/444-7275 for a reservation. Pick up an informational Angel Island map ($1) on the island, or send $2 to PO Box 866, Tiburon, CA 94920. Ferry service to the island is offered by the Red & White Fleet (at Pier 43½ in San Francisco's Fisherman's Wharf, 800/229-2784 or 415/435-2131) and by the Angel Island–Tiburon Ferry (at the pier on Main Street in downtown Tiburon, 415/435-2131). For more information on Angel Island, call 415/435-1915.

street, but behind a stretch of houses on the east side of San Rafael Avenue is **Belvedere Lagoon,** where residents sail, canoe, kayak, and mingle with their neighbors basking on their sunny waterside decks (you can get a peek at the lagoon just steps from the intersection of San Rafael Avenue and Windward Road).

San Rafael Avenue winds its way north to Tiburon Boulevard, which leads back to Highway 101. If you stay on Tiburon Boulevard and follow it past the highway on-ramps, it turns into E Blithedale Avenue and leads directly into the center of the lovely, sleepy town of **Mill Valley.** This is where many millionaires have forsaken bayside plots of land for the highly coveted real estate nestled in the redwoods. Introduce yourself to the town by walking along Throckmorton Avenue, the main shopping strip off Blithedale. Visit the popular **Depot Bookstore & Cafe** (87 Throckmorton Avenue, Mill Valley, 415/383-2665), where you can purchase some good reads and enjoy them with a glass of wine and a sandwich on the patio facing the town's central plaza. Hard-core coffee drinkers in search of the best cup in town should cross the street to **Peet's** (88 Throckmorton Avenue, Mill Valley, 415/381-8227). In the evening, stop by **Sweetwater** (153 Throckmorton Avenue, Mill Valley, 415/388-2820) for great live jazz, R&B, and rock 'n' roll.

No visit to Marin would be complete without a journey up **Mount Tamalpais** (pronounced tam-ul-PIE-us), commonly referred to as Mount Tam. You can drive to the top of this 2,586-foot peak (Marin's highest) and get an amazing bird's-eye view of the entire Bay Area, as well as the **Farallon Islands** 25 miles out at sea and the Sierra Nevada mountain range nearly 200 miles away. Follow Highway 1 (also called the Shoreline Highway) to the Panoramic Highway, turn right on Pan Toll Road, then right again on E Ridgecrest Boulevard, which leads to the mountain's east peak (it costs $5 to park in the lot, but you can park on any turnout in the road as long as you stay behind the white street line). To best appreciate the 6,400-acre **Mount Tamalpais State Park,** with its red-wood groves, streams, grassland, chaparral, deer, and even mountain lions, follow one of the 50 miles of well-maintained hiking and bicycling trails. If you don't have a map of the mountain (available in many Marin bookstores), invest a dollar for the trail map sold at the Pan Toll Camp/Mount Tamalpais Ranger Station. From Highway 101 north, take the Stinson Beach/Highway 1 exit, follow Highway 1 for 3 miles, make a sharp right onto Panoramic Highway, and follow this two-lane road until you reach a sign that says "Stinson Beach 4 miles, Mt. Tamalpais 4 miles"; the station is on the left side of the intersection; 415/388-2070.

You can pick up photocopies of Mount Tam trail maps for $1 at the **Mill Valley Chamber of Commerce** (85 Throckmorton Avenue, next to the Depot Bookstore, Mill Valley, 415/388-9700). The Mount Tamal-

A Museum for Kids

*Kids get a kick out of the **Bay Area Discovery Museum,** where they can sing and dance in the Discovery Theater, "pump" gas into a Model T in the Transportation Building, create a clay sculpture or paint a picture in the Art Spot, build a skyscraper in the Architecture & Design Building, dissect a squid in the Science Lab, and much more. This unique hands-on interactive learning center is designed for children ages 1 through 12—and it's a guaranteed kid-pleaser. Located at Fort Baker, under the north end of the Golden Gate Bridge, in Sausalito; call 415/487-4398 for directions and more information.*

Message to Mountain Bikers

Mount Tamalpais offers fantastic scenic trails for mountain bikers, but some trails are restricted to pedestrians only—and they're fiercely guarded. If you don't want to get slapped with a $200 fine for pedaling up the wrong path, ask a ranger for a list of legal bike routes, or look them up on a trail map.

pais Interpretive Association offers free guided walks of Mount Tam (ranging from 4 to 12 miles) every weekend starting at 9:30am, moonlight hikes on full-moon nights, and interesting astronomy programs on new-moon nights at Mount Tam's Mountain Theater; call 415/388-2070 or 415/258-2410 for more details or stop by the Mount Tamalpais Ranger Station. Another must-see in Marin is **Muir Woods National Monument,** the Bay Area's last remaining old-growth redwood forest. (For more information on Muir Woods and Marin's coastal areas, including Stinson Beach, see the North Coast chapter).

Cheap Eats

Jennie Low's Chinese Cuisine
38 Miller Avenue, Mill Valley ☎ 415/388-8868

Jennie Low, author of *Chopsticks, Cleaver and Wok,* a '70s bible of Chinese cooking, opened this restaurant in pastoral Mill Valley in 1987. Inspired by Cantonese, Mandarin, Hunan, and Sichuan cooking styles, Low's very personal cuisine features simple, reasonably priced, home-style dishes with velvety textures and sweet, subtle sauces. Start out with her rich rainbow chowder, a colorful mix of shrimp, crab, baby corn, green onions, carrots, and cellophane noodles. For entrees, anything preceded by the word "Jennie's" is a guaranteed winner. Other favored dishes include the crisp hot and spicy green beans sautéed in a garlic sauce, and the Snow White Chicken with mushrooms, snow peas, and spicy eggplant. Low also offers several "light creations"—dishes prepared without oil and with less salt. This place is perpetually packed, but Low and her family do a fine job managing the chaos. *AE, MC, V; no checks; lunch Mon–Sat, dinner every day; beer and wine.*

Piazza D'Angelo

22 Miller Avenue, Mill Valley ☎ 415/388-2000

When owners Paolo and Domenico Petrone renovated this restaurant in 1990, Piazza D'Angelo became one of Mill Valley's most popular restaurants—and it still is, with large (often noisy) crowds of Marinites packing the pleasant, airy bar. The menu abounds with familiar—though not always well-executed—fare, including numerous pasta plates and several juicy entrees from the rotisserie. The calzone, stuffed with fresh ingredients like ricotta, spinach, caramelized onions, mozzarella, and sausage, come out of the pizza oven puffy and light, and the pizzas make a good lunch. Desserts are made fresh daily, and if there's a crème brûlée on the tray, don't let your server take it away. *AE, DC, MC, V; no checks; lunch Mon—Fri, dinner every day, brunch Sat—Sun; full bar.*

Cafe Soleil

37 Caledonia Street, Sausalito ☎ 415/331-9355

If you're in the mood for something healthy, good, and cheap, stop for breakfast or lunch at Cafe Soleil, a bright, cheery little cafe just off Sausalito's main strip. Along with great smoothies, the kitchen also makes wonderful soups, salads, and sandwiches at low, low prices. A popular option is to order to-go at the counter, then walk a block over to the marina for a dock-side lunch. *No credit cards; local checks only; breakfast, lunch every day; no alcohol.*

Caledonia Kitchen

400 Caledonia Street, Sausalito ☎ 415/331-0220

On the north end of Caledonia Street is the Caledonia Kitchen, the kind of place you wish was in your neighborhood. For such a little cafe it offers a lot of great (and inexpensive) choices such as gourmet sandwiches made with fresh herbs and freshly baked bread, big salads, house-made soups and chili, and entrees like herbed roast

Tiburon Budget Breakfast

For Tiburon's best budget-minded breakfast, sit at one of the checkered-clothed tables at the pleasant New Morning Cafe, which serves the morning meal all day long (1696 Tiburon Boulevard, near Main Street, Tiburon, 415/435-4315).

Mill Valley Budget Breakfast & Lunch

*Mill Valley's most popular breakfast spot is the **Dipsea Cafe,** which flips huge, delicious buttermilk and whole-wheat blueberry pancakes every day of the week (200 Shoreline Highway/Highway 1, near Tam Junction, Mill Valley, 415/381-0298). For lunch, the best tacos in Mill Valley can be had at **Joe's Taco Lounge,** an exuberant Mill Valley taqueria with cherry-red counters where locals nosh on gordo soft tacos in sets of two for only $4.50 (382 Miller Avenue at Montford and La Goma Streets, Mill Valley, 415/383-8164).*

chicken or vegetarian lasagne for around $5. Inexpensive pastries and good coffee and espresso drinks are available as well. *No credit cards; checks OK; breakfast, lunch, early dinner (till 7pm) every day; beer and wine.*

Hamburgers

737 Bridgeway, Sausalito ☎ 415/332-9471

One of the best places to eat in Sausalito also happens to be one of the cheapest: a narrow little hamburger stand called simply "Hamburgers." Look for the rotating grill in the window off Bridgeway, then stand in line. For $5 and some change, you'll get one of the best burgers in Marin. The fresh grilled chicken burgers are particularly good. Order a side of fries, grab a bunch of napkins, then head over to the park across the street. *Cash only; lunch every day; no alcohol.*

Sam's Anchor Café

27 Main Street, Tiburon ☎ 415/435-4527

Enjoy spectacular views of the bay at the ever-popular Sam's restaurant, where Bay Area residents and boaters crowd the huge outdoor deck on sunny weekends for beer, burgers, and big baskets of fries. It's the kind of place where you and your buddies can take off your shoes, order a round of margaritas, and have a fun, relaxed lunch. Other menu items include sandwiches, salads, and seafood—typical seaside cafe stuff. It's all pretty good, but the main reason people come here is for the festive scene and to soak in some precious rays of sunlight (particularly when the city's fogged in). Be sure to assign a designated driver, because the cocktails can really catch up with you. *AE, MC, V; local checks only; lunch, dinner every day, brunch Sat–Sun; full bar.*

Sweden House Bakery-Café

35 Main Street, Tiburon ☎ 415/435-9767

This small Swedish-style cafe is the premier place to go on sunny mornings for breakfast. When you're seated at the terrace sipping a hot chocolate and gazing out over the bay, all is good in the world. The gingham-covered walls adorned with copperware and kitchen utensils add a homey touch, and the lingonberry, blueberry, or apple Swedish pancakes are dynamite. A full range of breakfast fare—eggs, bacon, omelets, etc.—are all accompanied by toasted Swedish limpa bread. At lunch, there's typical American fare—sandwiches, salads, and such—but most people come for the superb breakfast. *MC, V; local checks only; breakfast, lunch every day (open till 6pm); beer and wine.*

Cheap Sleeps

Compared to San Francisco's vast array of inexpensive lodgings, it's surprising Marin County has so few. You also won't get as much bang for your buck at the budget lodgings in Marin's inland cities, so consider slumbering in San Francisco or along the Pacific Coast instead. (Cheap sleeps in Marin's coastal towns are listed in the North Coast chapter.) The following accommodations are the only budget lodgings in Mill Valley and Sausalito (Tiburon has only one hotel, and it's definitely not cheap). If you're looking for an inexpensive sleep north of Mill Valley, you'll find a handful of dull chain hotels off Highway 101, particularly around San Rafael.

If you're interested in renting a room for one or more nights in a Marin resident's home, contact Suellen Lamorte at Bed & Breakfast Exchange of Marin, a referral and reservation service specializing in noncommercial "homestays." Rates range from $55 to $150 per night (45 Entrata Avenue, San Anselmo, CA 94960; 415/485-1971).

Fireside Motel

115 Shoreline Highway (Highway 1), Mill Valley, CA 94941 ☎ 415/332-6906

The rates at the crescent-shaped Fireside are comparable to what you'd pay at the Tamalpais Motel (see below), but they seem to change hourly, depending on the mood of the flippant manager (or perhaps on whether or not she likes your shirt?). Some of the 25 rooms are ragged and stained, with mildew in the lime-green tiled showers and ancient heaters that look as if they must violate some safety code, but others have been remodeled and sport sparkling

No-Cost Camping

Three rustic tent-camping sites are available for free in various locations in the lush Marin Headlands. Camping permits must be picked up in person at the Marin Headlands Visitor Center, and reservations are accepted no more than 90 days in advance; take the Alexander Avenue exit off the Golden Gate Bridge, make an immediate left, and follow the "Marin Headlands" signs. The visitor center is at Fort Barry, at the intersection of Field and Bunker Roads, 415/331-1540.

showers, big bathroom sinks, and color-coordinated bedspreads and drapes. Ask for room 20 if you want a queen-size bed, and try for room 5 if you prefer two doubles. El Rebozo, a pricey Mexican restaurant with an adjoining workingman's bar, sits in front of the Fireside's parking lot, but doesn't do much to buffer the highway noise. Perhaps the motel's best attribute is that it's steps away from the popular Buckeye Roadhouse, 415/331-2600, which doesn't have food at budget prices, but does have a beautiful bar where you can mingle with the locals. *AE, MC, V; no checks.*

Fountain Motel

155 Shoreline Highway (Highway 1), Mill Valley, CA 94941 ☎ 415/332-1732

If you're not interested in staying in a hostel and the Travelodge (see below) is booked, here's the runner-up. For about the same rate as a Travelodge room, the Fountain Motel offers a spacious room (in fact, larger than the rooms at the Travelodge) with a king- or queen-size bed, an electric-blue tiled bathroom with a tub shower, a phone, and a 25-inch TV with cable. There are also a table and a couple of chairs in each unit, or if you'd rather be outdoors, you can sit on one of the old white picnic benches and gaze at Mount Tam. Like the rest of the area's motels, the Fountain suffers from the hustle and bustle of the highway. *AE, MC, V; no checks.*

Tamalpais Motel

680 Redwood Highway (Highway 101), Mill Valley, CA 94941
☎ 415/381-4775

This is Marin's only-if-you're-desperate cheap sleep. As you zip along the Redwood Highway and glance over at the motel's light-pink exterior, baby-blue doors, and Spanish tile roof, you might think it looks like a respectable roadside stop. But look again. Perhaps in better hands this could be a cute little place, but it's been neglected over the years, and the $89 nightly rate is rather steep for a room with mildew on the bathroom walls. In addition, the motel hugs the side of the highway, so if you're not a super-sound sleeper, you might prefer a nice campsite in the woods. To get there, exit Highway 101 on Seminary Drive and head north. *AE, DIS, MC, V; no checks.*

Travelodge

707 Redwood Highway (Highway 101), Mill Valley, CA 94941

☎ **800/578-7878 or** ☎ **415/383-0340**

There's no competition between the Travelodge and Mill Valley's other budget motels—this one wins by a long shot. The 55 guest rooms have white walls and steel-blue carpeting, with color-coordinated bedspreads and comfortable, contemporary furnishings. Each unit also has air-conditioning and cable TV with a built-in alarm clock and radio. Reading lights are mounted on the wall on either side of the queen-size bed, and there are a couple of cushioned chairs, a desk, a phone, and a bathroom with a shower stall. Unfortunately, the Travelodge sits alongside a very busy highway, but that's true of every Marin cheap sleep; if you can't fall asleep to the sound of speeding cars, bring earplugs. To reach the Travelodge, exit Highway 101 on Seminary Drive and head south. *AE, DC, DIS, MC, V; no checks; www.travelodge.com.*

Marin Headlands Hostel

Fort Barry, Building 941, Sausalito, CA 94965 ☎ **415/331-2777**

Formerly known as the Golden Gate Hostel, the Marin Headlands Hostel sits high on a hill covered with evergreen trees and pink wildflowers and is an ideal hideaway if you prefer slumbering to the sounds of crickets and birds rather than to the hooting cars and night owls of city streets. The remote locale is gorgeous, but a car is really a necessity here. Building 941 was constructed in 1907 and served as the U.S. Army infirmary; now the aging complex has 66 bunks, a fully equipped kitchen, a spacious lounge with a piano and stereo, a laundry room, and a rather weathered rec room with a pool table, Ping-Pong table, TV, and VCR (videos available at no extra charge). In the summer of 1995 the hostel opened the doors of its neighboring Building 937, formerly a private residence. This beautiful addition is spiffier than its neighbor, with its polished hardwood floors, Oriental carpets, plush couches, four carved-oak fireplaces, and 37 bunks in rooms with views of the hills and, in some cases, the Pacific. Both buildings are closed from 9:30am to 3:30pm (so you must spend the day elsewhere), linens are rented for $1, and guests are expected to help with light chores. Rodeo Beach is only a short drive or a 15-minute walk away, and numerous trails wind throughout the scenic Marin Headlands. There are a few different ways to get to the hostel, which is about 5–10 minutes from the Golden Gate Bridge, so call for directions. Arriving before sunset? Be sure to ask for the scenic route. *DIS, MC, V; no checks; www.norcalhostels.com.*

Berkeley

You can still buy tie-dyed "Berserkley" T-shirts from vendors on Telegraph Avenue, but the wild days of this now-middle-aged, upper-middle-class burg are gone. There's nary a whiff of tear gas in the air; these days most UC Berkeley students seem more interested in cramming for exams than in organizing sit-ins. Thanks to the much-disputed People's Park (owned by the university, occupied by the homeless), occasional street battles still rattle Telegraph Avenue, though pillage, not protest, seems to be the order of the day. On the other hand, the city still has an official Peace and Justice Commission and sister cities in every politically correct corner of the globe.

Although PC politics still reign in Berkeley's city government, many of its well-heeled citizens seem more concerned about the plight of their palates than the plight of the poor. Luckily for them, Berkeley continues to hold its own as one of California's culinary hot spots. Alice Waters, owner-chef of Northern California's most famous restaurant, Chez Panisse, has been at the forefront of the California cuisine revolution since 1971, when she started cooking simple French meals for groups of friends, then opened her legendary restaurant. The crowds still come to Chez Panisse (1517 Shattuck Avenue, between Cedar and Vine Streets, 510/548-5049), as well as to the numerous wannabes nearby (and not all of them require dipping into your life savings to settle the tab). Even San Franciscans cross the Bay Bridge from time to time to indulge in a big Berkeley breakfast or lunch, followed by a tour of the city's terrific bookstores and unique shops.

Exploring

If you're a newcomer to Berkeley, start your tour of the town at the world-renowned **University of California at Berkeley** (also known as UC Berkeley and Cal), the oldest and second-largest of the nine campuses comprising the UC system. Driving through the campus is virtually impossible, so park on a side street and set out on foot. The university isn't so huge that you'd get hopelessly lost if you wandered around on your own, but without a guide you might miss some of the highlights. So pick up a self-guided walking packet at the UC Berkeley Visitor Information Center (open Monday through Friday), or attend one of the free 1½-hour tours held every Sunday, Monday, and Friday at 10am and 1pm and on selected Saturdays (2200 University Avenue at Oxford, University Hall, Room 101, 510/642-5215 or 510/642-INFO).

A few paces north of the intersection of Telegraph Avenue and Bancroft Way is the university's legendary **Sproul Plaza,** where the Free Speech Movement began in 1964. Walk up the famous steps of Sproul Hall, where many demonstrators stood (and still stand) to speak their piece; pass through the double doors, and just beyond the entrance you'll see a display of photos commemorating those exciting times. Several hundred feet north of Sproul Plaza is the pretty bronzed-metal and

Buy the Book

*As any local bookworm will tell you, most of the Bay Area's best bookstores are in Berkeley. Top of the list is **Cody's Books,** and most locals agree that if you can't find a book at Cody's, it probably isn't worth reading (2454 Telegraph Avenue at Haste, Berkeley, 510/845-7852). Almost every night, nationally known literary and political writers appear at Cody's and at **Black Oak Books,** a popular purveyor of new and used titles (1491 Shattuck Avenue at Vine, Berkeley, 510/486-0698). The four-story **Moe's Books** specializes in used books and remainders (2476 Telegraph Avenue, next to Cody's, Berkeley, 510/849-2087), and a **Barnes & Noble** megastore, complete with park benches for on-the-spot reading, offers discounts on New York Times best-sellers and stocks hundreds of periodicals (2352 Shattuck Avenue at Durant, Berkeley, 510/644-0861).*

white-granite **Sather Gate,** originally the main campus entrance until the university was expanded in the '60s. If you head northeast toward the center of things, you'll spot the **Campanile** (officially named Sather Tower, though nobody calls it that), a 307-foot clock tower modeled after St. Mark's Campanile in Venice, Italy. Built in 1914, this is Cal's best-known landmark; for only 50 cents you can take the elevator to the top for a stunning view of the Bay Area. The only original building still standing on campus is just southwest of the Campanile: **South Hall,** built in 1873. Walk north past the tower and turn east on University Drive, and you'll eventually see, on your left, the Beaux Arts beauty known as the **Hearst Mining Building.** Continue east on University Drive, and at the top of the hill in a eucalyptus grove is the **Greek Theatre,** which architect Julia Morgan (of Hearst Castle fame) modeled after the amphitheater in Epidaurus, Greece. The popular theater was presented in 1903 as a gift by newspaper publisher William Randolph Hearst.

A visit to Berkeley wouldn't be complete without a stroll down bustling **Telegraph Avenue,** still the haunt of students, street people, runaways, hipsters, professors, and tarot readers. If you want a cup of joe before you go, head east on Bancroft to **Caffe Strada** (Bancroft Way at College Avenue, 510/843-5282) and nab a seat on the sunny patio, where all the architecture students get their caffeine blasts before disappearing inside the gray monstrosity across the street known as Wurster Hall. If you prefer classical music with your coffee, go to the nearby **Musical Offering** (2430 Bancroft Way, west of Telegraph Avenue, 510/849-0211), which also sells sandwiches, soup, CDs, and tapes. Start your trek down Telegraph at Bancroft, and make a loop around all the friendly street vendors hawking everything from top-quality tie-dyed shirts, dresses, and boxer shorts to handmade earrings and hand-painted ties. Along this street are some great bookstores—including **Cody's Books** (2454 Telegraph Avenue at Haste Street, 510/845-7852)—and dozens of cheap eats ranging from food carts selling burritos and hot dogs for a little more than a dollar to pizza stands like the loud, raucous, and ever-popular **Blondie's** (2340 Telegraph Avenue, between Bancroft and Durant, 510/548-1129), where you can get a giant slice of greasy pizza from a purple-haired, tongue-pierced college student for only a couple of bucks.

On Dwight Way, between Telegraph and Bowditch, is **People's Park,** famous as a site of student riots, which first flared in 1969 when the university wanted to replace the park with a dormitory (the National

Facts by Phone

Want to know what time the museums open? Or where to take your fidgety 4-year-old? Or who's playing at the Greek Theatre next week? Call Berkeley's 24-hour information hot line, an up-to-date recording with all the answers to these questions and much, much more.

Berkeley's Information Hot Line: *510/549-8710*

Press:	
101	*This Week in Berkeley*
102	*Accommodations*
103	*Museums*
104	*Performing Arts*
105	*Theaters and Events by Facility*
106	*Places of Interest*
107	*Parks and Recreational Activities*
108	*Shops*
109	*Attractions for Kids*
110	*UC Berkeley Campus*
111	*Parking*
112	*Transportation*

Guard was called in by then-governor Ronald Reagan). The university never got its dorm, but in 1991 UC officials succeeded in placing a few sand volleyball courts and basketball courts in the park, although even that sparked several protests.

Farther south in Berkeley, near the Berkeley/Oakland border, is the small **Elmwood** neighborhood shopping district, which stretches along College Avenue and crosses over Ashby Avenue. Poke your head into the tiny **Tail of the Yak** boutique (2632 Ashby Avenue, west of College, 510/841-9891) for a look at the fabulous—though pricey—displays of Central American and other art treasures. Then stroll along College, where you can pet the lop-eared baby bunnies and squawk back at the beautiful parrots at **Your Basic Bird** (2940 College Avenue, north of Ashby, 510/841-7617); dip into the huge candy jars at **Sweet Dreams** (2901 College Avenue at Russell, 510/549-1211); munch on fantastic fresh-fruit cheese danish at **Nabolom Bakery** (2708 Russell Street at College, 510/845-BAKE); and shop for clothes at numerous boutiques along College Avenue.

Tucked away near the bay in West Berkeley is the **Fourth Street**

Creepy Crawly Critters

If you really want to impress the folks back home, leave the silly "I Left My Heart in San Francisco" souvenirs at the wharf and get your hands on a live 200-pound African rock python or a spider as big as a dinner plate. Thousands of snakes, lizards, spiders, and their vertebrate friends are crawling and slithering along the walls of **East Bay Vivarium,** *an only-in-Berkeley shop boasting the largest selection of reptiles and amphibians in the nation. Stop in and take a peek at the cold-blooded critters; the Vivarium is open every day (1827 5th Street at Hearst, Berkeley, 510/841-1400).*

shopping area, where you can find bargains galore at the Crate & Barrel Outlet Store (1785 4th Street, between Hearst and Virginia, 510/528-5500). Several purveyors of high-quality, high-priced gardening gadgets line this street, along with eclectic boutiques that are fun to browse.

Several excellent museums grace this little city as well, including the highly regarded **University Art Museum** (2626 Bancroft Way, between College and Bowditch, 510/642-0808), which has a small permanent collection of modern art and frequently hosts unusual but riveting exhibitions by such artists as Robert Mapplethorpe. The **Judah L. Magnes Museum** (2911 Russell Street, off Claremont Avenue, 510/849-2710), the third-largest Jewish museum in the West, offers numerous exhibitions. A vast array of anthropological artifacts is showcased at the **Phoebe Hearst Museum of Anthropology** (in UC Berkeley's Kroeber Hall, at the corner of College Avenue and Bancroft Way, 510/643-7648). Hands-on exhibits exploring the world of lasers, holograms, and cutting-edge computers are featured at the **Lawrence Hall of Science** (on Centennial Drive, near Grizzly Peak Boulevard, in the hills above UC Berkeley, 510/642-5133), and while you're there, duck outside to see (and hear) the giant, eerie wind chimes and take a peek at the Stonehenge-like solar observatory.

Berkeley Repertory Theatre (2025 Addison Street, 510/845-4700) has a national reputation for innovative new works and experimental productions of the classics and other plays. Every summer the **California Shakespeare Festival** (100 Gateway Boulevard, Orinda, 510/548-3422) performs in an outdoor theater (bundle up, it's usually quite cold) in the Berkeley hills near Orinda. Movie mavens appreciate the **UC Theatre** (2036 University Avenue, between Milvia and Shattuck, 510/843-6267), a revival movie house where the flicks change nightly,

Emeryville

*Slivered between Berkeley, Oakland, and the bay, the tiny town of Emeryville was once a dowdy industrial area, but 10 years of manic redevelopment has turned it into one of the most intriguing urban centers in the Bay Area; computer jockeys, artists, and biotechies now abound here in their live-work spaces. Emeryville's town center is a nouveau ultramall called the **Emeryville Public Market** (5800 Shellmound Street, off Powell, Emeryville, 510/652-9300). The mall offers great inexpensive ethnic food stands; a huge **Borders Books and Music**, 510/654-1633, with a cafe and espresso bar; and the hot **Kimball's East**, 510/658-2555, a jazz and blues supper club with national headliners (cover charges range from $15 to $25).*

and the **Pacific Film Archive** (2625 Durant Avenue, in the University Art Museum, 510/642-1412), which shows underground and avant-garde movies as well as the classics. For up-to-date listings of cultural events, pick up a free copy of *The Express,* the East Bay's alternative weekly, which is available at cafes and newsstands throughout the city.

For some toe-tappin' fun, visit **Pasand Lounge** (2284 Shattuck Avenue at Bancroft, 510/848-2009) for jazz and R&B, or get blasted at **Blake's** (2367 Telegraph Avenue at Durant, 510/848-0886) with modern rock, funk, and acid jazz. You can rock out to world beat and other ethnic music at **Ashkenaz** (1317 San Pablo Avenue, near Gilman Street, 510/525-5054), or mellow out at **Freight & Salvage** (1111 Addison Street, a half block east of San Pablo, 510/548-1761), the prime Euro-folkie hangout. Live rock, jazz, folk, reggae, and other concerts are frequently held at UC Berkeley's intimate, open-air **Greek Theatre** (on Gayley Road off Hearst, 510/642-9988), a particularly pleasant place for sitting beneath the stars and listening to music on warm summer nights. **Cal Performances** presents up-and-coming and established artists of all kinds—from Sting and Seal to superstar mezzo Cecilia Bartoli; call 510/642-9988 for a schedule of events.

When you're ready for more pastoral (and free) diversions, stroll through the **Berkeley Rose Garden** (on Euclid Avenue, between Bay View and Eunice), a terraced park with 3,000 rosebushes (250 varieties) and a stellar view of San Francisco, particularly at sunset. Or walk through the 30-acre **University of California Botanical Garden** (in Strawberry Canyon on Centennial Drive, 510/642-3343), where you'll see more than 12,000 plants, including a spectacular collection of cacti

Sake It to Me

*For free sips of sake and plum wine, visit the tasting room of **Takara Sake**, the largest sake brewery in America. (708 Addison Street, off University Avenue, Berkeley, 510/540-8250; and open daily).*

from around the world, a Mendocino pygmy forest, and a Miocene-era redwood grove; free guided tours are offered on weekends. The 2,065-acre **Tilden Regional Park** (off Wildcat Canyon Road), set high in the hills above town, offers picnic sites, forests, open meadows, and miles of hiking trails, plus a steam train, a pretty merry-go-round, and a farm and nature area for kids. Tilden also boasts a beautiful **Botanical Garden,** 510/841-8732, specializing in California native plants. For kite-flying, Frisbee throwing, and a very popular playground, drive to the west end of town to the **Berkeley Marina** (at the foot of University Avenue, Adventure Playground, 510/644-8623), which extends 3,000 feet into the bay, providing a stunning view of the San Francisco skyline, the Bay Bridge, and the Golden Gate Bridge.

Cheap Eats

Bette's Oceanview Diner

1807-A 4th Street, Berkeley ☎ 510/644-3230

The best breakfast in Berkeley is served at Bette's Oceanview Diner, a small, nouveau-'40s diner that doesn't have an ocean view (or any view, for that matter) but does have red booths, chrome stools, a checkerboard tile floor, hip waitresses, the best jukebox around, and damn good breakfasts. On weekends, bring the newspaper or a good book and expect a 45-minute, stomach-growling wait, but consider the payoff: enormous, soufflé-style pancakes stuffed with pecans and ripe berries, farm-fresh eggs scrambled with prosciutto and Parmesan, outstanding omelets, corned beef hash, and the quintessential huevos rancheros. If you can't bear the wait, pop into Bette's-to-Go (BTG) next door for a prebreakfast snack. Later in the day, BTG

Oakland

In an effort to help improve Oakland's image, former Oakland Mayor Elihu Harris ordered the city to change all of the vaguely threatening "Entering Oakland" signs to read "Welcome to Oakland." Some folks scoffed at the action and said improving the city's wretched schools or cutting its alarming murder rate would be a better way to improve the city's reputation (something city officials are also working on), but others appreciated the gesture. Most residents agree that Oakland gets a bad rap. While the media keeps close tabs on the body count, few seem to notice Oakland's peaceful, integrated neighborhoods and richly diverse cultural life.

Perhaps the only aspect of Oakland that gets as much publicity as its murder tally is its sports teams. This is the home of the tall guys of the **Golden State Warriors,** and you can watch them dribble the ball across the Oakland Coliseum Arena for as little as $10; 800/479-4667. Those hotshot boys of summer, the **Oakland As,** offer bleacher seats for about $5 and better seating for a few bucks more; 510/638-0500 or 510/762-BASS. And, after abandoning Oakland for a 13-year stint in Los Angeles, the **Oakland Raiders** football team is back. Most of the Raiders tickets are sold to season-ticket holders a year in advance, but a small number are set aside and sold on a first-come, first-served basis on game days; 510/569-2121.

Oakland's less publicized but equally entertaining attractions include the **Oakland Museum,** a spectacular specimen of modern architecture with tiered Babylonian-style roof gardens and innovative displays of the art, history, and ecology of California (1000 Oak Street, between 10th and 12th Streets,Oakland, 510/238-3401); the **Paramount Theatre,** a restored art deco masterpiece offering dance performances, concerts, plays, and films from Hollywood's golden age (2025 Broadway, at 21st Street, Oakland, 510/465-6400); the **Grand Lake Theatre,** a beautifully restored Egypto-deco movie palace where weekend screenings are kicked off by a live organist (3200 Grand Avenue, at Lake Park Avenue, Oakland, 510/452-3556); and **Jack London Square,** a vast open-air shopping center on the Oakland port's waterfront, where you can stroll the scenic boardwalk, catch a ferry to San Francisco, shop at the farmers market every Sunday from 10am to 2pm year-round, or listen to free live concerts on Thursday from 5:30pm to 7:30pm from May to mid-October (at Broadway and the Embarcadero, Oakland, 510/814-6000).

Berkeley's Gourmet Ghetto

Just northwest of the university on Shattuck Avenue is the area well known as the Gourmet Ghetto, thanks to the international reputation of Chez Panisse and other terrific neighborhood restaurants. Spend some time browsing through the upscale shops, most of which are concentrated on Shattuck between Virginia and Rose Streets and in Walnut Square on Vine Street, then chow down on some excellent yet inexpensive grub. If all the hoopla about Chez Panisse has you wondering if it's worth a splurge, first consider Alice Waters's much less expensive (but also wonderful) Cafe Fanny in West Berkeley (see review below). Other favored retreats in this neighborhood are Chester's Cafe (1508-B Walnut Square, off Vine Street, Berkeley, 510/849-9995), which serves breakfast all day, lunch, and weekend brunch—search for a seat on the upstairs deck, where you can look out at the bay and the Golden Gate; Saul's old-fashioned deli (1734 Shattuck Avenue at Vine, Berkeley, 510/848-DELI), which serves breakfast from sunrise to sunset as well as classic "regular or full-figured" sandwiches; and Cha Am (1543 Shattuck Avenue at Cedar, Berkeley, 510/848-9664) for good, reasonably priced Thai food served on a glassed-in patio under towering palm trees.

offers superlative focaccia sandwiches and California pizzas. *No credit cards; local checks only; breakfast, lunch every day; beer and wine.*

Cafe Fanny

1603 San Pablo Avenue, Berkeley ☎ 510/524-5447

A very popular breakfast and lunch spot in Berkeley is Alice Waters's diminutive Cafe Fanny. This corner cafe, nestled next to the famous Acme Bread Company, can handle fewer than a dozen stand-up customers at once, but that doesn't deter anyone. On sunny weekend mornings the adjacent parking lot fills with the overflow, with the luckier customers snaring a seat at one of the few tiny outdoor tables. Named after Waters's daughter, this cafe recalls the neighborhood haunts so dear to the French. Breakfast on crunchy Cafe Fanny granola, jam-filled buckwheat crepes, or perfect soft-boiled eggs served on sourdough toast with a side of homemade jam, and sip a café au lait from a big, authentically French, handleless bowl. For lunch, order a small pizza or one of the seductive sandwiches. You won't get trencherman portions, but you'll love every crumb. *MC, V;*

*checks OK; breakfast, lunch every day; beer and wine; lesliewilson_cafefanny@
msn.com; www.onlygourmet.com/.*

FatApple's

1346 Martin Luther King Jr. Way, Berkeley ☎ 510/526-2260

When Berkeley carnivores hear the call of the wild and nothing but a big, rare burger will do, they head for FatApple's, just a few blocks northwest of the famous Shattuck strip. A prime contender in the ongoing Berkeley burger wars, FatApple's makes its burgers of exceptionally lean, high-quality ground beef and serves them on homemade wheat rolls with a variety of toppings, including five very good cheeses (ask for the creamy crumbled blue cheese). The soups, such as the rich beef barley or creamy corn chowder, are usually winners, as is the delicious spinach salad tossed with feta, walnuts, red onions, marinated black beans, and a tart vinaigrette. Standout desserts include the flaky olallieberry or pecan pie, thick jumbo milk shakes, and cheese puffs (ethereal pastry pillows stuffed with baker's cheese and dusted with powdered sugar). FatApple's is also famous for its all-American breakfasts: fluffy egg dishes, waffles, pancakes, and the like. *Cash only; breakfast, lunch, dinner every day; beer and wine.*

Panini

2115 Allston Way, Berkeley ☎ 510/849-0405

A delicious yet cost-effective way to savor the fruits of Berkeley's obsession with all things gourmet, Panini's lunch menu offers an ever-changing array of creative sandwiches served on anise- and sesame-seed baguettes. Look for exotic collages such as prosciutto, sliced pears, creamy blue-veined Cambazola (similar to blue cheese), and basil, or a mix of melted mozzarella, capocollo (a thinly sliced dry-cured ham), tomatoes, chopped olives, greens, pesto, and sun-dried tomatoes. Fresh soups and a variety of salads round out a menu that also includes fresh-squeezed juices, strong espresso, and luscious pastries. Panini is operated with the efficiency of an assembly line, but the surroundings are sufficiently inviting to encourage lingering in either the airy dining room or the ivy- and trumpet-vine-laced courtyard. *No credit cards; checks OK; lunch Mon–Fri; no alcohol.*

Picante Cocina Mexicana

1328 6th Street, Berkeley ☎ 510/525-3121

Energetic and invested with an engaging neighborhood feel, Picante Cocina Mexicana (literally "spicy Mexican kitchen") packs 'em in because of both the *muy bueno* food and the *muy pequeño* prices. Jim Maser, owner of Cafe Fanny and brother-in-law of Alice Waters, studied cooking extensively in Mexico before taking over Picante in 1994 from the previous owners. His research shines in every bite: just about everything on the menu shows his passion for fresh ingredients and careful cooking, from tortillas made by hand throughout the day to the variety of savory sauces. The chiles rellenos are outstanding, as are the two types of tamales: a chicken version bathed in a tomatillo sauce and a vegetable tamale with butternut squash and roasted chiles poblano. Best seats in the house are at one of the big, comfortable booths or outdoors on the patio on a pleasant day. *MC, V; local checks only; lunch, dinner every day, brunch Sun; beer and wine.*

Zachary's Chicago Pizza

1853 Solano Avenue, Berkeley ☎ 510/525-5950

Where the northwest border of Berkeley meets the little town of Albany is Solano, home to one of the East Bay's best pizza joints, Zachary's Chicago Pizza. For years Bay Area transplants from the East Coast complained about the wretched local pizza. Then along came Zachary's with its tasty rendition of Chicago-style deep-dish: a

This Bread's for You

Most Berkeley residents go to Steve Sullivan's famous **Acme Bread Company** to stock up on the Bay Area's best loaves (1601 San Pablo Avenue at Cedar, Berkeley, 510/524-0880). When Acme sells out of its goods (and it always does), locals head over to the **Cheeseboard**, a collectively owned bakery and vast gourmet cheese shop (1504 Shattuck Avenue at Vine, Berkeley, 510/549-3183). Two Berkeley bagel shops rival Brooklyn's best: **Boogie Woogie Bagels** (1281 Gilman Street at Santa Fe, Berkeley, 510/524-3104) and **Noah's Bagels,** a wildly popular chain that started in Berkeley on College Avenue in 1989 and now has branches as far south as Los Angeles (3170 College Avenue at Alcatraz, Berkeley, 510/654-0944; 2344 Telegraph Avenue at Durant, Berkeley, 510/849-9951; and 1883 Solano Avenue at the Alameda, Berkeley, 510/525-4447).

deep-bottom crust packed with a choice of fillings, covered with a thin second crust, and topped with tomato sauce. (The bottom crust turns crisp in the oven; the top one melts into the filling.) Try the gooey spinach, cheese, and mushroom or the chicken and spinach in a whole-wheat crust. *Cash only; lunch, dinner every day; beer and wine.*

Cheap Sleeps

Berkeley is a college town, so bear in mind that just about every accommodation has been booked three to four months in advance for May graduations; this guaranteed booking period also prompts most lodgings to jack up their rates for that month.

Campus Motel

1619 University Avenue (between McGee Avenue and California Street), Berkeley, CA 94703 ☎ 510/841-3844

Located only 5 blocks from UC Berkeley, the Campus Motel is advertised as "squeaky-clean"—and that's no lie. Many of the lodgings lining University Avenue charge a few bucks less a night, but a mildewy shower and worn-out furnishings are usually part of the package. This eggshell-white motel with red adobe roof offers 23 well-maintained rooms, each with a double or queen-size bed framed by a pine headboard; amenities such as TV, phone, and coffeemaker; and a full bath with a gleaming tiled shower. The only thing the Campus Motel doesn't have is air-conditioning, but it's still one of the best cheap sleeps near the university. *AE, MC, V; no checks.*

Flamingo Motel

1761 University Avenue (at Grant Street), Berkeley, CA 94703 ☎ 510/841-4242

Is there a city in California that doesn't have at least one ugly pink motel with a black flamingo spray-painted on its side? Berkeley is no exception, and to make matters worse, this motel is even lined with bright green indoor-outdoor carpeting, making the whole place look like an oddly reconstructed miniature-golf course. In each of the 29 rooms the drapes droop, ancient yellow carpeting covers the floors, tacky art hangs lopsidedly over the beds, and air-conditioning is nonexistent. But you'll also find reasonably clean bathrooms with showers, as well as phones, TV, and proximity to the campus (only 4 blocks away). It may be worth suffering the dreadful decor. *AE, DIS, MC, V; no checks.*

The French Hotel

1538 Shattuck Avenue ☎between Cedar and Vine Streets), Berkeley, CA 94709 ☎ 510/548-9930

Because it's in the heart of Berkeley's famed Gourmet Ghetto, with a staggering array of specialty food purveyors on all sides, you could begin and end your trip to the Bay Area at the French Hotel. Simply haul an unending stream of goodies up to your room and stagger downstairs every now and then to quaff an espresso at the hotel's cafe, where you can relax at a sidewalk table while wondering what twist of fate turned a town from a hotbed of radicalism into a haven of haute cuisine in just a few short years. This North Berkeley hotel has 18 rooms, although unfortunately only one (room 101) qualifies as a cheap sleep. That room is Berkeley's best bargain accommodation, with modern, comfortable furnishings; a very large bathroom; and a private patio with a table and chairs (smoking is permitted, too). And if you're a university or government employee or a member of the California Alumni Association, you'll get fantastic rates for most of the hotel's other rooms. *AE, DC, DIS, MC, V; no checks.*

Golden Bear Motel

1620 San Pablo Avenue ☎between University Avenue and Cedar Street), Berkeley, CA 94702 ☎ 800/525-6770 or ☎ 510/525-6770

If the French Hotel's budget room is booked (see above), go to the 42-room, Spanish-style Golden Bear Motel. For less than $50 you'll get a clean, comfortable room with full bath and, best of all, you can walk across the street in the morning and be first in line when the famed Acme Bread Company and the adjoining Cafe Fanny open their doors. Golden Bear's beds are covered in shimmering Wizard-of-Oz-green bedspreads, and each room is equipped with TV and phone. The motel is 1.5 miles from UC Berkeley, 8 blocks from a BART station, and very near the Interstate 80 on-ramp leading to San Francisco. This part of town isn't the safest place to hang out at night, though, so beware. *AE, DC, DIS, MC, V; no checks.*

Travel Inn

**1461 University Avenue ☎between Sacramento and Acton Streets),
Berkeley, CA 94702 ☎ 510/848-3840**

Drive up at night and the first thing you'll see in the parking lot is a red neon sign that says "Quiet." Whether that's a command or an advertisement isn't quite clear, but given this lodging's location—on the edge of busy University Avenue—you should ask for a room in the back just to play it safe. The classic U-shaped pink stucco building (with turquoise doors, of course) looks somewhat dingy outside, but the 42 rooms are clean and the price is right: about $35 for two people. The furnishings are your basic flea-market specials—Naugahyde chairs and rickety nightstands—but each room has a color TV and phone. Ask for a nonsmoking room if the leftover smell of cigarettes makes you gag. Pricey but primo Andronico's supermarket is across the street, and a BART station is only 2 blocks away. *AE, MC, V; no checks.*

Travelodge

**1820 University Avenue (at Martin Luther King Jr. Way), Berkeley, CA
94703 ☎ 800/578-7878 or ☎ 510/843-4262**

When the temperatures soar in the summer, most savvy Berkeley visitors book a room at the Travelodge, the only budget sleep in town with air-conditioning. But that's not all this chain hotel has to offer. The 30 light, airy rooms are quite comfortable, the full bathrooms are sparkling clean, and rooms even have a table and a couple of chairs as well as TV, phone, and fax facilities. The Travelodge is within walking distance of the university and several cafes and ethnic restaurants. Ask for a room far from the street. *AE, DC, DIS, MC, V; no checks; www.travelodge.com.*

Wine
Country

sonoma valley
napa valley

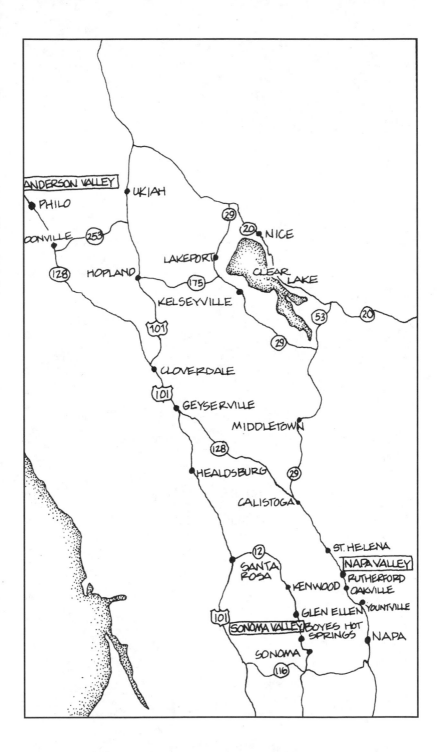

ANDERSON VALLEY
PHILO
UKIAH
29
20 NICE
OONVILLE 253
LAKEPORT
128 HOPLAND
CLEAR LAKE
175
KELSEYVILLE
53
20
101
29
CLOVERDALE
101 GEYSERVILLE
MIDDLETOWN
128
HEALDSBURG
29
CALISTOGA
ST. HELENA
12
NAPA VALLEY
SANTA ROSA
RUTHERFORD
KENWOOD
OAKVILLE
GLEN ELLEN
YOUNTVILLE
101
SONOMA VALLEY
BOYES HOT SPRINGS
NAPA
SONOMA
116

Sonoma Valley

M any California oenophiles would argue that when it comes to comparing Sonoma Valley with Napa Valley, less is definitely more: the Sonoma area is less congested, less developed, less commercial, and less glitzy than its rival. Smitten with the bucolic charm of the region, Sonomaphiles delight in wandering the valley's back roads, leisurely touring the wineries, and exploring the quaint towns along the way. Nestled between the Mayacama Mountains to the east and Sonoma Mountain to the west, the crescent-shaped valley is only 7 miles wide and 17 miles long.

But what an impressive and historical stretch of land: after all, this is where California's world-renowned wine industry was born.

The town of Sonoma, designed by Mexican general Mariano Vallejo in 1834, is set up like a Mexican pueblo, with a massive tree-covered central plaza that's often hopping with fiestas and family gatherings. Several historic adobe buildings hug the perimeter of the plaza, most of them housing wine stores, specialty food shops, boutiques, and restaurants. The plaza's most famous structure is the Sonoma Mission, the last and northernmost California mission built by Father Junípero Serra. A short drive north of Sonoma is the tiny, sleepy town of Glen Ellen, where Jack London spent the last years of his life. London fans flock here to peruse the famous author's Beauty Ranch, a vast expanse shaded by oaks, madronas, and redwoods.

Exploring

One of the joys of exploring the small city of Sonoma is that you can park your car and spend the day touring the shops and sites on foot. Begin your walk at the 8-acre Spanish-style **Sonoma Plaza,** a National Historic Landmark and the largest town square in California. In the mid-1800s the square was a dusty training ground for General Vallejo's troops, and at the turn of the 19th century a women's club transformed it into the lush park you see today, with more than 200 trees, rose gardens (look for the salmon-colored bloom called the Sonoma Rose), picnic tables and benches, a playground, and a pond swarming with ducks and their far-from-ugly ducklings. Sitting squarely in the center of the plaza is **Sonoma City Hall,** a stone Mission Revival structure built by San Francisco architect A. C. Lutgens in 1908. Note that all four sides of it are identical—Lutgens didn't want to offend any of the plaza merchants, so he gave them all the same view of his building. The city hall should look familiar to fans of the former prime-time hit "Falcon Crest," which featured it as the Tuscany County Courthouse.

Next to the city hall, on the plaza's east side, is the beautiful neo-classic brick building that houses the **Sonoma Valley Visitors Bureau** (453 1st Street E, Sonoma, 707/996-1090; open daily). Stop here for info on special events such as the annual Ox Roast, held in June, and the Valley of the Moon Vintage Festival, held in September. For $3.50 you can also get the League for Historic Preservation's self-guided walking-tour map, which outlines a one-hour stroll to 59 historic plaza buildings.

Many people come to Sonoma simply to browse the dozens of shops and galleries circling the plaza. A couple of notable establishments are **Robin's Nest** (116 E Napa Street, Sonoma, 707/996-4169), a small discount store that sells high-quality crockery, cooking utensils, and such oddities as decorative freeze-dried carrots and grapefruits; and **Readers' Books** (127 E Napa Street, on the plaza's southeast corner, Sonoma, 707/939-1779, www.readersbooks.com), a strangely configured but pleasant bookstore that stocks many of its tomes in two hard-to-find rooms in the back. This is the place to shop for best-sellers, travel guides, and children's books. For used books, stroll south of the plaza to **Chanticleer Books** (552 Broadway, on the street's east side, Sonoma,

Free Wine Country Maps by Mail

It pays to plan in advance. For a free guide to the Sonoma Valley—complete with maps to wineries, historical sites, and lodgings—just send your request to the Sonoma Valley Visitors Bureau (453 1st Street E, Sonoma, CA 95476, 707/996-1090, www.sonomavalley.com). If you wait until you get to Sonoma to pick one up, it'll cost $1.50, or $5 for the deluxe guide.

707/996-5364), which has a table stacked with good reading material at prices ranging from 50 cents to $5.

The town's beloved **Mission San Francisco Solano de Sonoma** (a.k.a. the Sonoma Mission) sits on the northeast corner of the plaza, and for a nominal fee you can tour the interior of this early 19th-century adobe structure (114 E Spain Street at 1st Street E, Sonoma, 707/938-9560). Your ticket into the mission also gives you access (provided you use it the same day) to the nearby **Sonoma Barracks** (1st Street E and E Spain Street, Sonoma), a two-story adobe structure built between 1836 and 1840 to house Mexican army troops, as well as to General Vallejo's well-preserved, yellow-and-white Victorian home, known as **Lachryma Montis**—Latin for "tears of the mountain," a reference to a mineral spring on the property (W Spain Street at 2nd Street W, Sonoma, 707/938-9559). Scattered locations notwithstanding, all of these historic structures are part of the **Sonoma State Historic Park,** 707/938-1519.

The ever-popular **Sebastiani Vineyards** (389 4th Street E, Sonoma, 800/888-5532 or 707/938-5532, www.sebastiani.com) is only 4 blocks from the Sonoma Plaza. After indulging in a few (or more) free sips of wine, walk or bicycle through the vineyards on the easy 3.25-mile paved path that leads to General Vallejo's home.

When you're ready to venture beyond the town of Sonoma, drive north about 10 miles to Jack London territory. In Sonoma County there are more places and things named after Jack London than there are women named Maria in Mexico, and this cult reaches its apex in **Glen Ellen.** This is where the author of *The Call of the Wild, The Sea Wolf,* and some 50 other books and numerous articles built his aptly named Beauty Ranch, an 800-acre spread now known as **Jack London State Historic Park** (2400 London Ranch Road, off Highway 12 and Arnold Drive, Glen Ellen, 707/938-5216, www.parks.sonoma.net). London's vineyards, piggery, horse stalls, and other ranch buildings are here, as

Sonoma Wineries

Franciscan fathers planted California's first vineyards at the Mission San Francisco Solano de Sonoma in 1823 and harvested the grapes to make their sacramental wines. Thirty-four years later, the state's first major vineyard was planted with European grape varietals by Hungarian Count Agoston Haraszthy at Sonoma's revered Buena Vista Winery. Little did the count know, however, that one day he would become widely hailed as the father of California wine—wine that is now consistently rated as some of the best in the world. Today more than 30 wineries dot the Sonoma Valley, most offering pretty picnic areas, free tours of their wine-making facilities, and, unlike many of their Napa Valley competitors, free tastings. Here's a roundup of some of Sonoma's best:

Buena Vista Winery: *California's oldest premium winery (founded in 1857) has a large estate set in a forest, picnic grounds and supplies, tours of the stone winery and the hillside tunnels, and a gallery featuring locals' artwork (18000 Old Winery Road, Sonoma, 707/938-1266).*

Château St. Jean: *This beautiful 250-acre estate with tastings in the mansion and stunning views has a self-guided tour and a picnic area (8555 Highway 12/Sonoma Highway, Kenwood, 707/833-4134, www.chateaustjean.com).*

Ferrari-Carano Vineyards and Winery: *Good chardonnay, fumé blanc, and cabernet are available in this cutting-edge facility (8761 Dry Creek Road, Healdsburg, 707/433-6700).*

Geyser Peak Winery: *This stone winery covered with ivy has pleasant gewürztraminer and riesling, beautiful hiking trails, and a great picnic area available by reservation (22281 Chianti Road, Geyserville, 800/255-9463, www.peakwines international.com).*

Gloria Ferrer Champagne Caves: *Interesting subterranean cellars offer complimentary tapas served in the tasting room and an excellent tour (23555 Highway 121, Sonoma, 707/996-7256, www.gloriaferrer.com).*

well as the cottage where he wrote (and where he died) and a beautiful stone house-turned-museum called the House of Happy Walls. Lining those walls are pieces from London's interesting and worldly art collection and personal mementos, including some of the 600 rejection letters he received from publishers (such as one from a hotshot at the *San Francisco Chronicle*), who surely must have fallen over backward in their cushy corporate chairs when London later became the highest-paid author of

Gundlach-Bundschu Winery: This grand, historic building on impressive grounds is known primarily for its red wines; picnic facilities are available (2000 Denmark Street, Sonoma, 707/938-5277, www.gunbun.com).

Kenwood Vineyards: Renowned for its reds, this winery has quaint wooden barns (9592 Highway 12/Sonoma Highway, Kenwood, 707/833-5891, www.kenwood vineyards.com).

Korbel Champagne Cellars: This ivy-covered brick building set in a redwood forest with a view of the Russian River offers informative winery tours and extensive flower gardens open for tours May through September (13250 River Road, Guerneville, 707/887-2294, www.korbel.com).

Kunde Estate Winery: This century-old winery set on 2,000 gorgeous acres of rolling hills is one of Sonoma County's largest grape suppliers and has a tasting room (10155 Highway 12/Sonoma Highway, Kenwood, 707/833-5501, www.kunde.com).

Matanzas Creek Winery: It is a beautiful drive to the winery, which has attractive facilities, outstanding chardonnay and merlot, guided tours, and picnic tables (6097 Bennett Valley Road, Santa Rosa, 707/528-6464, www.matanzas creek.com).

Sebastiani Vineyards: Sonoma's largest premium-variety winery has tours of the redwood cellar, featuring an interesting collection of carved-oak cask heads, a tasting room, and picnic tables (389 4th Street E, Sonoma, 800/888-5532 or 707/938-5532, www.sebastiani.com).

Viansa Winery and Italian Marketplace: These buildings and grounds modeled after a Tuscan village are owned by the Sebastiani family; good sauvignon blanc, chardonnay, and cabernet are offered along with gourmet Italian picnic fare and beautiful hillside picnic grounds (25200 Highway 121, Sonoma, 707/935-4700, www.viansa.com).

For a list of highly recommended Napa wineries, see the "Napa Valley Wineries" box in the Napa Valley section of this chapter.

his time. There's a $6-per-car fee to enter the park (and it's worth spending an extra buck to get the informative park map), or you may hike or ride your bike or horse in for free. Your dog can come along, too ($1 fee), though canines are restricted to certain areas.

The park is a pretty place for a **picnic,** with tables and barbecues set out under the oak and eucalyptus trees (a short walk from the parking lot). Carry your lunch to London's cottage to find the park's best table:

Russian River Valley

Mother Nature reigns supreme in Sonoma County's Russian River Valley, where folks prefer to sip their cabernets and chardonnays amid the company of redwoods, fruit orchards, and sandy river beaches instead of chichi restaurants and wineries bustling with city slickers. Everything moves at a leisurely pace here, from the weekend revelers floating down the river in inner tubes to the cars cruising the winding roads. Pack a picnic and spend the day touring some of the 60 wineries sprinkled throughout the vast valley, or plunk down in a beach chair along the river and call it a day. If you decide you like this region so much you want to stay a night or two, you can get budget-lodging and campground referrals through the Russian River Region Visitor Information Center (14034 Armstrong Woods Road, Guerneville, CA 95446, 800/253-8800 or 707/869-9212) or the Sonoma County Convention & Visitors Bureau (5000 Roberts Lake Road, Suite A, Rohnert Park, CA 94928, 800/326-7666 or 707/586-8100). For a free copy of the excellent "Russian River Wine Road" map, which provides a summary of the valley's wineries, contact Russian River Wine Road, PO Box 46, Healdsburg, CA 95448, 707/433-6782.

__Healdsburg__ is the heart of the Russian River Valley, and it's one tourist town whose charm seems completely unforced. Boutiques and bakeries surround a pretty, tree-lined plaza where you can sit and read the newspaper while munching on pastries from the marvelous Downtown Bakery & Creamery (308-A Center Street, Healdsburg, 707/431-2719). In summer, nothing beats paddling down the glorious Russian River past vineyards and secret swimming holes in a canoe or kayak rented from W. C. "Bob" Trowbridge Canoe Trips (20 Healdsburg Avenue, Healdsburg, 800/640-1386 or 707/433-7247, www.trowbridgecanoe.com). Come evening, catch a flick at the Raven Theater, the Wine Country's best movie house for new releases and art films (115 North Street, Healdsburg, 707/433-5448).

Southwest of Healdsburg is the Russian River Valley town of __Guerneville,__ which was explored by the Russians in the 1840s and grew into one of the busiest logging centers in the West by the 1880s. More recently, it was a haven for bikers (the sort who wear leather, not Lycra) before becoming a hangout for hippies. Now it's a summer mecca for gays and lesbians as well as naturalists drawn by the beauty of the land. The town is a good place to kick off a nature expedition or a tour of the area's wineries. __Armstrong Woods State Reserve__ boasts a peaceful grove of spectacular ancient redwoods and a variety of hiking trails (17000 Armstrong Woods Road, Guerneville, 707/869-2015). Equestrians should saddle up at Armstrong Woods Pack Station, which offers half- and full-day horseback rides *with gourmet lunches by reservation only; 707/579-1520. Check out Johnson's Beach, which is home to the wildly popular Russian River Jazz Festival, held every September; 707/869-3940. Another crowd pleaser is the annual Stumptown Days Parade and Russian River Rodeo held on Father's Day weekend; 707/869-1959. For a good, simple meal, grab a bite at **Burdon's** (15405 River Road, Guerneville, 707/869-2615) or **Sweet's River Grill** (16521 Main Street, Guerneville, 707/869-3383).*

*Farther south on Highway 116 is **Forestville**, a tiny hamlet surrounded by redwoods. From here you can launch an all-day canoe trip down the gentle Russian River, where you'll see turtles, river otters, egrets, and great blue herons. Set forth from Burke's Canoe Trips, 707/887-1222, from May through September, and someone there will pick you up 10 miles down the river and take you back to your car. While you're in the area, visit Koslowski Farms (5566 Gravenstein Highway, Forestville, 707/887-1587), a family farm that has turned into a gourmet-food business. Try their apple butter, jam, vinegar, and—what they're most famous for—fresh berries.*

sitting next to a goldfish pond overlooking the grapevines. Hard-core hikers should plan to spend the day trekking to Bathhouse Lake and up Sonoma Mountain's steep slopes (carry water), which are blanketed with grassy meadows and forests of madrona, manzanita, redwood, and Douglas fir. Or consider letting the friendly folks at the Sonoma Cattle Company (based in the park) saddle up a horse for you. Call for the lowdown on their **guided horseback trips** (reservations are required, 707/996-8566, www.thegrid.net/trailrides). A ticket to Jack London Park allows you free entrance (on the same day only) to the spectacular 2,700-acre **Sugarloaf Ridge State Park** (2605 Adobe Canyon Road, 3 miles east of Highway 12, Kenwood, 800/444-7275 for camping reservations, www.reserveamerica.com), a 20-minute drive north. Sugarloaf has 25 miles of hiking and horseback-riding trails (with great views from the ridge), guided horseback rides, 50 tent campsites, and a horse corral.

Cheap Eats

Café Citti

9049 Sonoma Highway, Kenwood ☎ 707/833-2690

Café Citti (pronounced CHEAT-ee) is a roadside Italian trattoria that serves hearty, home-cooked Italian fare for low, low prices. It's a sort of do-it-yourself place: first you order from the huge menu board displayed above the open kitchen, then find a vacant table inside or at the shaded patio, and wait for a server to bring you your food. Some of our favorite dishes are the focaccia sandwiches, tangy Caesar salad, green bean salad, and the roasted rotisserie chicken stuffed with rosemary and garlic. There's also an array of freshly made pastas that come with a variety of sauces such as zesty marinara. Everything on the menu is available to go and makes for excellent picnic fare. *MC, V; no checks; lunch, dinner every day; beer and wine.*

Basque Boulangerie Café

460 1st Street E, Sonoma ☎ 707/935-7687

One of the most popular cafes in the town of Sonoma is the Basque Boulangerie Café, where every morning you'll always find locals lining up for a light breakfast and strong coffee. Just about everything on the menu is made in-house: quiche, sandwiches, cookies, soups, pastries, desserts, cinnamon bread, salads, and—their specialty— sourdough Basque breads. There are also daily lunch specials, which are listed on the chalkboard out front, such as a grilled veggie sandwich with smoked mozzarella cheese for under $5. There's not much seating aside from a few tables on the sidewalk, so order to-go and dine alfresco at the pretty plaza across the street. *No credit cards; local checks only; breakfast, lunch every day; beer and wine.*

Cucina Viansa

400 1st Street E, Sonoma ☎ 707/935-5656

There's certainly no shortage of wonderful things to snack on at this classy deli and wine bar owned by Sam and Vicki Sebastiani (the same couple who own and run Viansa Winery). A small cadre of young men are behind the counter slicing meats, pouring wines, and

Cheesy but Free

There may be no such thing as a free lunch, but in Sonoma there are free snacks. When you tour the historic plaza, amble over to the north side and step into the **Sonoma Cheese Factory,** *where more than a dozen cheeses are made on the premises and set out for you to sample. Try their famous Sonoma Jack, creamy Havarti, tender Teleme, and a variety of Jack cheeses spiked with hot peppers, onions, caraway, and pesto. The Viviani family has been making cheese here since 1931, and you can watch as workers in navy aprons and white hard hats whip up a batch in the 10,000-pound-capacity vats in the back. Call ahead for cheese-making schedules (2 W Spain Street, Sonoma, 707/996-1931, www.sonoma cheese.com).*

scooping gelato for the numerous locals and tourists who fill the place daily. First sample the preserves and jams near the entrance, then decide what you want for lunch today: roasted turkey sandwich on herbed focaccia; herb-marinated rotisserie chicken, lamb, duck, pork, rabbit; pasta; salad; fruit; cheese—the list goes on. On the opposite side of the deli is a wine bar featuring all of Viansa's current releases for both tasting and purchase. There's also a small selection of microbrewed beers on tap, a *gelateria* offering rich Italian ice cream, and live jazz music on Friday and Saturday nights. *AE, DIS, MC, V; no checks; lunch, dinner every day; beer and wine.*

La Casa

121 E Spain Street, Sonoma ☎ 707/996-3406

Enchiladas, chimichangas, fajitas, and numerous other south-of-the-border favorites are served steaming hot at this popular Mexican restaurant on the Sonoma Plaza. On sunny days ask for a table on the patio and start the feast with their great black-bean soup or their ceviche made of fresh snapper marinated in lime juice with cilantro and salsa, served on crispy tortillas. The house-made tamales—stuffed with tender chicken and topped with a mild red-chili sauce—and the deep-dish chicken enchiladas are *muy bueno* as well. One thing's for sure: you won't leave hungry. *AE, DIS, MC, V; no checks; lunch, dinner every day; full bar.*

Wild Thyme Cafe

165 W Napa Street, Sonoma ☎ 707/996-0900

The Wild Thyme Cafe is a newcomer to Sonoma, and from the local feedback we're getting, it's a welcome one. It's a sort of upscale deli—replete with earthen tile flooring, rough-hewn wood furniture, lots of sunshine—that serves inexpensive yet high-quality foods for here or to go. For breakfast, which is served from 7am to 11am, try their fantastic old-fashioned waffles served with real maple syrup; the Sonoma sourdough French toast and fresh poached eggs also do the trick. Being a deli, there's the usual array of sandwiches—such as roast turkey on focaccia with jalapenos, jack cheese, and arugula—as well as pastas, soups, salads, and a short selection of heartier items like roast chicken, baby back ribs, and meatloaf served with a side of garlic mashed potatoes and fresh green beans. WTC also carries the requisite Sonoma wines, olive oils, and cheeses, in addition to coffee drinks, pastries, and picnic supplies. When the sun's out be sure to find a vacant table in the back patio surrounded by a rose garden. *MC, V; local checks only; breakfast, lunch, dinner Sun—Tues; beer and wine.*

Cheap Sleeps

*Note: If you're having trouble finding an affordable accommodation (and there are very few in the Wine Country), call the **Sonoma Valley Visitors Bureau** (707/996-1090). They might be able to find a budget lodging that has a vacancy. You can also try the **Bed-and-Breakfast Association of Sonoma Valley** (800/969-4667) which will refer you to one of their member B&Bs. Be aware, however, that most Wine Country B&B rates start at well over $100.*

Jack London Lodge

13740 Arnold Drive, Glen Ellen, CA 95442 ☎ 707/938-8510

For those who really want to get away from the city scene, this white, two-story, wisteria-draped lodge offers 22 quiet rooms next to rippling, tree-lined Sonoma Creek. The lodge is a short drive from the town of Sonoma, near several wineries and the beautiful Jack London State Historic Park. The rates are reasonable, but as usual in Wine Country, they creep above the Cheap Sleeps price range in the summer. Ask for one of the upstairs rooms, with a view of the trees. The decor is simple if somewhat bland, and each unit has a brass bed (either one king-size or two queen-size), private bath, cable TV, a portable radiator, and air-conditioning. A continental breakfast is included on weekends and holidays, and daily in the summer. The swimming pool sits alongside the creek, but its surrounding chain-link fence is an eyesore in spite of the vines of red roses planted all around. Next door is London's Grill, an attractive, moderately priced restaurant, and the wonderful Jack London Saloon, where you can admire London memorabilia and hoist a glass to the author's memory. *MC, V; checks OK.*

Best Western Sonoma Valley Inn

5550 2nd Street W, Sonoma, CA 95476 ☎ 800/334-5784 or ☎ 707/938-9200

Okay, so Sonoma's Best Western isn't exactly romance central, but it's relatively inexpensive, it's in a good location near the town plaza, kids are welcome, and on summer weekends it may be the only place left with a vacancy. Although the guests rooms are woefully plain, the free benefits are many: continental breakfast delivered to your room each morning, a gift bottle of white table wine from Kenwood Vineyards sitting in the refrigerator, cable TV with HBO, and either a balcony or deck overlooking the inner courtyard. The hotel also has an enclosed pool and gazebo-covered spa, which come in really handy on typically scorching-hot summer afternoons. *AE, CB, DC, MC, V; no checks.*

El Pueblo Inn

896 W Napa Street, Sonoma, CA 95476 ☎ 800/900-8844 or ☎ 707/996-3651

If you're looking for just an inexpensive place to stay and you're not too concerned with prime location and goose-down pillows, consider the El Pueblo Inn, a modest little hotel located about 8 blocks west of Sonoma Plaza. The guest rooms' exposed-brick walls, light-wood furnishings, and post-and-beam construction lend a sort of ersatz rusticity to them (but not much). The usual budget accommodation perks are included, such as air-conditioning, television, coffeemaker, and use of the inn's outdoor heated pool. Since this is one of the only budget lodgings in town, be sure to make reservations as far in advance as possible. *AE, DIS, MC, V; no checks.*

Sonoma Chalet

18935 5th Street W, Sonoma, CA 95476 ☎ 707/938-3129

On the outskirts of downtown Sonoma lies this secluded Swiss-style farmhouse overlooking a 200-acre ranch. It's quite the bucolic setting with its roving ducks, geese, and chickens, and the guest-room decor—country quilts, woodstoves, cozy furnishings—fit the theme well. Although the private cottages are well out of budget range, the Chalet does have two relatively inexpensive guest rooms that share a bath. The $85 rate may seem steep, but it includes a breakfast of fruit, yogurt, pastries, and cereal, which is served either in the country kitchen or in your room. *AE, MC, V; checks OK; www.sonomachalet.com.*

Sonoma Valley Inn

550 2nd Street W (off W Napa Street), Sonoma, CA 95476 ☎ 800/334-5784 or ☎ 707/938-9200

This 75-room hotel is part of the Best Western chain and is located off a busy street across from a supermarket, but you won't care about all that once you see how spacious, tidy, and well appointed the rooms are. Standard features include a private bath, cable TV, air-conditioning, mini-fridge, gift bottle of wine, continental breakfast delivered to your door, and a tiny enclosed patio. The floral bedspreads obviously didn't come from Sears, and even the art is more upscale than you'd expect in a chain hotel. In addition, most rooms have a wood-burning fireplace. The landscaped courtyard with a swimming pool, fountain, and gazebo-covered Jacuzzi will prompt you to scratch your head and wonder if you can actually afford to stay here. Well, if you come in the off-season, it'll cost only about $75 a night (peak-season customers pay triple those rates). *AE, DC, DIS, MC, V; checks OK; www.sonomavalleyinn.com.*

Napa Valley

Despite the plethora of nouveau chateaus, fake French barns, and gimcrack stores selling cabernet-flavored jelly beans, Napa Valley is still one of Northern California's most magical spots. In early spring, the hills are a vibrant green, bright-yellow mustard blossoms poke up between the grapevines, and stands of fruit trees burst into showy flower. In summer, tourists flood the valley and its 250 wineries, cranking up the energy level a few notches and conferring a patina of glamour and excitement that some locals delight in and others deplore. Later, after the grape harvest, the vineyards turn a bright autumnal scarlet, and the region's quaint, Old West–style towns assume a more relaxed, homey atmosphere. At any time of year, the Napa Valley is a great area for wine tasting, hiking, picnicking, shopping, eating, exploring historic sites, and soaking in mud baths or hot springs—activities that won't leave you bankrupt as long as you bypass the ritzier resorts and restaurants.

The 35-mile-long valley is home to some of the most famous wineries in the world. Many of them are clustered along scenic Highway 29 and the verdant Silverado Trail, two parallel roads running the length of the region and through such quaint little towns as Yountville, Oakville, St. Helena, and Calistoga. The valley is a zoo on weekends—especially in summer and early fall, when traffic on narrow Highway 29 rivals rush hour in the Bay Area. Wise Wine Country visitors plan their trips here for weekdays, the misty months of winter, or early spring, when room rates are lower and everything's less crowded, but the valley is no less spectacular.

Exploring

At the southernmost end of Napa Valley is the pretty, sprawling town of **Napa,** where about half the county's 114,800 residents live. Although its name is synonymous with wine, most of the wineries are actually several miles north of town. The city, founded in 1848, is well known for its imposing Victorian structures, many of them in the downtown area near the Napa River. Introduce yourself by taking a self-guided walking tour of downtown Napa's architectural gems. A detailed map highlighting everything from a Victorian Gothic church to an art deco brewery and a Beaux-Arts bank is available for free at the **Napa Valley Conference and Visitors Bureau** (1310 Napa Town Center, between Pearl and Clay Streets, Napa, 707/226-7459, www.napavalley.com), or you may choose from a half dozen 25-cent walking-tour maps sold by **Napa County Landmarks** (1026 1st Street at Main Street, in the Community Preservation Center, Napa, 707/255-1836). If you have time for only a quick tour, walk along Main Street, which crosses the river. At the south end of Main, adjacent to Veteran's Park on the river's west bank, is a handsome century-old building that's now home to **Downtown Joe's Restaurant and Brewery** (see Cheap Eats below), a great place to have a beer and relax on the outdoor patio.

A couple of blocks north on Main the locals kick back at the **Napa Valley Coffee Roasting Company** (948 Main Street at 1st Street, Napa, 707/224-2233), a great little spot for a cup of freshly brewed java. Across the street at **Copperfield's** (1005 1st Street, Napa, 707/252-8002), you'll find new and used books at reasonable prices.

About 9 miles north of Napa, just off Highway 29 where the hills are covered with grapevines, is the tiny town of **Yountville,** home of Moet et Chandon's Napa Valley–based winery, **Domaine Chandon.** Yountville was founded in the mid-19th century by pioneer George Clavert Yount, reportedly the first American to settle in Napa Valley, and it's now the site of some of the best (and priciest) restaurants in Wine Country. In the heart of Yountville is the beautiful brick complex now known as **Vintage 1870** (6525 Washington Street, Yountville, 707/944-2451, www.vintage 1870.com), a touristy mall with a few dozen overpriced shops and a handful of restaurants. The building was erected in 1870 as a winery, and

Clear Lake

Clear Lake, California's largest freshwater lake, once had more than 30 wineries ringing its shore, but Prohibition put an end to all that in 1919. The land was converted to walnut and Bartlett-pear orchards, and only in the last few decades have the grapes (and the wineries) been making a comeback. This area north of Napa County may one day become as celebrated as Napa and Sonoma, but unlike these trendy stepsisters to the south, there ain't nothin' nouveau about Clear Lake. Country music wafts from pickup trucks, bored (and bared) youths wander the roads (perhaps in search of their shirts), and there's generally not a lot going on until the weekend boaters and fishers arrive. Clear Lake's annual blowout is the Fourth of July festival, when thousands of born-again patriots amass (and timorous locals split) for a three-day, sunburnt orgy of flag-waving, fireworks, and water-skiing.

If you want to dive into the aquatic activities, boats of all shapes and sizes—as well as Jet Skis, Toobies, and Wave-Runners—can be rented at **Mike's Watersports** (6235 Old Highway 53, Clearlake, 707/994-6267) or from **On the Waterfront** (60 Third Street, Lakeport, 707/263-6789). Clear Lake also draws crowds eager to snag some of its largemouth bass, catfish, perch, and crappie. Although the lake has earned the title of "Bass Capital of the West," there aren't any shops renting fishing equipment, so you'll have to tote your own or purchase gear at K-Mart (2019 S Main Street, Lakeport, 707/263-9305).

With its small, old-fashioned downtown, **Lakeport** is the prettiest town on Clear Lake. Formerly known as Forbestown (after early settler William Forbes), the area is usually very peaceful until people from outlying cities pack up their all-terrain vehicles and caravan out here in the summer for fishing, camping, swimming, water-skiing, and wine tasting. **Clear Lake State Park,** on the southwest side of the lake, is one of the area's main draws, with its campground, miles of hiking trails, and beaches (on Soda Bay Road, south of Lakeport, 707/279-4293). Folks also flock to Lakeport every Labor Day weekend for the Lake County Fair, featuring 4-H exhibits, livestock auctions, horse shows, and a carnival (Lake County Fairgrounds, 401 Martin Street, Lakeport, 707/263-6181). Wine lovers stop at Kendall-Jackson Winery, one of the most popular wineries in Lake County, for a taste of the barrel-fermented chardonnay, Johannisberg riesling, sauvignon blanc, and cabernet sauvignon and a picnic in the gazebo (600 Matthews Road, off Highland Springs Road, Lakeport, 707/263-9333).

For more information on Clear Lake and its surrounding towns and wineries, call or drop by the **Lake County Visitor Information Center** (875 Lakeport Boulevard, Vista Point, Lakeport, 800/LAKESIDE or 707/263-9544, www.lakecounty.com).

Napa Valley Wineries

Ever since Napa's wineries became world-renowned, millions of people from all over have journeyed here each year to see their favorite vintners in action. Most of the wine makers love the attention, although the onslaught of visitors has prompted many to charge a small wine-tasting fee. In addition, some wineries now require reservations for taking a tour (but don't be deterred—it's mainly to control the crowd and make sure someone's there to show you around).

As you whiz along the road past signs for some of the most famous wineries in the world, it's tempting to pull over at every one. But do yourself a favor and follow a tip from veteran tasters: pick out the four or five wineries you're most interested in visiting over a two-day period, and stick to your itinerary. Touring more than two or three a day overwhelms and exhausts even the most intrepid connoisseur, although if you really want to cover several in a short period, skip the tours and stick to the tastings. If you're new to the wine-touring scene, rest assured that you won't ever be pressured to buy any of the wines you've sampled—the vintners are just delighted to expose you to their products (besides, you'll often find much better prices at some of the good wine stores in town). Here's a roster of some of Napa's most popular wineries, many of which offer free tours:

Beaulieu Vineyards: *This historic estate—nicknamed "BV"—is famous for its cabernet (1960 St. Helena Highway, Rutherford, 707/963-2411, www.bv-wine.com).*

Beringer Vineyards: *As Napa Valley's oldest continuously operating winery, this stately, old Rhineland-style mansion has good tours of the vineyards and caves and is well known for its chardonnay and cabernet (2000 Main Street, St. Helena, 707/963-7115).*

Château Montelena Winery: *A stunning French château-style winery built of stone is in a beautiful setting including a lake with two islands; celebrated for its chardonnay (1429 Tubbs Lane, Calistoga, 707/942-5105, www.montelena.com).*

now it's listed on the National Register of Historic Places.

If you continue north on this scenic stretch of Highway 29, you'll drive smack through the center of **St. Helena,** which has come a long way since its days as a rural Seventh-Day Adventist village. On St. Helena's Victorian Old West–style Main Street (a.k.a. Highway 29), farming-supply stores now sit stiffly next to chic women's clothing boutiques and upscale home furnishings stores. It's a great place to shop—if you've got money to spare. If you don't, take a picnic lunch or supper

Clos Pegase: *This stunning, modern facility designed by architect Michael Graves has grand outdoor sculpture, a "Wine in Art" slide show, and interesting guided tours of the winery, caves, and art collection (1060 Dunaweal Lane, Calistoga, 707/942-4982, www.clospegase.com).*

Domaine Chandon: *Here you'll find good sparkling wine, a handsome building and location with four-star (expensive) dining room, and fantastic guided tours (1 California Drive, Yountville, 707/944-2280, www.dchandon.com).*

The Hess Collection Winery: *This stone winery in a remote, scenic location is well known for its cabernet sauvignon and chardonnay, contemporary American and European art showcased in a dramatic building, and a good self-guided tour (4411 Redwood Road, Napa, 707/255-1144).*

Merryvale Vineyards: *This historic stone building offers daily tastings and informative and thorough tasting classes on Saturday mornings by appointment; Merryvale is known for its chardonnay (1000 Main Street, St. Helena, 707/963-7777, www.merryvale.com).*

Robert Mondavi Winery: *This huge, world-famous winery in a Mission-style building has excellent tours and a famous cooking school (7801 St. Helena Highway, Oakville, 707/226-1335, www.robertmondaviwinery.com).*

Schramsberg Vineyards: *Attractive, historic facilities and extensive caves offer first-rate sparkling wines and interesting, educational guided tours (1400 Schramsberg Road, Calistoga, 707/942-4558, www.schramsberg.com).*

Sterling Vineyards: *An excellent self-guided tour through an impressive, white Mediterranean-style complex perched high on a hill is accessed via an aerial tramway (for a fee) offering splendid views; the vast tasting room also has great views (1111 Dunaweal Lane, Calistoga, 707/942-3344, www.sterlingvineyards.com).*

For a list of highly recommended Sonoma wineries, see the "Sonoma Valley Wineries" box in the Sonoma Valley section of this chapter.

to **Lyman Park** (on Main Street, between Adams and Pine Streets, St. Helena), and sit on the grass or in the beautiful white gazebo, where bands sometimes set up for free summer concerts. You can also rent bicycles for about $7 an hour (or $25 a day) at **St. Helena Cyclery** and pedal your way around the valley (1156 Main Street, St. Helena, 707/963-7736; open daily).

Leaving downtown St. Helena and heading north toward Calistoga, you'll pass under the **Tunnel of the Elms** (also called the Tree Tunnel), a fantastic row of dozens of elm trees arched across Main Street (Highway

29) in front of **Beringer Vineyards.** The trees were planted by the Beringer brothers more than 100 years ago, and their interlaced branches form a gorgeous canopy about a quarter mile long. Beyond Beringer are two parks popular for hiking and picnics. **Bale Grist Mill State Historic Park** (3369 Highway 29 at Bale Grist Mill Road, 3 miles north of St. Helena, 707/963-2236) holds a historic flour mill built in 1846 by a British surgeon named Bale. The 36-foot wooden waterwheel still grinds grain into meal and flour on weekends. If the park looks familiar, perhaps you saw it featured in the 1960 film *Pollyanna.* Next door is the 1,800-acre **Bothe-Napa Valley State Park,** offering about 100 picnic spots with barbecues and tables, a swimming pool open from mid-June through Labor Day, and 50 campsites (call 707/942-4575 for general information and 800/444-PARK for camping reservations, www.cal-parks.ca.gov). You can even hike from one park to the other by following the moderately strenuous 1.2-mile History Trail.

Water-sports enthusiasts and anglers in search of trout, bass, crappie, catfish, and silver salmon should make the long haul east to Napa Valley's **Lake Berryessa,** the second-largest artificial lake in the state (after Shasta). The 21-mile-long, 3-mile-wide lake has boat launches, berths, picnic areas, campsites, 168 miles of shoreline, and marinas with boat and fishing rentals (on Berryessa Knoxville Road, via Steel Canyon Road or Pope Canyon Road, Napa Valley).

Sitting pretty at Napa Valley's northernmost end is the charming little spa town of **Calistoga,** where mud baths, mineral pools, and massages are still the main attractions. The city was founded in the mid-19th century by California's first millionaire, Sam Brannan, who had made a bundle of cash provisioning miners during the Gold Rush. Brannan quickly recognized the value of Calistoga's mineral-rich hot springs, and in 1859 he purchased 2,000 acres of the Wappo Indian hot springs land, built a first-class hotel and spa, named the region Calistoga (a combination of the words California and Saratoga), and watched his fortunes grow as affluent San Franciscans paraded in for a relaxing respite from city life. Generations later, spa-seeking city slickers are still doing that; these days, however, more than a dozen enterprises touting the magical restorative powers of mineral baths line the town's Old West–style streets. You'll see an odd combo of stressed-out CEOs and earthier types shelling out their dough for a chance to soak away their worries and get the kinks rubbed out of their necks. While Calistoga's spas and resorts are far from glamorous, many offer body treatments

Mind Your Beezwax

Kids and candle collectors alike get a kick out of a quick roadside stop at Hurd Beeswax Candles, where you can peer through a small window at thousands of honeybees working in their hive. Look for the little brown doors covering the hive in the center of the shop, pull them open to let in the light, and then watch (the busybodies like to do their thing in the dark). On the other side of the store you can see how candle makers turn the beeswax into luminaries of all shapes and sizes (3020 St. Helena Highway, in the Freemark Abbey complex near Brava Terrace restaurant, 2 miles north of St. Helena, 707/963-7211; open daily).

and mud baths you won't find anywhere else in this part of the state. If you decide to splurge on a spa treatment, first check for discount coupons in the town's free publications, such as "California Visitors Review" and "Inside Napa Valley," distributed in area hotels, businesses, and visitors bureaus.

After you've steamed or soaked, head over to the **Calistoga Inn**'s (1250 Lincoln Avenue, at the bridge, Calistoga, 707/942-4101, www. napabeer. com) pretty outdoor patio for a tall, cool drink, or try one of their home-brewed beers and a sandwich from the grill. Once you're rejuvenated, stroll down the main street and browse through the numerous quaint shops marketing everything from French soaps and antique armoires to silk-screened T-shirts and saltwater taffy. The **Calistoga Bookstore** (1343 Lincoln Avenue, Calistoga, 707/942-4123) carries a great selection of travel guides and kids' books, and provides a browser-friendly couch in back. For a look back at Calistoga's pioneer past, stop by the **Sharpsteen Museum** (1311 Washington Street, off Lincoln Avenue, Calistoga, 707/942-5911), created by Walt Disney animator and Oscar-winning producer Ben Sharpsteen.

Just outside of town you can marvel at the **Old Faithful Geyser** (1299 Tubbs Lane, 2 miles north of Calistoga, 707/942-6463, www.old faithfulgeyser.com; open daily), which faithfully shoots a plume of 350-degree mineral water 60 feet into the air at regular intervals. Other natural wonders abound at the **Petrified Forest** (4100 Petrified Forest Road, off Highway 128, 6 miles north of Calistoga, 707/942-6667, www. petrifiedforest.org; open daily), where towering redwoods were turned to stone by a volcanic eruption about 3 million years ago. You can read all about the fascinating event and the world's largest petrified trees at the museum in the gift shop.

For a splendid view of the entire valley, hike through the beautiful, rugged redwood canyons and oak-madrona woodlands in **Robert Louis Stevenson State Park** to the top of 4,343-foot **Mount St. Helena**—a rigorous 10-mile hike round-trip, so carry water. The impoverished Stevenson and his wife, Fanny Osbourne, spent their honeymoon here in an abandoned Silverado Mine bunkhouse in 1880, a site that inspired Stevenson's *Silverado Squatters*. The author was so taken by Mount St. Helena, the highest point in Napa County, that he used it as his model for Spyglass Hill in *Treasure Island*. The park is just off Highway 29, 8 miles north of Calistoga, 707/942-4575.

Cheap Eats

Bosko's

1364 Lincoln Avenue, Calistoga ☎ 707/942-9088

Bosko's is exactly the kind of place we budget-minded travelers are always searching for: a friendly, casual restaurant serving big portions of hot, tasty Italian food for well under $10 a plate. The sawdust on the floor is the first clue that Bosko's ain't ritzy; that, and you have to place your own order and find your own table. You can dine at either the huge U-shaped counter or at one of the tables topped with red-and-white-checkered tablecloths. The menu offers 16 versions of pasta that are made to order, as well as 10 kinds of pizzas, several types of hot sandwiches, fresh salads, and darn good minestrone soup. Wine? Sure, just pick a bottle from the wine rack and serve yourself. *MC, V; local checks only; lunch, dinner every day; beer and wine.*

Pacifico

1237 Lincoln Avenue, Calistoga ☎ 707/942-4400

The Pacifico Mexican restaurant in Calistoga doesn't look like much from the outside, but inside it sports quite the fiesta atmosphere with its colorful Latino artwork, enormous potted palm trees, and an elaborately decorated bar offering 40 different kinds of premium tequilas. The extensive menu goes beyond the standard Mexican fare, offering reasonably priced regional cuisine such as Enchiladas del Ray (filled with Chihuahua cheese and covered with *chile verde* sauce),

Tacos de Oaxaqueños (grilled, marinated chicken tacos topped with *guajillo chile* salsa), and Mole del Pueblo—chicken mole with chayote and potato, served with rice and tortillas. Gorge yourself on reduced-priced margaritas and tacos during Fiesta Hour, which happens every Monday through Friday from 4:30 to 6pm. *MC, V; local checks only; lunch, dinner every day; full bar.*

Smokehouse Café

1458 Lincoln Avenue, Calistoga ☎ 707/942-6060

The Smokehouse Café is a meat-eater's paradise, offering a great selection of house-smoked meats and addictively good spareribs. We always start off the gluttony with an order of Sacramento delta crawfish cakes and then move on to husk-roasted Cheyenne corn, a half slab of ribs, and a side of house-made sausages. For dessert, try the Smokehouse slow pig sandwich. The clincher, though, is the fresh-baked, all-you-can-eat cornbread dipped in pure cane syrup that comes with every meal. *MC, V; local checks only; breakfast, lunch, dinner every day (closed Tue–Wed Jan and Feb); beer and wine.*

Alexis Baking Company and Café

1517 3rd Street, Napa ☎ 707/258-1827

A Napa favorite for breakfast, lunch, and early dinner is the Alexis Baking Company and Café (or ABC, as the locals call it). You can bet that there's a line out the door on weekend mornings, and once you sample their breakfast specialties, such as pumpkin pancakes with sautéed pears or pumpkin-spice muffins, you'll know why. The lunch dishes range from fusilli pasta to roast lamb sandwiches, grilled chicken, and lentil-orzo salad. For dessert try the ultradecadent chocolate-caramel cake. The ABC is also a great place to pack your picnic basket. *No credit cards; checks OK; breakfast, lunch every day; beer and wine.*

Downtown Joe's Restaurant and Brewery

902 Main Street, Napa ☎ 707/258-2337

Downtown Joe's may sound pedestrian, but its key downtown location, great microbrews, hearty food, and inviting outdoor patio have made it one of the most popular restaurants in town. The menu offers a wide array of dishes ranging from omelets and oysters to fresh seafood specials, pasta, burgers, and steaks at reasonable prices. For the best brew prices, come during happy hour from 4 to 6pm Monday through Friday for $2.50 pints and free appetizers, plus a drawing every half hour to win free stuff. Downtown Joe's even makes its own root beer and ginger ale. *AE, DC, DIS, MC, V; no checks; breakfast, lunch, dinner every day; beer and wine.*

Oakville Grocery Co.

7856 St. Helena Highway, Oakville ☎ 707/944-8802

Just up the highway from Yountville is the itsy-bitsy town of Oakville, where you'll find our favorite Wine Country lunch stop: the Oakville Grocery Co., a gourmet deli disguised as an old-fashioned country grocery store. Inside you'll find a fine variety of local wines (many that are available by the glass or for tasting), a small espresso bar tucked in the corner that sells breakfast and lunch items and house-baked pastries, and pricey but fantastic deli items ranging from pâté and caviar to turkey sandwiches and freshly made sweets. You'll marvel at the quality of ingredients that go into everything they make, including house-made preserves, smoked Norwegian salmon, and wonderful breads—all the makings for a gourmet picnic. Or, if you give the staff a day's notice, you can have them prepare a picnic basket for you. *AE, MC, V; local checks only; breakfast, lunch every day (9am–6pm); beer and wine; www.oakvillegrocery.com.*

Cantinetta Tra Vigne

1050 Charter Oak Avenue, St. Helena ☎ 707/963-8888

If you want to savor the famous fare of Ristorante Tra Vigne for lunch but don't have the bucks to pay for it, visit the adjoining Cantinetta Tra Vigne, which is both a casual cafe and a gourmet food shop. It's

Virgin Oil

The family-run Napa Valley Olive Oil Manufacturing Company produces high-quality California olive oil (pure and extra-virgin) and sells it at bargain prices in a tiny, off-the-beaten-path shop in St. Helena. You'll also find a wealth of Italian gourmet foodstuffs ideal for a picnic in the park: salami, prosciutto, fresh mozzarella, dried fruit, fresh-baked bread, biscotti, and more. Look for the white barn at the intersection of Charter Oak and Allison Avenues (at the end of the long block behind Ristorante Tra Vigne, St. Helena, 707/963-4173; open daily).

open only for lunch, but that's the best time to relax at the beautiful enclosed patio and nosh on the Cantinetta's outstanding focaccia pizzas, Italian sandwiches, interesting soups and salads, pastas topped with smoked salmon and other delights, as well as a variety of sweets. It's also a good place to stock up on picnic fare and wine. *DC, DIS, MC, V; no checks; lunch every day; beer and wine.*

Tomatina

1016 Main Street (at the Inn at Southbridge), St. Helena ☎ 707/967-9999

Tomatina is St. Helena's best bet for the budget traveler, offering great pizzas, pastas, and other freshly prepared Italian dishes at low prices. The specialty here is "Apizza," a folded pizza filled with a variety of gourmet toppings such as fennel sausage, fresh clams, sundried tomatoes, house-made pepperoni, baby spinach, and many more (the same toppings are available on the standard pizzas as well). There's also a lengthy list of wines by the glass for about half of what most other places charge. The cafe has an outdoor patio as well as a pool table and big-screen TV to keep the kids entertained. *DC, DIS, MC, V; checks OK; lunch, dinner every day; beer and wine.*

The Diner

6476 Washington Street, Yountville ☎ 707/944-2626

Great cheap eats are rare in Yountville, with the exception of the ever-popular Diner. It's the place to go in Napa Valley when you've brought along the kids; want a tasty, informal meal; or have an uncontrollable urge for a buttermilk shake—it tastes just like cheesecake! Terrific, belly-packing breakfasts (don't pass up the huevos rancheros) have secured this restaurant's reputation for years, but lunches and dinners are good, too, with hearty, well-prepared Mexican dishes and seafood specialties supplementing the typical diner fare. *No credit cards; checks OK; breakfast, lunch, dinner Tues–Sun; beer and wine.*

Cheap Sleeps

Note: The Napa Valley has become so popular that true budget lodgings just don't exist anymore. During the peak tourist season you can consider yourself lucky to find any room under $100, so you might want to either visit during the off-season or stay in Sonoma *(which has gotten much more expensive as well). The following lodgings are the best budget accommodations in Napa Valley, but you still won't find anything for under $65 a night— those days are long gone.*

Calistoga Inn

1250 Lincoln Avenue (next to the bridge), Calistoga, CA 94515
☎ 707/942-4101

The Calistoga Inn is probably best known for the homemade brews it serves on its beautiful, flower-covered patio, but its 18 very reasonably priced rooms merit attention, too. Each has a double bed and pretty white-wicker, floral-print decor and furnishings. Nasturtiums overflow from window boxes, and some rooms overlook Calistoga's main street and the inn's towering trees. There are no phones or TVs, and all baths are shared. The inn is one of the few B&Bs in Wine Country that doesn't have a two-night minimum on weekends during peak season, although hot summer nights are tough to tolerate here (there's no air-conditioning, only fans). The simple grilled fare served on the outdoor patio (weather permitting) is better (and cheaper) than the food on the menu in the inn's handsome restaurant. There's a small beer-and-wine bar on the first floor. *AE, MC, V; no checks; calistoga@napabeer.com; www.napabeer.com.*

Calistoga Village Inn & Spa

1880 Lincoln Avenue (next to the Ford Dealership), Calistoga, CA 94515
☎ 707/942-0991

Located at the northernmost end of the valley, the Calistoga Village Inn & Spa is a one-story, 41-room, sprawling white inn trimmed in slate blue, with baskets of colorful begonias hanging out in front. The rooms are spare but comfortable and spacious and include a private bath, air-conditioning, a queen-size or double bed, and a TV. The least expensive ones are in back, facing a parking lot and the rear of the Calistoga water–bottling plant. A natural mineral well supplies the hot water to the inn's swimming pool, wading pool, and 12-person Jacuzzi, which is set under a handsome natural-wood and glass-block gazebo. The pools aren't always as sparkling-clean as others in the neighborhood, but they're still inviting. You can also get the full gamut of body treatments here—from mud baths to salt scrubs—although, as elsewhere in the valley, most cost as much as a night's lodging in a cheap sleep. *AE, DC, DIS, E, MC, V; no checks; greatspa@ napanet.net; www.greatspa.com.*

Golden Haven Hot Springs

1713 Lake Street (off Grant Street at Arch Way), Calistoga, CA 94515
☎ 707/942-6793

If only Golden Haven Hot Springs were as colorful as its name, perhaps it would be a more pleasant place to spend the night. The least expensive rooms are carpeted with a mottled brown shag, navy spreads cover the queen-size beds, and when you open the gray plastic drapes, you'll get an eyeful of the oak tree–lined asphalt parking lot. At least there's a full (though aging) bathroom, a color TV, and air-conditioning. An unimpressive natural mineral-water pool and

Hiding out at Harbin Hot Springs

For a suntan without tan lines, head over to **Harbin Hot Springs,** *a clothing-optional retreat nestled in a very secluded valley near Middletown, 30 minutes north of Calistoga. The nonprofit hot springs retreat has a sauna, two warm mineral pools, and a hot and a cold mineral pool, as well as dressing rooms, showers, and plenty of spacious redwood sundecks. You can come for the day or stay the night; the New Age resort offers clean, comfortable, and reasonably priced lodgings ranging from a dormitory with communal bathrooms to private cabins with full baths. Or camp out for about the same price as a day pass. The pretty 1,100-acre property is covered with meadows, spring-fed streams, and groves of oak and pine, with several hiking trails winding throughout the terrain.*

Guests have access to a new gourmet restaurant, which was recently added to the resort, featuring vegetarian dishes as well as chicken and fish entrees. Harbin also offers free movies every evening, along with activities like meditations, moon ceremonies, and massages. Although the resort has a definite touchy-feely, aging-hippie flavor, it attracts plenty of more conventional types who just want to relax (albeit in the nude). The Harbin staff takes great pride in the tranquil environment it has created (telephones, TVs, and alarm clocks are purposely kept out of the rooms) and, indeed, it's so peaceful you're apt to see deer and their fawns lounging alongside guests on the lush lawns. If you're not comfortable around a lot of nudity, though, Harbin is not for you. For more information, contact 800/622-2477 (Northern California only), 707/987-2477, or www.harbin.org.

Jacuzzi are housed in an adjacent barnlike metal structure. None of the 26 rooms are reserved for nonsmokers. There's a two-night minimum on weekends, a three-night minimum on holiday weekends, and children under 12 are not allowed on weekends or holidays. If you decide to indulge in one of Golden Haven's spa treatments—they do have private side-by-side mud baths for couples and a full range of body treatments—look for the discount coupons frequently featured in the free Wine Country magazines distributed throughout the valley. *AE, MC, V; checks OK; www.goldenhaven.com.*

Nance's Hot Springs

1614 Lincoln Avenue, Calistoga, CA 94515 ☎ 707/942-6211

Many Bay Area residents escape the hustle and bustle of city life by hiding out at Nance's, a very reasonably priced, comfortable hotel just steps from Calistoga's shops and cafes. The color scheme leaves a bit to be desired (dark-green shag carpeting clashing with turquoise-and-navy bedspreads), but in a second-floor room, with a balcony overlooking the tree-covered hills, such issues fade in importance. Each room has a kitchenette, a cushioned chocolate-brown Naugahyde chair, air-conditioning, cable TV (with HBO), and a phone. What more do you need? Nance's even offers massages, mud baths, and blanket wraps, and all guests have access to the 102-degree indoor mineral pool. *AE, DIS, MC, V; checks OK.*

The Chablis Lodge

3360 Solano Avenue (off Highway 29), Napa, CA 94558 ☎ 800/443-3490 or ☎ 707/257-1944

Two reasonably priced inns sit side by side on Napa's Solano Avenue, and while both offer similar amenities, the Chablis Lodge edges out the Napa Valley Budget Inn (see below) by a notch or two. The 34-room Chablis looks a little older, but its rooms are larger and more comfortable (and a little more expensive). Each unit has a king- or queen-size bed, phone, TV, wet bar, and small refrigerator; some have kitchenettes. The small heated swimming pool and spa—a godsend during the sweltering summer months—are surrounded by cement, but the potted flowers and baby-blue-and-white umbrellas add a little zip. Small dogs are welcome. Ask for a room facing away from Highway 29. *AE, DC, DIS, MC, V; no checks.*

Napa Valley Budget Inn

3380 Solano Avenue (off Highway 29), Napa, CA 94558 ☎ 707/257-6111

The runner-up to the Chablis Lodge offers just what it says—rooms at budget rates, about $10 to $15 cheaper per night during the week and just a tad cheaper on weekends than those at the Chablis. Both require a two-night minimum stay if a Saturday is included. But you get what you pay for, and in this case the 58 cramped rooms don't provide much beyond the basics—queen-size bed, cable TV, a solitary chair, and a phone. The inn had a former life as a Motel 6, which accounts for the uninspired (i.e., cheap) architecture. The large heated swimming pool is clean but rather dreary-looking, with its bare, fenced-in cement patio. Busy Highway 29 runs behind Solano Avenue, so request a room that doesn't get too much traffic noise. The inn does allow small pets. *AE, DIS, MC, V; no checks; NVBI@aol.com.*

El Bonita Motel

195 Main Street, St. Helena, CA 94574 ☎ 800/541-3284 or ☎ 707/963-3216

Thanks to an extensive remodeling, El Bonita is indeed *bonita*. Hand-painted grapevines grace many of the room entrances, and inside, the walls are colored a faint pink, with floor-length baby-blue drapes and pink-and-baby-blue floral bedspreads. Each of the 41 rooms has a private bath, color TV, and phone; for a little more money, you can have cable TV, microwave, refrigerator, and even a kitchen and a whirlpool bath. Huge oak trees surround the motel, a heated kidney-shaped swimming pool sits in front, and there's a sauna and an outdoor whirlpool on the premises (massages are available by appointment). The rates vary from month to month (depending on business), but in general you (and your pet) can get a reasonably priced room Sunday through Thursday year-round. El Bonita fronts Highway 29, so try to get a room as far from the street as possible. St. Helena's shopping district is a short drive (or a 20-minute walk) away. *AE, DC, DIS, MC, V; no checks; elbonita1@aol.com; www.elbonita.com.*

Hotel St. Helena

1309 Main Street (Highway 29), St. Helena, CA 94574 ☎ 707/963-4388

Those who'd like to stay in the heart of charming St. Helena need look no further. Unfortunately, you may be able to afford only a winter weekday stay, since the rates are twice as much the rest of the year. But even if you don't book a room, take a peek at the amazing lobby, which looks like someone transported all the props from Disneyland's "It's a Small World After All" and deposited them here. Hundreds of elaborately decorated dolls and marionettes are draped over the furniture and hung from the ceiling. Fortunately, the excessive doll theme doesn't continue in the rooms, which are decorated in rich tones of burgundy, gold, and mauve, with polished antique furnishings (no smoking allowed). Most of the 18 units have private baths, although some have shared baths and run a bit cheaper. If you look hard enough beyond the lobby's dollscape, you'll see a small coffee-wine-and-beer bar tucked in the back, where—with the wide-eyed plastic faces staring at you from all angles—you'll never drink alone. *AE, DC, DIS, MC, V; no checks.*

White Sulphur Springs Resort & Spa

3100 White Sulphur Springs Road (off Spring Street), St. Helena, CA 94574 ☎ 707/963-8588

This 330-acre resort is only a 3-mile winding drive from St. Helena's Main Street, but it's nestled in such a secluded canyon covered with hundreds of beautiful redwood, madrona, and fir trees that you'd swear you were 100 miles from anywhere. Founded in 1852, White Sulphur Springs is the oldest operating resort in California. The proprietors have successfully maintained its rustic charm and beauty, offering a variety of lodgings—from large, fully equipped creekside cottages to little rooms with shared baths—that suit a world of budgets and tastes. The most affordable rooms are in the Carriage House (where you'll share bathrooms) and the Inn (which offers rooms with a half or full bath). The Carriage House has a kitchen and refrigerator available to resort guests who'd like to prepare their own meals. One of the resort's highlights is the series of hiking trails that wind alongside rippling creeks and waterfalls; another don't-miss attraction is the natural sulphur soaking pool, which maintains an 85–87°F temperature year-round. There's also a Jacuzzi and a mineral pool, along with massages, volcanic mud wraps, and other pricey luxuries. *MC, V; no checks; www.whitesulphursprings.com.*

Napa Valley Railway Inn

6503 Washington Street (at Yount Street), Yountville, CA 94599

☎ 707/944-2000

Sitting on the original tracks of the Napa Valley Railroad are three turn-of-the-century cabooses and six railcars that have been converted into one-room suites with private entrances, skylights, and bay windows. The vintage slate-blue and brick-red railcars are actually more interesting on the outside, with some of their original fixtures intact and their "Southern Pacific Lines" and "Great Northern Railway" logos painted on the side. Inside, each car has dated but comfortable furnishings, including a queen-size brass bed, an armchair and a love seat that look like '60s remnants, a pair of reading lights, and some tacky artwork (no phones or TVs). But these granny-style interiors probably help keep the rates down, and at least there are private baths and air-conditioning. The Railway Inn is conveniently located in the center of tiny Yountville, with many of Napa Valley's most popular wineries and restaurants a short drive away. The inn's west side faces Highway 29, with a small strip of vineyards planted in between, and the opposite side overlooks a parking lot, which is partially shaded by eucalyptus trees and vines of star jasmine. Rates vary depending on the season, during peak season there is a two-night minimum when you stay on a Saturday, but between November and May you usually can get a room for less than the rate sheet suggests. *MC, V; checks OK; www.bestlodgings.com.*

North Coast

**stinson beach &
point reyes national seashore**

bodega bay & jenner

mendocino & fort bragg

eureka & arcata

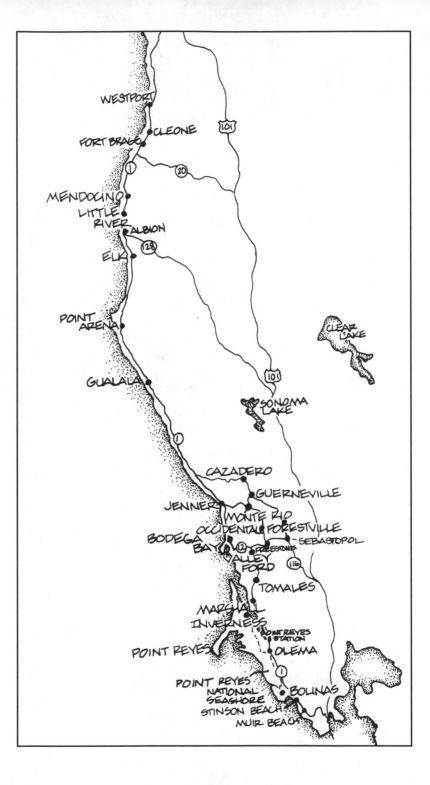

Stinson Beach & Point Reyes National Seashore

On those treasured weekend days when the fog has lifted and the sun is scorching the Northern California coast, blurry-eyed Bay Area residents grab their morning paper and beach chairs, pile into the car, and scramble to the sandy shores of Stinson Beach—the North Coast's nice-try answer to the fabled beaches of Southern California. Natural wonders abound at every hairpin turn, from the magnificent redwoods (the tallest living organisms in the world) of Muir Woods to the brilliant wildflowers carpeting the rolling hills.

If you're looking for a stellar strip of the coast where you can ditch the beer-guzzling surfer set and the Bart Simpson family scene, keep driving north to Point Reyes National Seashore, where miles of spectacular windswept beaches are practically deserted every day of the year. Point Reyes also offers thousands of acres of lush meadowlands, chaparral ridges, valleys, and forests, none of which have been defaced by a burger emporium, condo complex, or used-car dealership. And because commercial excess has taken a backseat to land and animal preservation, Point Reyes is crisscrossed with the footprints of tule elk, deer, raccoons, and squirrels, and the playful sea lions, harbor seals, and gray whales still swim near the pristine shore.

Exploring

Half the fun of going to Stinson Beach and its neighboring nature areas is the wild, wonderful drive getting there. Stinson Beach is located right off Highway 1 at the base of Mount Tamalpais in Marin County, and although it's only 10 miles from San Francisco as the crow flies, those without feathers must negotiate 20 miles of steep turns before they finally arrive. From the Bay Area, take the Stinson Beach/Highway 1 exit off Highway 101 just north of Sausalito, and follow Highway 1. As the road descends toward the shore, it forks; take the left fork, which is the continuation of Highway 1, leading to the beach. The fork to the right veers toward **Muir Woods National Monument,** a 560-acre fern-filled sanctuary of ancient redwoods dedicated to legendary conservationist John Muir. People flock to Muir Woods (many in tour buses) to walk the miles of well-marked trails—and spectacular trails they are. The 250-foot tall, 800-year-old trees (the Bay Area's only large, intact stand of old-growth redwoods) provide a solid canopy of shade for the ferns, wildflowers, Sonoma chipmunks, moles, bats, birds, black-tailed deer, and Pacific giant salamanders that live here (it's typically a cool, damp environment, so dress appropriately). Although the park can get absurdly crowded on summer weekends, you can usually circumvent the masses by hiking up the Ocean View Trail, returning via Fern Creek Trail. Admission to Muir Woods is free; picnicking is not allowed, but there's a snack bar at the entrance (open from 8am to sunset daily; on Muir Woods Road, off the Panoramic Highway via Highway 1, 415/388-2595).

Past Muir Woods, along Highway 1, is another tempting detour: a small, crescent-shaped cove called **Muir Beach.** Littered with bits of driftwood and numerous tide pools, Muir Beach is a more sedate alternative to the beer 'n' bikini crowds at Stinson. If all you want is a sandy, pretty place for some R&R, park the car right here and skip Stinson altogether (but be aware that swimming isn't allowed at Muir Beach because of the strong rip currents). Should you build up a thirst for a cold mug of beer, the very British **Pelican Inn,** with its dartboards and dark, intimate pub, is just a short walk away (off Highway 1 at the entrance to Muir Beach, 415/383-6000).

A wickedly curvaceous, 6-mile drive north takes you to **Stinson**

Kayaking on Tomales Bay

If the best things in life are free, then the next-best things must be in the $40 range, which is about how much you'll need to rent a sea kayak from the friendly folks at Tomales Bay Kayaking. The kayaks are very stable and you won't have to contend with any waves on beautiful, placid Tomales Bay, a haven for migrating birds and marine mammals. Rental prices start at about $35 for a half day ($45 for a double-hulled kayak), and guided day trips, sunset cruises, and romantic full-moon outings are also available. Instruction, clinics, and boat delivery are offered, and all ages and ability levels are welcome. The launching point is on Highway 1 at the Marshall Boatworks in Marshall, 8 miles north of Point Reyes Station. Open Friday through Sunday, 9:30am–5:30pm, and by appointment. For more information, call 415/663-1743.

Beach, one of Northern California's most popular sun-and-surf spots. Although overrun with Bay Area refugees on summer weekends, the wide stretch of beige sand offers enough elbow room for everyone to spread out their beach blankets, picnic baskets, and toys. Swimming is permitted, but notices giving detailed instructions on how to escape a raging riptide tend to make folks think twice about venturing too far into the water (then again, so do the toe-numbing temperatures and the threat of sharks). The town of Stinson Beach, sustained purely by the influx of fun-loving beach bums, is only a few blocks long and can be toured entirely on foot in less than 30 minutes. A couple of recommended stops are **Stinson Beach Books** (3455 Highway 1, Stinson Beach, 415/868-0700), which has a great selection of children's books and toys, and the **Parkside Café,** Stinson's best (and coincidentally its cheapest) restaurant, which serves breakfast, lunch, and dinner and is perpetually packed (see Cheap Eats below).

A short drive north of town on Highway 1 leads to **Bolinas Lagoon,** a placid expanse of salt water that serves as a refuge for numerous shorebirds and harbor seals. Nearby is the **Audubon Canyon Ranch's Bolinas Lagoon Preserve,** a 1,014-acre wildlife sanctuary that supports a major population of great blue herons and great egrets. This is the prime spot along the Pacific Coast to watch the immense, graceful seabirds as they court and mate and rear their young, all accomplished on the tops of towering redwoods. Admission is free, although donations are requested; open from mid-March to mid-July on Saturdays, Sundays, and holidays, 10am to 4pm, and by appointment for groups

If You Like to Bike

As most ardent Bay Area mountain bikers know, Point Reyes National Seashore has some of the finest mountain-biking trails in the region—narrow, winding dirt paths that lead through densely forested knolls, ending with spectacular Pacific vistas. What, forgot to bring your $2,000 custom-built graphite Cannondale with GripShifters and Rock Shocks? No problem: for less than $30 a day, you can rent a quality mountain bike at Pacific Currents in the town of Olema. Binoculars are also a popular rental item here, and you'll wish you had a pair when you reach the Sea Lion Overlook (10155 State Highway 1, Olema, 415/663-0333).

(4900 Highway 1, Stinson Beach, 415/868-9244).

At the north end of the lagoon is the unmarked turnoff to the town of **Bolinas,** home to a handful of famous writers and '60s rock stars, as well as the requisite number of former hippies. In an attempt to preserve their town's reclusive mystique, residents regularly take down any directional or identifying highway sign (an act that, ironically, has created more publicity for Bolinas than any sign ever would). Set in a forested knoll between the ocean and the lagoon, the artsy community has a thriving cultural scene, including numerous dance, music, and theatrical performances held at the **Bolinas Community Center** (14 Wharf Road, Bolinas, 415/868-2128). **Smiley's Schooner Saloon** is also a happening spot on weekends, when the live jazz, country, blues, or rock music kicks in (41 Wharf Road, Bolinas, 415/868-1311).

For those who are tired of driving and want to stretch their legs, three local side trips offer some adventurous exercise. The **Duxberry Reef Nature Reserve** is a rocky outcropping with numerous tide pools harboring a healthy population of sea stars, sea anemones, snails, sea urchins, and other creatures. During low tide, you are allowed to admire and touch the marine life as long as you don't remove anything from its home (from downtown Bolinas, head north a few miles, then turn left on Mesa Road, left on Overlook Road, and right on Elm Road). About a mile up the coast is the **Point Reyes Bird Observatory,** established in 1964. Here ornithologists keep an eye on more than 400 species, and visitors may observe the banding of birds' legs; free admission, open daily 7am to 5pm (near the west end of Mesa Road, Point Reyes, 415/868-0655). At the very end of Mesa Road is the **Palomarin Trailhead,** the start of a popular hiking path that leads into the south entrance of Point Reyes National Seashore. The 6-mile round-trip trek—one of Point

Reyes's prettiest—passes several small lakes and meadows before it reaches Alamere Falls, a freshwater cascade that rushes down a 40-foot bluff onto Wildcat Beach.

Ten miles north of Bolinas is the main entrance to **Point Reyes National Seashore,** a 71,000-acre playground of forested hills, deep-green pastures, and gorgeous windswept beaches. Before exploring, stop at the big, wooden barn–style Bear Valley Visitors Center, which happens to sit alongside the **San Andreas Fault Zone** (on Bear Valley Road, off Highway 1—look for the small sign just north of the town of Olema, 415/663-1092). Grab a free Point Reyes trail map and a newsletter listing the several daily park events, and take a look at the center's exhibits, which include a seismograph. The visitors center is also the starting point for several spectacular hiking, mountain-biking, and equestrian trails. The popular, flat **Bear Valley Trail** (8.2 miles round-trip) begins just a few steps away from the visitors center parking lot and winds through a lush creek canyon rimmed with ferns, flowers, and towering trees. The trail ends at Arch Rock, a natural arch in the seaside cliffs that visitors can walk through at low tide (but be careful not to get stranded on the other side at high tide).

Athletic sorts will want to test their stamina on the 308 stone steps leading down to the **Point Reyes Lighthouse**—one of the West Coast's few surviving lighthouses—where you can see (and hear) sea lions battling for basking space. When the fog burns off (a rare occurrence, unfortunately), the lighthouse and headlands provide a fantastic lookout point for spotting **gray whales** during their annual 5,000-mile round-trip migration from the Arctic Sea to their Baja California, Mexico, breeding grounds; they swim south from December through February and return north in March and April. Visitors have access to the lighthouse steps from 10am to 4:30pm Thursday through Monday (no fee), barring hazardous high winds or rain (for more information, call

Snack Attack

*For some great, inexpensive road snacks, stop by the **Bolinas Bay Bakery** (20 Wharf Road, Bolinas, 415/868-0211), renowned for its cinnamon buns made with organic flour, as well as croissants, breads, pizzas, and pasta salads. Or load up on fresh, organically grown fruits and vegetables at the **Bolinas People's Store** (14 Wharf Road, Bolinas, 415/868-1433).*

the lighthouse visitors center at 415/669-1534).

The 10-plus miles of pristine Point Reyes beaches include **Limantour Beach,** excellent for bird-watching and swimming (although the water is always chilly) and **Drake's Beach,** another good swimming spot, thanks to its protected cove (there's also a small cafe on shore). Be forewarned, however, that many Point Reyes beaches are unsafe for swimming due to pounding surf and treacherous riptides and undertows; consult the Bear Valley Visitors Center (see above) for a guide to the safest spots. Those who'd rather stroll than swim should not miss **Kehoe Beach** in spring, when a riotous display of violets, larkspur, California poppies, wild roses, fuchsias, and many other wildflowers blanket the terrain.

Cheap Eats

The Gray Whale

2781 Sir Francis Drake Boulevard, Inverness ☎ 415/669-1244

The Gray Whale Inn in downtown Inverness is the place to go for a good, inexpensive meal for lunch or dinner. The small, homey, vegetarian-friendly cafe serves a wide array of sandwiches (our favorite is the roasted eggplant with pesto and mozzarella), pizza (try the Californian with artichoke hearts, fresh basil, and tomatoes), soups, salads, pastas, and gourmet coffee. On sunny days you'll appreciate the outdoor seating on the shaded patio overlooking the blocklong town of Inverness. *MC, V; checks OK; lunch, dinner every day; beer and wine.*

The Station House Café

11180 Shoreline Highway, Point Reyes Station ☎ 415/663-1515

For more than two decades the Station House has been a favorite stop for West Marin residents and San Francisco day-trippers. Breakfast

Picnic Tip

*The **Bovine Bakery**, with its "udderly divine" sandwiches, pastries, and breads, is an ideal stop for picnic supplies. It's located at 11315 Main Street (Highway 1) in downtown Point Reyes Station, 415/663-9420.*

items range from French toast made with Il Fornaio bakery's sweet challah to buckwheat pancakes and roasted-vegetable frittatas. For lunch or dinner, some of the best dishes are also the least expensive: the fish-and-chips with country fries and cole slaw, and probably the best hamburger we have ever had (seriously). There's a good selection of wines, too. If the weather is warm, sit outside in the shaded garden area—particularly if you're eating breakfast here on a sunny day. In the summer, barbecued oysters are often served on the patio. *DIS, MC, V; local checks only; breakfast, lunch, dinner every day; full bar.*

Taqueria la Quinta

11285 Highway 1, Point Reyes Station ☎ 415/663-8868

Mexican folk music fills the air and bright colors abound at this exuberant restaurant, where most of the fare costs less than *seis dólares*. La Quinta (Spanish for "the country house") offers a large selection of Mexican-American standards—tacos, burritos, tostadas—as well as vegetarian dishes and weekend seafood specials. The service is fast, the food is fresh, the salsa is *muy caliente. No credit cards; local checks only; lunch, dinner Wed—Mon; beer only.*

The Parkside Café

43 Arenal Avenue, Stinson Beach ☎ 415/868-1272

During the day this popular neighborhood cafe bustles with locals and Bay Area beachgoers who stop for an inexpensive breakfast or lunch before shoving off to Stinson Beach around the corner. Morning favorites are the omelets, blueberry pancakes, and the not-to-be-missed

Aw, Shucks

Johnson's Oyster Farm, located in the heart of Point Reyes National Seashore, offers you the golden (if also odoriferous) opportunity to see briny bivalves being harvested. The farm doesn't look like much—a cluster of trailer homes, shacks, and oyster tanks surrounded by huge piles of shells—but that doesn't detract from the taste of right-from-the-water oysters dipped in Johnson's special sauce. Eat 'em on the spot or buy a bag for the road; either way, you're not likely to find California oysters as fresh or as cheap anywhere else (off Sir Francis Drake Highway in Point Reyes National Seashore, about 6 miles west of Inverness, 415/669-1149; open Tuesday through Sunday).

raisin-walnut bread. For lunch there are basics like burgers, grilled sandwiches, and soups, as well as a few daily specials. The evening menu includes a wide variety of dishes ranging from lamb chops and roast chicken to mussel linguine, seafood pizza, and baked eggplant. On sunny days, dine alfresco on the brick patio; otherwise, cozy up to the fire. For a quick bite to go, the cafe's snack bar sells great burgers, fries, and shakes daily from March through September, and on weekends from October through February. *AE, MC, V; local checks only; breakfast, lunch every day, dinner Thurs–Mon; beer and wine.*

Cheap Sleeps

Motel Inverness

12718 Sir Francis Drake Boulevard, Inverness, CA 94937 ☎ 415/669-1081

Recently remodeled, Motel Inverness offers Tomales Bay–front accommodations at the high end of Cheap Sleeps rates. Each of the seven lovely rooms has a color TV and private bath, and if you actually reach a point where you just can't take any more of nature's wonders, you can play pool or pinball in the huge rec room or lounge in front of the big-screen TV. *AE, DIS, MC, V; checks OK; www.coastaltraveler.com/motelinverness.*

Knob Hill

40 Knob Hill Road, Point Reyes Station, CA 94956 ☎ 415/663-1784

Janet Schlitt built her rustic-looking home in 1990 with an eye toward providing lodgers with a lovely, economical setting for a stay on the North Coast—complete with a dramatic view across the Point Reyes Mesa and Inverness Ridge. Schlitt offers a one-room cottage with queen-size bed and wood-burning stove (unfortunately, priced too high for the budget-minded), but the small room adjoining the main house is certainly a bargain. Accessed by its own stairway and entrance, and complete with double bed, private bath, and a door leading to a tiny garden, this cheap sleep rents for $60–$95 (depending on the season), in an area where such charming accommodations are difficult to find. *No credit cards; checks OK; www.knobhill.com.*

Point Reyes Hostel

Point Reyes National Seashore, Point Reyes Station, CA 94956

☎ 415/663-8811

Formerly a working ranch house, this popular hostel off Limantour Road in the national seashore area has 45 dormitory-style bunks that are often filled with college students and foreign travelers (there's also a separate room that will accommodate a family). The location is idyllic—isolated deep inside the park and surrounded by numerous hiking trails, including a beautiful 2-mile walk to Limantour Beach. The two common rooms are each warmed by woodstoves, and there's a large, fully equipped kitchen, outdoor barbecue, and patio. If you don't mind sharing sleeping quarters with strangers, this is a $12-per-person deal that can't be beat (children under age 17 only $6 per night if accompanied by a parent). Reservations (and earplugs) are strongly recommended. Reception is open from 7:30am to 9:30am and 4:30pm to 9:30pm daily. *MC, V; checks OK.*

Green Gulch Farm Zen Center

1601 Highway 1, Sausalito, CA 94965 ☎ 415/383-3134

When was the last time your bodhisattva ("the spirit of kindness") had a vacation? Green Gulch Farm, a Soto Zen practice center hidden in a verdant valley off Highway 1 near Muir Beach (10 minutes west of the Muir Woods turnoff), offers fantastically priced "guest practice retreats" for those interested in learning the art of Zen meditation. Retreat participants are offered a minimum three-night stay (Sunday through Thursday only), and they're expected to attend early morning meditations (i.e., 5am) and then go to work (usually in the farm's expansive organic gardens) until noon. After that, you're on your own to wander down to Muir Beach, hike through Muir Woods or on nearby trails, attend classes on Buddhism, or do whatever else your heart desires. Rates are an enlightening $30 per person per day ($50 for double occupancy), including, amazingly, three square meals and snacks. Nightly lodgings are also available without program participation, but they cost about twice as much. *No credit cards; checks OK; www.sczc.com.*

Stinson Beach Motel

3416 Highway 1, Stinson Beach, CA 94970 ☎ 415/868-1712

A gravel walkway leads through a garden setting to six small rooms in this pleasant motel in the heart of downtown Stinson Beach. The rooms, all with private baths, are individually decorated with aging yet homey furnishings. Prices start at about $80 for a studio. Try to reserve room 7, which is located apart from the rest and is therefore more private. And if you're tired of sunbathing at the beach, the motel's garden area offers a shady retreat. *DIS, MC, V; no checks.*

Steep Ravine Environmental Cabins

Mount Tamalpais State Park ☎ 800/444-7275 (California Campground Reservations)

How much would you expect to pay for a night in a rustic, romantic redwood cabin just steps from a small, secluded beach? $200? $300? How about a paltry 30 bucks? Three Andrew Hamiltons buy you and your party a night at one of 10 bare-bones cabins that were once the private getaways of powerful Bay Area politicians and their cronies (they lost their long-term leases in a battle with the state). The cabins are now available to those who are lucky enough to snag a reservation (which are taken only up to eight weeks in advance) and who don't mind bringing their own sleeping bags and pads. Platform beds, running water, wood-burning stoves, and outhouses are provided, but there's no electricity and firewood costs an extra $4. Each cabin sleeps up to five (all for the same $30-a-night rate), but only one car per cabin is allowed. Cabins are located off Highway 1, a mile south of Stinson Beach; look for a paved turnout and a brown metal sign. *DIS, MC, V; no checks; www.cal-parks.ca.gov/districts/marin/mtsp239.htm.*

Bodega Bay
& Jenner

Alfred Hitchcock probably wouldn't recognize Bodega Bay these days. When the filmmaker directed *The Birds* here, Bodega Bay was little more than a tiny, white-clapboard seacoast town. Today it's more of a vacation destination than a sleepy little fishing village. But although more than 30 years have passed since Hitchcock yelled "Action" in the streets of Bodega Bay and the neighboring town of Bodega, thousands of his fans still flock here every year to try to identify buildings and landscapes from his classic flick.

The true star attraction, however, has nothing to do with Hollywood—it's Mother Nature. Dramatic ocean vistas are punctuated by towering sea stacks, natural arches, teeming tide pools, and crescent-shaped coves. The birds—not Hitchcock's spooky movie versions, but wild great blue herons, snowy egrets, brown pelicans, and other fine-feathered friends—are also a big crowd pleaser. Strolling the beach, picnicking, hiking, fishing, clamming, and whale-watching are favorite local pastimes—and virtually free. Unfortunately, inexpensive accommodations are extremely limited, except for the sleeping-bag-and-tent variety, and even campsites get booked up far in advance during peak season (although some are available first-come, first-served). If you can't find a place to sleep, don't despair—just head farther north.

A short drive north of Bodega Bay is the tiny, charming town of Jenner, where the Russian River spills into the sea. Jenner marks the beginning of the most beautiful, cliff-hugging stretch of coastal Highway 1. A few campgrounds dot the beaches and forests on either side of this narrow, scenic road, and a three-hour drive north leads to Mendocino and Fort Bragg, an area much richer in budget accommodations and cafes (see the Mendocino and Fort Bragg section of this chapter). But if sunset is near and the fog is rolling in, don't risk the dizzying hairpin turns just to find a bed; instead, go east from Jenner into the nearby Russian River Valley.

Exploring

No matter what direction you're coming from, getting to Bodega Bay is a rather long haul, because there are no fast, direct routes. From the San Francisco area, the easiest way is via **Petaluma.** From Highway 101, take the Bodega Bay/Central Petaluma exit and turn left toward the town. After a straight shot though the center of Petaluma, you'll spend about 45 minutes driving through a countryside of rolling emerald-green hills dotted with grazing sheep and whitewashed farmhouses. Eventually the deep-blue Pacific appears on the horizon.

Just before you reach the ocean, take a quick detour through the town of **Bodega** (not to be confused with the town of Bodega Bay a few miles farther on). On Bodega Road is the hauntingly familiar schoolhouse

Bodega Bay Bash

For a festive time in Bodega Bay, visit on the last weekend of April, when as many as 25,000 partiers let loose at the Fisherman's Festival, a two-day orgy of lamb and oyster barbecues, Sonoma County wine tastings, craft fairs, pony rides, bathtub races, parades, kite-flying contests, live music, and dancing. The festival highlight is the Blessing of the Fleet, a colorful, jubilant boat parade in which clergymen stand on a vessel and bless the fishing fleet as it floats by. For more information, call the Bodega Bay Chamber of Commerce at 707/875-3422.

immortalized in Hitchcock's *The Birds* (it's now a bed-and-breakfast). The two or three boutiques in Bodega entice a few visitors to park and browse, but most seem content with a little rubbernecking and finger-pointing as they snake through town.

Rolling into Bodega Bay, keep an eye out for the local **Chamber of Commerce** (850 Highway 1, Bodega Bay, 707/875-3422) in the center of town. Load up on free maps, camping information, guides, and brochures, including the "Bodega Bay Area Map & Guide," which pinpoints all the town's attractions.

Next, take the short drive to the sea at **Bodega Head,** the small peninsula that shelters the bay (from Highway 1, turn west on Eastshore Road, then right at the stop sign onto Bay Flat Road and follow it to the end). This is one of the premier whale-watching points along the California coast; the annual migrations of the humpback and California gray run from December through April. Two superb walking trails begin here, too. From the park's west parking lot, a 4-mile round-trip trail leads past the Bodega Marine Preserve and ends at the sand dunes of Salmon Creek Beach. An easier, 1.5-mile round-trip walk begins in the east parking lot and encircles Bodega Head, branching off for an optional side trip to the tip of the point for a spectacular 360-degree view.

In the afternoon, be sure to spend some time at the docks watching the fishing boats returning and unloading their catches. **Tides Wharf** (835 Highway 1, Bodega Bay, 707/875-3652) has the most active dock scene, including a viewing room near the processing plant that lets you witness the fish's ultimate fate—a swift and merciless gutting by deft

Something to Spout About

Sure, spotting gray whales from shore is exciting, but nothing compares to getting within listening distance of a 40-ton cetacean—so close you can actually hear the blast from the blowhole. Fishing charters offer whale-watching trips from late December through April, typically charging about $15–$25 per person (it pays to shop around) to take you as close to the whales as legally permitted. Excursions last about three hours (seemingly forever if you get seasick). While nobody can guarantee you'll see or hear a whale, most people get at least a glimpse of these majestic mammals, and the boat trip alone, with its view of the shore from a whale's perspective, is worth the price. Several companies offer morning and afternoon trips departing daily from Bodega Bay.

Fishy Suave

If you're the kind of person who spends a weekend fishing, only to return home with an empty ice chest and a bad cold, well, here's your chance to catch a mess of big, beautiful rock cod, ling cod, salmon, halibut, or albacore. It's this simple: (1) Get on a fishing boat in Bodega Bay; (2) grab a prerigged fishing pole; (3) lower your line in the water when everyone else does; and (4) reel in the fish. All the rest, from taking the fish off the hook to cleaning it, is handled by the friendly deckhands. Then you get to take your haul home and indulge in a feeding frenzy of your own.

On the fish-and-crab combination trips (even more fun than the straight fishing jaunts), you get to keep not only your finned catch but also a few of the enormous Dungeness crabs caught in traps set out the previous day. Both the fishing and fish-crab-combo trips cost approximately $55–$65 per person (rod-and-reel rental is an additional $7.50), and almost everyone takes home a sack so full of seafood it's nearly too heavy to lift off the boat. For information and reservations, call Bodega Bay Sportfishing Center at 707/875-3344.

hands, followed by a quick burial in ice. Just outside, sea lions linger by the dock hoping for a handout.

Linking Bodega Bay and nearby Jenner are the **Sonoma Coast State Beaches,** 16 miles of pristine sand-and-gravel beaches, tide pools, rocky bluffs, and hiking trails. A few campgrounds are located nearby; call the Salmon Creek Ranger Station, 707/875-3483, for more information, and Reserve America, 800/444-7275, for reservations. The southernmost beach is tranquil **Doran Park Beach,** just south of Bodega Bay. This is also one of the safest spots for kids—when the water's rough everywhere else, Doran is still calm enough for swimming, clamming, and crabbing. Bird-watchers should stake out the Doran mudflats, a favorite haunt of egrets, big-billed pelicans, and other seabirds, while tide-pool trekkers ought to visit the north end of **Salmon Creek Beach** (off Bean Avenue, 2 miles north of town) or **Shell Beach,** a small low-tide treasure trove (10 miles north of Bodega Bay, near Jenner).

About 16 miles north of Bodega Bay on Highway 1 is **Jenner,** a hamlet built on a bluff rising from the mouth of the Russian River. It's a small jewel of a town, comprised of little more than a gas station, three restaurants, two inns, and a deli, but Jenner is (ironically) well known as Northern California's "secret" spot for getting away from the masses. One of the local highlights is beautiful **Goat Rock Beach,** which is also a breeding ground for harbor seals. "Pupping season" begins in March and lasts till June, and orange-vested volunteers are usually on hand to protect the seals (which give birth on land) from dogs and overzealous tourists. They'll also answer questions about the playful animals and even lend binoculars for a closer look.

From Jenner, follow Highway 1 north for a winding, spectacular 12-mile stretch to **Fort Ross State Historic Park** (19005 Highway 1, Jenner, 707/847-3286), a beautifully restored redwood fort built by Russian fur traders in 1812 and partially destroyed by the great 1906 earthquake. About 3–4 miles north of the fort on Highway 1 are **Timber Cove,** one of photographer Ansel Adams's favorite places, and the 3,500-acre **Salt Point State Park,** 707/847-3221, which offers 139 campsites in the redwoods and numerous day-hike trails that zigzag through coastal woodlands, wildflower-filled meadows, and rocky beaches. Within the state park lies the 317-acre **Kruse Rhododendron Preserve,** an uncultivated native garden bursting with shocking-pink and purple flowers that grow up to 30 feet tall in the shade of a vast redwood canopy; the peak blooming period varies yearly, but April is usually the best time to see them.

Cheap Eats

Breakers Café
1400 Highway 1, Bodega Bay ☎ 707/875-2513

Bodega Bay's Breakers Café is a welcome alternative to the over-priced and overrated fish restaurants on the wharf. For breakfast, park your fanny among the numerous plants in the sun-filled dining room and feast on yummy Belgian waffles topped with hot spiced peaches and whipped cream. Lunch is mostly sandwiches, burgers, and house-made soups; dinner items range from fresh seafood to chicken, pasta, and low-fat vegetarian dishes. If the weather's warm, ask for a table on the patio. *MC, V; local checks only; breakfast every day (May 1–Sept 30), lunch, dinner every day (year-round); beer and wine.*

Dig 'n' Dine

How often do you have a legitimate, legal excuse to get down and dirty on a public beach? Well, as long as you're on the hunt for a sack of fresh clams, you can do it year-round at Bodega Bay. The only skill required is digging; the only equipment, a shovel and a sturdy bag. The rest is childishly straightforward: find a good spot (hint—try the western side of the bay); wait for low tide; search the sand closest to the water for a small, bubbling siphon hole; then dig like heck with whatever's handy (a narrow clammer's shovel works best). What you'll discover is a long "neck" leading to a horseneck clam, the most abundant bivalve in Bodega Bay. A fishing license is required for anyone over 16 (one-day licenses are available at most sporting-goods stores and bait shops).

Lucas Wharf Deli

595 Highway 1, Bodega Bay ☎ 707/875-3562

Few tourists come to Bodega Bay just for the seafood, as you'll soon discover if you spend more than a day here. There are only two "seafood" restaurants in town, Tides Wharf and Lucas Wharf, and both do little to excite the palate. Your best bet is to skip both restaurants and go next door to Lucas Wharf Deli, which most visitors don't even give a glance as they head into the adjacent restaurant. Order a $6 pint of ultrafresh crab cioppino or, when it's not crab season, a big ol' basket of fresh fish-and-chips and make a messy picnic of it on the dock. It's what we do every time we're in town. *AE, DIS, MC, V; checks OK; picnic items to go every day; beer and wine.*

River's End

1104A Highway 1, Jenner ☎ 707/865-2484

Aside from the Sizzling Tandoor, this is the only restaurant anywhere near Jenner. The menu is still decidedly eclectic, with entrees ranging from Indian curries to beef Wellington, seafood, and steaks (and probably out of your price range). Lunch, however, is more down to earth, with reasonably priced burgers, sandwiches, and salads. Most tables have a wonderful view of the ocean, as does the small outside deck—the perfect spot for a glass of Sonoma County wine. *MC, V; no checks; lunch, dinner Thur–Mon; full bar.*

Sizzling Tandoor

9960 Highway 1, Jenner ☎ 707/865-0625

When the weather is warm and sunny, Sizzling Tandoor is the best place on the Sonoma coast to have lunch. This Indian restaurant is perched high above the placid Russian River, and the view, particularly from the outside patio, is fantastic. Equally great are the inexpensive lunch specials: huge portions of curries and kebabs served with vegetables, soup, *pulao* rice, and superb naan (Indian bread). Even if you don't have time for a meal, drop by and order some warm naan to go. *AE, DIS, MC, V; no checks; lunch, dinner every day (closed Mon in winter); beer and wine.*

Cheap Sleeps

Bodega Harbor Inn

1345 Bodega Avenue, Bodega Bay, CA 94923 ☎ 707/875-3594

A homey old-timer in a town of mostly modern motels, the Bodega Harbor Inn consists of seven clapboard buildings (with a total of 16 guest rooms) set on a large lawn overlooking the harbor. The small, tidy rooms have private baths, cable TV, double beds, and access to a private yard where you can kick back in the lawn chairs. Rates are often at the very top of the Cheap Sleeps price range, but they're the best deal in town and, to be fair, the rates stay the same year-round. If you're willing to shell out a bit more, ask for room 12 or 14 and you'll get a partial ocean view and a small deck. The inn, located off Highway 1 at the north end of Bodega Bay, also rents seven houses and cottages, some located on the property, and others scattered throughout the town. *MC, V; checks OK; www.bodegaharborinn.com.*

Jenner Inn & Cottages

10400 Highway 1, Jenner, CA 95450 ☎ 800/732-2377 or ☎. 707/865-2377

When people say they stayed at the cutest little place in Jenner, they're talking about Jenner Inn & Cottages. Unfortunately, most of the rooms are out of the Cheap Sleeps range, but since this is the only lodging in Jenner, it's here or in a tent. The 16 guest rooms are dispersed within a cluster of cottages and houses perched above the

Russian River or the ocean. The houses are subdivided into separate suites that are rented out individually, and all have private baths, separate entrances, and antique and wicker furnishings. An extended continental breakfast, served in the main lodge, is included in the room rate. Don't expect the Ritz if you opt for the lower-priced rooms, which are far from fancy but still a great deal for oceanfront property. *AE, MC, V; checks OK; innkeeper@jennerinn.com; www.jennerinn.com.*

Mendocino & Fort Bragg

The village of Mendocino has managed to retain more of its gracious, small-town allure than most picturesque coastal getaway spots. Founded in 1852, this classic New England–style fishing village, complete with a white-spired church, is still home to a few fishers and loggers, but writers, artists, therapists, and other urban transplants now outnumber the natives. Springtime is Mendocino's best season, when the streets aren't flooded with tourists and the climbing tea roses and wisteria are in full bloom. The village is so compact you can abandon your car and tour it on foot, visiting the quaint rows of shops that form the heart of Mendocino.

Fort Bragg, Mendocino's working-class cousin 10 miles to the north, was built in 1855 as a military outpost supervising the Pomo Indian Reservation. Now it's primarily a logging and fishing town (as well as the largest city along the Mendocino coast), although gentrification is slowly creeping in with the relentless rise of the tourist trade. If it weren't for Fort Bragg, however, the budget traveler would be hard pressed to find an affordable hotel room within 50 miles. Most cost-conscious vacationers browse the boutiques and galleries of pretty-yet-pricey Mendocino by day, then dine and recline in inexpensive Fort Bragg by night.

Exploring

Like many towns hugging the Northern California coast, Mendocino's premier attractions are provided gratis (or nearly so) by Mother Nature and the Department of Parks and Recreation. **Mendocino Headlands State Park,** the grassy stretch of land between Mendocino village and the ocean, is one of the town's most popular attractions. The park's flat, 3-mile-long trail winds along the edge of a heather-covered bluff, providing spectacular sunset views and good lookout points for seabirds and California gray whales. A few miles south of Mendocino off Highway 1 is **Van Damme State Park,** 707/937-0851, a 2,072-acre preserve blanketed with ferns and second-growth redwoods. The park has a small beach, a museum, and a campground, but its main attraction is the 15 miles of spectacularly lush trails—ideal for a stroll or a jog—that start at the beach and wind through the tree-covered hills. **Fern Canyon Trail** is the park's best, an easy, incredibly scenic, 2.5-mile hiking and bicycling path that crosses over the Little River. You may also hike or drive (most of the way) to Van Damme's peculiar **Pygmy Forest,** an eerie scrub forest of waist-high stunted trees that grew on a limestone deposit (by car, follow Highway 1 south of the park and turn up Little River Airport Road, then head uphill for about 3.5 miles).

On the opposite side of Mendocino, about 2 miles north of town off Highway 1, lies the often photographed, 1,500-acre **Russian Gulch State Park,** 707/937-5804, a paradise for sunbathers, fishers, bird-watchers, and snorkelers. Pick up a trail map at the park's entrance, then walk down the path to **Devil's Punch Bowl**—a 200-foot-long tunnel carved by the sea, with an immense blowhole that's particularly spectacular during

Hurray for Mendo-Wood

If the house on the corner of Little Lake and Ford Streets in Mendocino looks familiar, perhaps that's because it was the set for the hit TV show "Murder, She Wrote," starring Angela Lansbury. Mendocino's Cape Cod–style architecture and beautiful landscapes have made it to the big screen, too. Did you recognize them in East of Eden, Summer of '42, Same Time Next Year, and Forever Young?

Shopping Strategies

You can spend more time shopping and less time walking if you pick up a free copy of the handy "Guide to Shops & Galleries, Restaurants & Lodgings." The guide provides a map and a brief description of most stores in the area; the Mendocino edition is available at the Ford House Visitor Center (735 Main Street, next to the public rest rooms, Mendocino, 707/937-5397). For the Fort Bragg edition, go to the Fort Bragg–Mendocino Coast Chamber of Commerce (332 N Main Street, Fort Bragg, 800/726-2780 or 707/961-6300).

a storm. For another good hike (or bike ride), follow the Falls Loop Trail to the Russian Gulch Falls. Farther north on Highway 1, 1.5 miles north of the town of Caspar, is **Jug Handle State Reserve's Ecological Staircase Trail,** 707/937-5804. Hike up the series of naturally formed, steplike bluffs—each one about 100 feet higher and 100,000 years older than the one below—and observe how the trees and soil differ dramatically on each "ecological step."

The top beachcombing spot in the area is at **MacKerricher State Park,** 707/937-5804, 3 miles north of Fort Bragg off Highway 1. Here you'll find an 8-mile stretch of sandy beaches speckled with tide pools, as well as numerous sand dunes, miles of hiking trails, and even an underwater park for divers. Within the state park is **Laguna Point,** one of the region's best spots for viewing harbor seals and gray whales.

If you have a passion for plants and pretty scenery, spend a few dollars to take the self-guided tour of the **Mendocino Coast Botanical Gardens** (18220 Highway 1, 2 miles south of Fort Bragg, 707/964-4352). The nonprofit gardens feature 47 acres of native plants—from azaleas and rhododendrons to dwarf conifers and ferns—as well as a picnic area and a restaurant. You can even purchase some of your favorite flower and plant species at the nursery.

Outdoor enthusiasts willing to dole out money for adventure find plenty of recreation in the Mendocino/Fort Bragg region. **Ricochet Ridge Ranch** (24201 Highway 1, Fort Bragg, 707/964-PONY) offers guided horseback rides (English or Western saddle) along the beach and in the redwoods. At **Lost Coast Adventures** (19275 S Harbor Drive, Fort Bragg, 707/937-2434) you can rent an ocean kayak to explore the shoreline, coastal rivers, or—along with a guide—sea caves that are nearabouts.

To rent mountain bikes for exploring nearby Van Damme and Russian Gulch State Parks, or to rent a kayak, canoe, or outrigger for a leisurely

Comfort Camping

Like to camp along the coast, but hate the hassle of pitching tents and picking grains of sand out of your food? Here's the solution: call North Coast Trailer Rentals, 619/648-7509, and ask them to set up one of their self-contained, fully equipped trailers for you and your friends. You select the seaside campground (it must be in the Fort Bragg/Mendocino area); they take care of the rest. There's a three-night minimum, and prices start at about $65 a night—a real deal for beachfront property.

paddle up the Big River, go to **Catch a Canoe & Bicycles, Too!** (at Highway 1 and Comptche-Ukiah Road, a half mile south of Mendocino, 707/937-0273).

Between December and April, the migrating California gray whales and humpback whales make their annual appearance along the North Coast. Although they're visible from the bluffs, you can meet the 40-ton cetaceans face-to-face by boarding one of the whale-watching boats in Fort Bragg; the **Tally Ho II** (in the Old Fish House, N Harbor Drive, Fort Bragg, 707/964-2079) charter offers two-hour tours for about $20. Another great way to get out on the ocean is to book a trip on one of the numerous fishing charters that depart from Fort Bragg's Noyo Harbor. For approximately $55 per person, which includes rod, bait, and a one-day fishing license, **Anchor Charter Boats,** 707/964-4550, takes you on a five-hour salmon or bottom-fishing trip. Equipment, instruction, and fish-cleaning services are provided.

You can give your tired dogs a break from beating up and down those coastal trails by booking passage aboard Fort Bragg's popular **Skunk Train** (so named because the odoriferous mix of diesel and gasoline once used to fuel the train allowed you to smell it before you could see it roaring down the tracks). Depending on which day you depart, a steam-, diesel-, or electric-engine train takes you on a scenic six- to seven-hour round-trip journey through the stupendous redwoods to the city of **Willits** and back again (or you can take the four-hour round-trip excursion to Northspur). Reservations are recommended, especially in summer (100 Laurel Street Depot, Fort Bragg, 707/964-6371).

The North Coast has never been famous for golf or tennis, but if you get the urge to smack a ball across the range or over the net, head for the **Little River Inn Golf and Tennis Club** (7750 Highway 1, Little River, 707/937-5667). Located a few miles south of Mendocino on Highway

Budget Lunch Tip #1

*The **Little River Market**, 707/937-5133, located across from the Little River Inn on Highway 1, has a great little deli serving inexpensive sandwiches, bagels, tamales, and even an assortment of just-baked breads from the famed Mendocino eatery Café Beaujolais. Three small tables in the back overlook a gorgeous view of the bay. Open 8am–7pm daily.*

1, the club has a regulation nine-hole course, driving range, lighted tennis courts, and a pro shop—all open to the public.

Recreational shoppers should whip out their Gold Cards and head straight for **Mendocino.** The majority of its stores and boutiques are sandwiched between a 4-block stretch of Ukiah and Main Streets. The village is well known for its classy jewelry shops and stylish clothing boutiques; a couple others that shouldn't be missed are **Mendocino Jams & Preserves** (440 Main Street at Woodward Street, Mendocino, 707/937-1037), a town landmark that offers free tastings of marmalades, dessert toppings, mustards, chutneys, and other spreads; and the **Gallery Bookshop** (Main Street at Kasten Street, Mendocino, 707/937-2665), which has wonderful selections for kids, cooks, and local-history buffs.

Mendocino also has two museums with changing exhibitions that are worth a brief visit: the **Ford House** (735 Main Street, between Kasten and Lansing Streets, Mendocino, 707/937-5397), one of the area's oldest homes, and the **Kelly House** (45007 Albion Street at Lansing Street, Mendocino, 707/937-5791). The highly regarded, nonprofit **Mendocino Art Center** (45200 Little Lake Street, between Williams and Kasten Streets, Mendocino, 707/937-5818), where scenes for the James Dean flick *East of Eden* were filmed, offers art classes, poetry readings, storytelling sessions, and occasional concerts.

After you've explored the village and headlands, walk down to the east end of Ukiah Street and treat your tired body to one of **Sweetwater**

Budget Lunch Tip #2

*Seafood doesn't get any fresher than the tasty cod-cheeks-and-chips from the deep fryers of **Eureka Fisheries Inc.**, 707/964-1600, at Fort Bragg's Noyo Harbor. There's even live entertainment—watching the sea lions vie for dock space. Open daily 11am–5:30pm.*

Garden's (955 Ukiah Street, Mendocino, 800/300-4140 or 707/937-4140) private or group hot tubs and saunas. Or for some true TLC, blow your budget on a soothing Swedish massage.

If you've browsed all over Mendocino and still have the shopping bug, head to downtown **Fort Bragg,** which has enough shops and galleries—all within walking distance of one another—to keep you entertained for hours. Another good place for a spree is the **Fort Bragg Depot** (401 Main Street at Laurel Street, Fort Bragg, 707/964-4367), a 14,000-square-foot marketplace with more than 20 shops and restaurants, as well as a historical logging and railroad museum.

After a full day of adventuring, why not top off the evening with a little nightcap and music? If you appreciate classical tunes and warm snifters of brandy, take a stroll down Mendocino's Main Street to the elegant bar and lounge at the **Mendocino Hotel and Restaurant** (45080 Main Street, Mendocino, 707/937-0511). If blue jeans and baseball caps are more your style, hang out with the guys at **Dick's Place** (45080 Main Street, next to the Mendocino Hotel, Mendocino, 707/937-5643), which has the cheapest drinks in town and the sort of jukebox 'n' jiggers atmosphere you'd expect from this former logging town's oldest bar. For a rowdy night of dancing and drinking, head a few miles up Highway 1 to **Caspar Inn,** the last true roadhouse in California, where everything from rock and jazz to reggae and blues is played live Thursday through Saturday nights starting at 9:30pm (take the Caspar Road exit off Highway 1, 4 miles north of Mendocino and 4 miles south of Fort Bragg, 707/964-5565).

Cheap Eats

North Coast Brewing Company

444 N Main Street, Fort Bragg ☎ 707/964-3400

This homey brew pub is the most happening place in town, especially at happy hour, when the bar and dark wood tables are occupied by boisterous locals. The pub is housed in a dignified, century-old redwood structure, which in previous lives has functioned as a mortuary, an annex to the local Presbyterian Church, an art studio, and administration offices for the College of the Redwoods. Beer is brewed on

Deluxe Dining Tip

Tuesday through Thursday, the nationally acclaimed Café Beaujolais (961 Ukiah Street, Mendocino, 707/937-5614) offers a prix-fixe country menu for only $25.

the premises, in large copper vats displayed behind plate glass. You'll like the menu, too, which offers above-average pub grub—hamburgers, ribs, roast chicken, chili—as well as more exotic fare ranging from Mayan roast pork to seafood crepes. *DIS, MC, V; checks OK; lunch, dinner Tues–Sun; beer and wine.*

Viraporn's Thai Café
500 S Main Street, Fort Bragg ☎ 707/964-7931

When Viraporn Lobell opened this tiny Thai cafe in 1991, Asian-food aficionados on the North Coast breathed a communal sigh of relief. Born in northern Thailand, Viraporn attended cooking school and apprenticed in restaurants there before coming to the United States. After moving to the North Coast with her husband, Paul, she worked for a while at Mendocino's most popular restaurant, Café Beaujolais. A master at balancing the five traditional Thai flavors of hot, bitter, tart, sweet, and salty, Viraporn works wonders with refreshing Thai classics such as spring rolls, satays, pad thai, lemongrass soup, and a wide range of curry dishes. *No credit cards; checks OK; lunch Mon, Wed–Fri, dinner Wed–Mon; beer and wine.*

Bay View Café
45040 Main Street, Mendocino ☎ 707/937-4197

This homey, lively, and reasonably priced cafe is one of the most popular eateries in town for breakfast. Be sure to request a table on the second floor, which has a sweeping view of the headlands and ocean. Breakfast ranges from the basic bacon 'n' eggs to eggs Florentine and omelets to more inciting options such as honey-wheat pancakes. The lunch and dinner menu offers pseudo-Southwestern selections (the marinated chicken breast is hugely popular) as well as an array of sandwiches (try the hot crabmeat with avocado slices), fish-and-chips, and the fresh catch of the day. *No credit cards; checks OK; breakfast, lunch, dinner Fri–Sun (winter, no dinners); full bar.*

Lettuce Rejoice

Long before "pesticide-free" became the mantra of California growers, organic gardening was the modus operandi of Mendocino-area farmers. For years, they've catered to such health- and quality-conscious clients as the famous chefs of Mendocino's Café Beaujolais; although the produce is pricey, you'll pay less for it if you forgo the stores and buy direct from the growers. From May through October, they sell their luscious strawberries, asparagus, melons, and other goodies to the public at the Mendocino Farmers Market on Fridays, from noon to 2pm (Howard Street, between Main and Ukiah Streets), and at the Fort Bragg Farmers Market on Wednesdays, from 3:30pm to 5:30pm (Laurel Street, between Franklin and McPherson Streets).

Lu's Kitchen

45013 Ukiah Street, Mendocino ☎ 707/937-4939

For a quick, healthy bite to eat while touring Mendocino, keep an eye peeled for a small shack with a few plastic tables around it on Ukiah Street between Lansing and Ford Streets. The mostly Mexican menu—burritos, tacos, salads, and quesadillas—is all vegetarian, organically grown, and a real deal. *No credit cards; checks OK; lunch every day; no alcohol.*

Mendo Burgers

10483 Lansing Street, Mendocino ☎ 707/937-1111

One of the best burger-and-fries combos in California is at Mendo Burgers, located behind the Mendocino Café. Also cheap and filling are the scrumptious beef, chicken, fish, turkey, and veggie burgers served with a side of fresh-cut fries and plenty of napkins. It's a bit hard to find—head for the back patio of the Mendocino Café—but if you love a good, juicy burger, it's worth the search. *No credit cards; checks OK; lunch, early dinner every day; no alcohol.*

Mendocino Café

10451 Lansing Street, Mendocino ☎ 707/937-2422

The Mendocino Café is one of the last vestiges of the Mendocino of the '60s. Everyone, from nursing mothers to tie-dyed teenagers to Gap-clad couples, queues up for the cafe's eclectic mix of Asian and Mexican specialties, served fresh and fast. The hands-down winner is the Thai burrito, a steamed flour tortilla filled with brown rice, sautéed vegetables, a healthy dash of the cafe's fresh chili sauce, and a choice of smoked chicken, pork, or beef. The hot Thai salad, spicy nachos, and barbecued half chicken are also good bets. Xenophobes needn't worry: there's also good ol' American food like salads, steaks, and fresh fish, as well as macaroni and cheese for the kids. If the weather's mild, grab a table on the deck. *DC, DIS, MC, V; checks OK; lunch Mon–Fri, dinner every day, brunch Sat–Sun; beer and wine.*

Tote Fete Bakery

10450 Lansing Street, Mendocino ☎ 707/937-3383

Tote Fete Bakery, located on the corner of Albion and Lansing Streets in downtown Mendocino, has a wonderful little carry-out booth offering an array of inexpensive eats such as foil-wrapped barbecued-chicken sandwiches, pizza by the slice, focaccia bread, and twice-baked potatoes. The deli has a small dining counter, but a better idea is to order it all to go and have a picnic at the headlands just down the street. *No credit cards; checks OK; lunch, early dinner every day; no alcohol.*

Cheap Sleeps

Jug Handle Creek Farm

Highway 1, south of Jug Handle Beach, Caspar, CA 95420 ☎ 707/964-4630

If you bring along your sleeping bag, you can rent some floor space and a foam mat or a bed in a private bedroom for a night at this beautiful century-old farmhouse in Caspar, a tiny town hidden off Highway 1 between Mendocino and Fort Bragg. The farmhouse offers only 20 sleeping spaces, so reservations are recommended; you also may pitch a tent on the 39-acre property or, if you're lucky enough to get a vacancy, rent one of the farm's two small cabins for a reasonable rate. Guests are expected to do one hour of chores for each night they stay—or, instead, pay an additional $5 a night. The basic nightly rate also includes cooking privileges in the huge kitchen—another way to cut costs on meals. *MC, V; checks OK; www.jughandle.creek.org.*

Beachcomber Motel

1111 N Main Street, Fort Bragg, CA 95437 ☎ 800/400-7873
or ☎ 707/964-2402

If all those fancy B&Bs in Mendocino are way out of your price range, the Beachcomber Motel has just what you're looking for. Okay, so the rooms aren't exactly reeking with ambience, but they are certainly spacious, comfortable, and equipped with the basic necessities such as cable TV and private bathrooms. Not that it matters much, since you'll be spending most of your time on the huge back deck that overlooks the cool blue Pacific (at sunset it's a veritable postcard view). Directly across from the motel is MacKerricher State Park's miles of beaches and dunes. Those in the know get a room with a kitchenette, stock up on groceries, and make use of the barbecue area. Rates range from $59 for a standard room with no ocean view to $195 for the deluxe suite with king bed, hot tub, fireplace, and ocean view. Pets are welcome but cost you an extra $10. A huge 45-room expansion was completed in May 1999. *AE, DIS, MC, V; no checks.*

Coast Motel

18661 Highway 1, Fort Bragg, CA 95437 ☎ 707/964-2852

Even if there aren't any cheap sleeps in Mendocino, Fort Bragg's Coast Motel is only 6 miles away. Located off Highway 1 at the southernmost end of town, this motel's 28 rooms have all the standard amenities—color TV, private bath, double bed, desk—plus a few extra perks, such as a heated pool, 4 acres of woods that children enjoy exploring, and—hold on to your tackle box—a fish-cleaning facility. Many rooms have refrigerators; three have kitchenettes. The motel isn't within walking distance of any restaurants or shops, but it offers more seclusion and serenity than the motels along Fort Bragg's Main Street. And for an extra $5, you can bring your pooch. *MC, V; no checks.*

Columbi Motel

647 Oak Street, Fort Bragg, CA 95437 ☎ 707/964-5773

Without a doubt, the Columbi is one of the least expensive motels on the North Coast. Yet, ironically, this 21-room motel has more amenities than any other in Fort Bragg. Most of the rooms come with cable TV, double or queen-size bed, private bathroom, full-size fridge, stove, sink, small desk, and your own carport. If you're traveling with the family or a large group, reserve one of the two-bedroom units or suites that sleep up to six. The motel is located 5 blocks from Main Street in a quiet residential neighborhood, and it's within steps of a laundry, a taqueria, and the Columbi Market, which is where the motel's guests check in and out. *MC, V; no checks.*

Fort Bragg Motel

763 N Main Street, Fort Bragg, CA 95437 ☎ 800/253-9972 or ☎ 707/964-4787

The 48-room Fort Bragg Motel is only a 3-block stroll from Glass Beach, and within staggering distance of the North Coast Brewing Company. While it earns zero points for character, it scores a perfect 10 for cleanliness. Each of the "soundproof" rooms is equipped with a queen-size bed, lamp, chair, phone, TV, and bathroom—all the creature comforts of home. *AE, MC, V; no checks.*

Ocean Breeze Lodge

212 S Main Street, Fort Bragg, CA 95437 ☎ 707/961-1177

Husband-and-wife owners Linda and Tino Tarantino work hard to keep their gleaming peach-colored lodge in pristine shape. The eight-room Ocean Breeze is located on the main strip of downtown Fort Bragg, so it's plagued by the steady drone of traffic, but if a large, comfy bed, spotless bathroom, TV, and reasonable room rate are enough to keep you content for a night or two, then you won't be disappointed. Linda pours complimentary coffee for guests each morning and is happy to offer sight-seeing suggestions. *MC, V; no checks; www.oceanbreezelodge.com.*

Eureka & Arcata

One can only wonder what city officials in the early 19th century were thinking when they named this town after the popular gold-mining expression "Eureka!" (Greek for "I have found it"). They certainly never found any gold in these parts. Perhaps the Eureka of yesteryear offered more to get excited about, but today the North Coast's largest city (population 27,000) has little for the visitor except a slew of inexpensive motels, fast-food restaurants, and a somewhat entertaining Old Town dignified by stately Victorian buildings. Most travelers take advantage of Eureka's budget prices and bunk down here for the night, then head north to Arcata and the Lost Coast for more stimulating explorations.

Just up the highway from Eureka is the much smaller and inviting community of Arcata, home to Humboldt State University (the northernmost college of the California State University system). As with most college towns, everyone tends to lean toward the left: environmentalism, artistry, and good beads and bagels are indispensable elements of the Arcatian philosophy, as is a cordial disposition toward tourists, making this one of the more interesting and visitor-friendly towns along the North Coast.

Exploring

The heart of Eureka is **Old Town,** a 13-block-long stretch of shops, restaurants, and hotels, most of which are housed in painstakingly preserved Victorian structures (a favored architectural style in these parts).

Talk of the Town

Worried about getting lost in the Lost Coast? Curious about Eureka's Victorian architectural heritage? Let loquacious historian Ray Hillman lead the way on one of his reasonably priced guided tours offered from May through September; 800/400-1849.

Bordered by 1st and 3rd Streets, between C and M Streets, the neighborhood takes only about an hour or two to ramble through, although bookworms might get sidetracked at the **Booklegger** (402 2nd Street, Eureka, 707/445-1344), a marvelous store with thousands of used paperbacks (especially mysteries, westerns, and science fiction) as well as children's books and cookbooks. For a look at one of the country's finest examples of Victorian architecture, visit the multi-gabled-and-turreted **Carson Mansion** (corner of 2nd and M Streets, Eureka), built of redwood in 1886 for lumber baron William Carson, who initiated the construction to keep mill workers occupied during a lull in the lumber business. Although the three-story, money-green mansion is closed to the public (it's now a snooty men's club), you can stand on the sidewalk and click your Kodak at one of the state's most-photographed houses.

History buffs should stroll through the **Clarke Memorial Museum** (240 E Street at 3rd Street, Eureka, 707/443-1947), which has one of the top Native American displays in the state, showcasing more than 1,200 examples of Hupa, Yurok, and Karuk basketry, dance regalia, and stonework. A block away, there's more Native American artwork, including quality silver jewelry, at the **Indian Art & Gift Shop** (241 F Street at 3rd Street, Eureka, 707/445-8451), which sells many of its treasures at reasonable prices.

Just south of Eureka is the **Humboldt Bay National Wildlife Refuge,** a bird-watcher's paradise that is open to the public year-round for hiking, bird-watching, boating, and fishing. More than 200 species of birds feed, rest, or nest in the 2,200 acres of wetlands, marshes, mudflats, and open bay that are accessible by two short, easy foot trails. To get there, take the Hookton Road exit off Highway 101 south of Eureka and turn west on Ranch Road. A free guide to the refuge is available at the Ranch Road entrance. For more information, call 707/733-5406.

Six miles north of Eureka on Highway 101 lies **Arcata,** about half the size of Eureka but with twice the appeal. **Arcata Plaza** (at 8th and G Streets) marks the center of this seaside community, and a statue of

Moveable Feats

Arcata is a festival-happy town, and its wackiest event is the World Championship Great Arcata to Ferndale Cross-Country Kinetic Sculpture Race. The three-day event, held every Memorial Day weekend, draws more than 10,000 spectators, who come to watch about 50 crazy competitors try to slog through 38 grueling miles of sand, swamp, and salt water in their custom-made, people-powered amphibious crafts. Contestants start in Arcata Plaza, pass though Eureka, and finish (if they're lucky) in the town of Ferndale. Cheating and bribery are part of the rules, provided they're done with "proper style and panache."

President McKinley stands guard over the numerous shops and cafes housed in the historic buildings. At the plaza's southwest end is its flagship structure, **Jacoby's Storehouse** (791 8th Street at H Street, Arcata, 707/822-2434), a handsomely restored 1857 pack-train station that now holds shops, offices, and restaurants. Also worth a look is the **Tin Can Mailman** (1000 H Street at 10th Street, Arcata, 707/822-1307), a terrific used-book store with 130,000 hard- and soft-cover titles, including a few collector's items.

Once you've toured the downtown, it's time to explore Arcata's numerous parks and preserves. A two-minute drive east on 11th Street takes you to the town's beloved 20-acre **Redwood Park,** an ideal picnic spot with a playground guaranteed to entertain the tots. Adjoining the park is the **Arcata Community Forest,** 600 acres of second-growth redwoods favored by hikers, mountain bikers, and equestrians; before you go, pick up free guides to the forest's mountain-biking and hiking trails at the Chamber of Commerce (1062 G Street at 11th Street, Arcata, 707/822-3619). Across town is the 154-acre **Arcata Marsh and Wildlife Preserve,** a 154-acre sanctuary for hundreds of egrets, marsh wrens, and other waterfowl (as well as joggers), and including Arcata's integrated wetland wastewater treatment plant. A free, self-guided walking-tour map is available at the Chamber of Commerce (see above), or join the Audubon Society's free one-hour guided tours, held rain or shine, on Saturday at 8:30am (meet at the south end of I Street, Arcata, 707/826-7031).

To kill some time without killing your budget, investigate Arcata's small-town diversions, such as attending a **Humboldt Crabs game;** this local semipro baseball team plays in the charming Arcata Ballpark (at the corner of 9th and F Streets, Arcata). Most games are in the evening

Down the Hatch

When you take the 75-minute narrated bay cruise aboard the M.V. Madaket, you'll not only be riding on the oldest continuously operating vessel in the United States, you'll be ordering drinks from the smallest licensed bar in California. Sip your spirits while you watch the seals play, and listen to veteran Captain Leroy Zerlang's witty—well, after you've had a few gin-and-tonics, he's witty—and well-rehearsed narrative of Eureka's tempestuous maritime past. The ship departs several times daily from the foot of C Street in Eureka's Old Town; 707/445-1910.

throughout the summer; the schedule is posted at the Chamber of Commerce and in shops and restaurants around town. For a wide range of first-run and classic repertory flicks, queue up at the **Arcata Theatre** (1036 G Street at 10th Street, Arcata, 707/822-5171) or the **Minor Theatre** (1013 H Street at 10th Street, Arcata, 707/822-5171), both of which charge below-average prices—particularly for matinees. You can see (and touch!) 3.66-billion-year-old fossils and view various California flora and fauna at **Humboldt State University's Natural History Museum** (13th and G Streets, Arcata, 707/826-4479). The university also offers art exhibits and theater, dance, and musical performances on campus year-round (14th Street and L. K. Wood Boulevard, Arcata, 707/826-3011).

For more information about Eureka, Arcata, or Humboldt, contact the **Eureka/Humboldt County Convention and Visitors Bureau** (1034 2nd Street, Eureka, 800/346-3482 or 707/443-5097) or the **Eureka Chamber of Commerce** (2112 Broadway, Eureka, 800/356-6381 or 707/442-3738).

Cheap Eats

Humboldt Brewing Company
856 10th Street, Arcata ☎ 707/826-BREW

Heaven on earth is a full pitcher of Red Nectar Ale and a big ol' jumbo burger (medium rare) at the Humboldt Brewing Company, located at the corner of 10th and G Streets in downtown Arcata. You'll immediately love this classic brew pub with its profusion of well-worn wood furnishings, giant beer-making machinery, and seemingly endless pitchers of their award-winning Pale Ale. On weekend nights stop by for some great live country, folk, or blues music. Brewery tours are offered as well (call for times). *AE, DIS, MC, V; no checks; dinner Wed–Sat; beer and wine.*

Los Bagels

1061 I Street, Arcata ☎ 707/822-3150
403 2nd Street, Eureka ☎ 707/822-3150

In 1987 bagel companies all over the country sent their doughy products to NBC's "Today Show" to vie for the title of Best Bagel. The verdict: the best bagel outside of New York City was made by Los Bagels in Arcata. This emporium is a popular town hangout, where you'll see lots of folks scanning the morning paper while they munch on bagels layered with smoked salmon, smoked albacore, or lox. Try some fresh-baked challah or, if you're feeling particularly adventurous, a poppy-seed bagel topped with jalapeño jam and cream cheese, or a multigrain bagel smeared with hummus or guacamole. Owing to Los Bagels's brisk business, the owners opened a second location in Eureka. *No credit cards; local checks only; breakfast, lunch Wed–Mon; no alcohol.*

Samoa Cookhouse

79 Cookhouse Lane, Eureka ☎ 707/442-1659

Visiting the Eureka area without a stop at the Samoa Cookhouse is like visiting Paris without seeing the Eiffel Tower. This venerable dining spot is the last surviving cookhouse in the West (it's been in operation for more than a century) and a Humboldt County institution, where guests are served lumber camp–style in an enormous barnlike building at long tables covered with checkered tablecloths. Few decisions are required—just sit down, and the food will come until you say uncle. Breakfast typically features sausages, biscuits, scrambled eggs, and potatoes as well as a choice of French toast, hash browns, or pancakes (not to mention all the coffee and OJ you can drink). Lunch and dinner include potatoes and the meat of the day, which might be ham, fried chicken, pork chops, roast beef, barbecued chicken, or fish. Mind you, the food isn't great (except for the delicious bread, which is baked on the premises), but there's plenty of it. And just when you think you're about to burst, along comes the fresh-baked pie. After your meal, spend a few minutes waddling

Beet of a Different Grower

If purple potatoes, cylindra beets, and other fancy foods are on your shopping list, you'll find them at the farmers markets held weekly in Eureka and Arcata. Most of the produce is grown along the local Eel, Mad, and Trinity Rivers, and is sold at bargain prices at Arcata Plaza on Saturdays 9am–1pm, May to November; in Eureka Mall (800 W Harris Avenue, at the south end of town) on Thursdays 10am–1pm, June to October; and in Eureka's Old Town on F Street on Tuesdays 10am–1pm, July to October.

through the adjoining logging museum. *AE, DIS, MC, V; checks OK; breakfast, lunch, dinner every day; no alcohol.*

Tomaso's Tomato Pies

216 E Street, Eureka ☎ 707/445-0100

This family-style Italian pizza parlor reeks so divinely of baked garlic and olive oil that you can smell it a block away. At the top of the list of Tomaso's favored fare are the calzone and the spinach pies, both guaranteed to make garlic lovers (and their dining partners) swoon. Other popular plates include the chicken cannelloni and the square pizza with a whole-wheat crust. For a proper Italian finale, order a Cremosa: a blend of milk, soda water, and whipped cream infused with a fruity Torani Italian syrup. *AE, DIS, MC, V; local checks only; lunch Mon–Sat, dinner every day; beer and wine.*

Cheap Sleeps

Fairwinds Motel

1674 G Street, Arcata, CA 95521 ☎ 707/822-4824

Aside from the Arcata Crew House dormitory, the Fairwinds Motel is the only budget accommodation in Arcata. Located 2 blocks from Humboldt State (Highway 101 at 17th Street), this motel has 27 plain but pleasant rooms, all with direct-dial phones, cable TV, and double or queen-size beds. Although the hotel has been around for a few decades and its age lines are showing, the rooms have been completely remodeled, with new beds and modern furnishings and prints. *AE, DIS, MC, V; no checks.*

Bayview Motel

2844 Fairfield Street, Eureka, CA 95501 ☎ 707/442-1673

The Bayview Motel is Eureka's best motel and so squeaky-clean you could eat off the floor. Perched on a knoll high above noisy Highway 101, the Bayview *does* have a view of the bay, but you have to look really hard past the industrial park to see it. Each of the 17 "minisuites" has a private bath, remote-control TV, and queen-size bed; rates are about $75 a night, but it's worth the extra few dollars. The motel's best views are actually of the lovely, meticulously manicured lawn and garden. If you feel like splurging, request a room with a Jacuzzi or fireplace. Family units are also available. *AE, DIS, MC, V; no checks.*

Downtowner Motel

424 8th Street, Eureka, CA 95501 ☎ 707/443-5061

You can't judge a book by its cover, but you can usually judge a Eureka motel by its exterior. Of the town's 40 or so budget lodgings, only a handful aren't really run-down, and the Downtowner is one of them. The motel's best asset is its location—well off the noisy main strip (between E and F Streets) yet within walking distance of Old Town. It also has great amenities, including a heated pool, sauna, Jacuzzi, and a funky cocktail lounge. The 72 plain-Jane rooms are decorated in brown tones and equipped with queen-size beds, remote-control cable TV, and direct-dial phones. Rates include a continental breakfast. *AE, DIS, MC, V; checks OK.*

Fireside Inn

1716 5th Street, Eureka, CA 95501 ☎ 707/443-6312

If Eureka's Downtowner and Bayview Motels are full, try the Fireside Inn, which is certainly more hospitable than its Cheap Sleeps competitors along Highway 101. Each of the 65 rooms has a refrigerator and cable TV, and some have a microwave oven. Family and kitchen units are also available, and the inn's tiny laundry room is open to guests. Located at the north end of downtown, the motel is a short walk from Old Town shops and restaurants. *AE, DIS, MC, V; no checks.*

Cascade Range

mount shasta
lassen volcanic national park

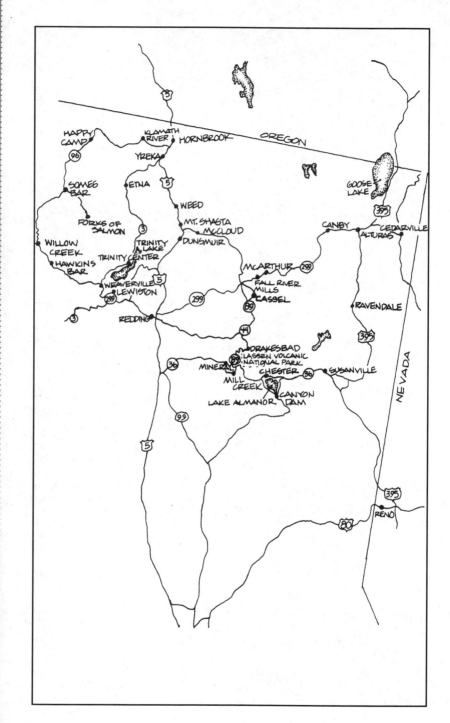

Mount Shasta

Magnificent, snowcapped Mount Shasta soars 14,162 feet into the sky, making it the tallest mountain in California's Cascade Range and the largest volcano in the contiguous 48 states. Shasta is a dormant volcano: not dead, just sleeping until it decides to blow its snowy stack—something it hasn't done since the late 1700s. While it may seem long overdue for an eruption, fear not; geologists constantly monitor movement within the volcano and claim they will be able to predict an eruption well in advance—early enough for you to pack your bags and safely skedaddle.

Shasta is only the fifth-highest peak in the state, but unlike its taller cousins, which are clustered with other large mountains, this volcano stands alone, a position that seems to intensify its grandeur. "Lonely as God and white as a winter moon" is how author Joaquin Miller described this solitary peak in the 1870s. The mountain dominates the horizon from every angle, and on clear days it's visible from as far away as 150 miles.

Some Native Americans who lived in its shadow believed Mount Shasta was the home of the Great Spirit and vowed never to disrespect it by climbing its sacred slopes. Today, men and women from around the world pay tribute to the volcano by making the spectacular trek to the top. This is not a mountain for novice hikers, however; its many tremendous crevasses have swallowed careless climbers, and the extreme, unpredictable weather changes at high altitudes make expert equipment a must. But with some basic mountain-climbing instruction and a good study of Shasta's various routes, physically fit adventurers can safely reach its stunning summit. ("It's just like climbing stairs nonstop from 9 to 5," says one veteran climber.)

This region of Northern California is actually known for its "three Shastas": Shasta Dam, the second-largest and -tallest concrete dam in the nation (containing enough concrete to build a 3-foot-wide sidewalk around the world); Shasta Lake, the largest reservoir in California; and the mighty mountain itself. Together they make for an immense recreational playground that draws hikers, rock climbers, fishers, campers, houseboaters, snow skiers, water-skiers, river rafters, bird-watchers, and many other outdoor enthusiasts. Fortunately, this northernmost region of California is so vast it's possible to escape the summer crowds by backpacking into the wilderness, where your only companions will be bald eagles, black bears, Rocky Mountain elk, and the other numerous critters that call the Shasta area home.

Exploring

As you zip along Interstate 5 heading north, keep an eye out for the monolithic **Shasta Dam,** a great place to pull over for a lengthy pit stop. Granted, the visitors center and viewing area are rather ho-hum, but the free 45-minute tour of the dam is outstanding (tours are held from 9am to 4pm daily; call ahead for winter and holiday hours). The tour kicks off with a speedy elevator ride down into the chilly bowels of the 15-million-ton, 602-foot-high structure (definitely not recommended for claustrophobes). Next comes a brief spiel on what it takes to make the behemoth dam function, followed by a look at the ominous spillway and inner workings of this impressive power plant. All in all, it's one of the best and most entertaining free tours in Northern California (kids love it) and a great way to beat the summer heat; from Interstate 5, take

A Houseboating Hiatus

Most savvy Northern Californians agree that renting a houseboat and basking in the sun on Shasta Lake is one of the not-to-be-missed recreational activities of this region. So what are you waiting for? Smooth-talk your beer-guzzling, bass-fishing, book-reading buddies into chipping in on a big ol' Shasta Cruiser. Prices range from about $150 to $300 a day, which means if you get five friends together, that's only $30 a night each for prime lakefront property. Houseboats are in high demand during summer, so make reservations very early (deposits are required). Shasta Lake rental companies include Antlers Marina, 800/238-3924; Bridge Bay Resort, 530/275-3021; Holiday Harbor, 800/776-2628; Lakeshore Marina, 530/238-2301; Lakeview Marina, 530/223-3003; Packers Bay Marina, 800/331-3137; and Shasta Marina, 800/959-3359.

the Shasta Dam Boulevard exit and follow the signs (about 50 miles south of Mount Shasta, Shasta Lake, 530/275-4463).

About 10 miles up the highway is another popular attraction: guided tours of the impressive, crystal-studded stalagmites and stalactites in the **Lake Shasta Caverns** (you'll have to fork over $15 per adult and $7 per child over 3 for this two-hour excursion). Getting there is an adventure in itself; after you pull off the highway and check in at the cavern headquarters, you'll hop aboard a ferry for a 15-minute trip across Shasta Lake, then climb onto a bus for a white-knuckle ride up to the caverns, open daily year-round (from Interstate 5, take the Shasta Caverns Road exit and follow the signs, Shasta Lake, 530/238-2341).

Back on the highway, continuing toward the town of Mount Shasta, you'll see many arms of **Shasta Lake,** which is fed primarily by the Sacramento, Pit, and McCloud Rivers. Plagued by years of drought, the enormous lake—with 370 miles of shoreline—was something of an eyesore until recent floodings brought it back to normal levels. Although a haven for houseboaters and fishers who arrive by the thousands in summer, most of the lake is accessible only by boat, which limits many budget travelers' options to a free swim (and sunburn) and some picnicking. A better bet is to continue north along Interstate 5 to **Castle Crags State Park,** one of California's geologic wonders. The enormous 6,500-foot spires of ancient granite are visible from the highway, but they deserve a much closer look. If you're anxious to really stretch your legs, hike up the park's moderately strenuous 2.7-mile **Summit Dome Trail** to the base of the crags—the view of Mount Shasta alone is worth

The Bald Eagle Returns

If ever there were a reason to keep your eye on the sky while traveling through the Shasta Cascades, it's to catch a glimpse of the nation's symbol, the bald eagle. Shasta Lake is currently the home of 18 pairs of the endangered birds—the largest nesting population of bald eagles in California. The largest bird of prey in North America, the eagle mates for life, replacing a partner only if it dies. The majestic birds return to the same nest every January or February to breed. To spot an adult, look for a white head and tail, dark-brown body, and a 6- to 7½-foot wingspan.

the trip. Less adventurous souls can stroll along the 1-mile Root Creek or Indian Creek Trails or picnic among the pines and wildflowers—a refreshing break from the long, hot drive (from Interstate 5, take the Castle Crags State Park exit, about 13 miles south of Mount Shasta, 530/235-2684).

If ever a community owed its existence to a 14,162-foot pile of volcanic rock (albeit a pretty pile of rock), it's the friendly town of **Mount Shasta.** The downtown area's shops, motels, and restaurants all cater to the thousands of climbers, skiers, naturalists, and spiritualists who make the long journey here each year. And fortunately for the low-budget traveler, just about every hotel and restaurant offers small-town prices (most rooms start at about $30 a night, and it's not hard to find a meal for less than $7). After securing a hotel room, head right over to the Mount Shasta Visitors Bureau to pick up a free copy of the "Things to See & Do" brochure and the informative "Lodging & Dining Guide," which features a map showing the location of every hotel and restaurant in the area (300 Pine Street at Lake Street, Mount Shasta, 800/926-4865).

For years Mount Shasta has been hailed by spiritualists as one of the seven "power centers" of the world. Although city council members are loathe to admit it (and you certainly won't see the words "channeling" or "crystal" in any Chamber of Commerce brochure), a large percentage of visitors are spiritual pilgrims who have come from around the world to bask in the majestic mountain's mysterious energy. If you're interested in learning about the mountain's alleged mystical powers, visit the delightfully funky **Golden Bough Bookstore** (219 N Mount Shasta Boulevard at Lake Street, Mount Shasta, 530/926-3228), where the staff can give you the spiritual lowdown and direct you to tapes, books, and all manner of info on the topic.

A couple of free attractions in town include the **Sisson Museum,** which showcases changing exhibits on local history, nature, geology, and Native American life, and the adjacent **Mount Shasta Fish Hatchery,** the oldest hatchery in the West, where thousands of rainbow and brown trout, including a few biggies, fill the holding ponds. For only 25 cents you can get some fish food and incite a fish-feeding frenzy (take Lake Street across the freeway, turn left on Hatchery Road, and head to 3 N Old Stage Road, Mount Shasta, 530/926-2215 for hatchery, 530/926-5508 for museum).

The highlight of Mount Shasta is, of course, the mountain itself. If you're fit and raring to climb the snow-topped volcano, make sure you have a well-thought-out plan of action before making the steep ascent. The views from the mountain's peak are unbelievably beautiful, but the steep climb isn't without its perils; crevasses cover the mountain, and avalanches and whiteouts are common at certain times of year (for a mountain report, call 530/926-5555). If you're a newcomer, go to the **Mount Shasta Ranger District office** (204 W Alma Street off N Mount Shasta Boulevard, Mount Shasta, 530/926-4511) for plenty of climbing literature as well as friendly advice. Fill out the free (but mandatory) hiking permit while you're there, so the rangers will know how long you'll be on the mountain (permits are located in a small booth outside the front door and are $15 if you go above 10,000 feet). You also must sign off on your permit after you return from your climb so no one sends a rescue team to search for you.

Next stop is the **Fifth Season** sports store, where you can buy a good map of the mountain and rent crampons, an ice ax, and sturdy, insulated climbing boots; equipment can be reserved in advance. If you have any questions the rangers couldn't answer, ask the store's experienced and helpful staff (300 N Mount Shasta Boulevard at Lake Street, Mount Shasta, 530/926-3606).

To Summit All Up

If you're eager to climb Mount Shasta but you don't know a crampon from a crayon, call the folks at Shasta Mountain Guides. For a reasonable fee, they'll give you an all-day lesson in basic mountain-climbing skills, including how to use an ice ax, crampons, and ropes. For more information and reservations, call Shasta Mountain Guides, 530/926-3117.

Rolling on the River

For an experience you'll never forget, blow your budget and splurge on a guided whitewater-rafting day trip down the mighty Klamath River. Daredevils can soar down the narrow, steep chutes appropriately called Hell's Corner and Caldera, while saner souls (including children) can navigate the much-less-perilous forks. Prices range from $82 to $116 (multiday trips are also available). For more information, call the Turtle River Rafting Company in Mount Shasta, 530/926-3223.

Now you should be ready to load up your gear, drive to the mountain, and psych yourself up for the climb. Most hikers set up a base camp at **Horse Camp** (although the best—and easiest—routes vary with the seasons). They begin their ascent at about 4:30am the next day, and it's a 7-mile journey to the top, which takes at least seven to eight hours of steady climbing. Bring plenty of water, food, warm and waterproof clothing (sudden thunderstorms are not unusual near the peak), glacier goggles, a first-aid kit, and the strongest sunscreen money can buy.

Psst . . . if all this climbing sounds a wee bit intimidating, there is an easier way. For the past 10 years, many folks have made their way up Mount Shasta via a chair lift (though it doesn't reach the peak) and their way down on skis. For about $32 (less on weekdays) you can purchase an all-day lift ticket at **Mount Shasta Ski Park,** which offers mostly intermediate runs with nary a mogul in sight. Ski Park also has a ski and snowboard rental/repair shop, restaurant, snack bar, and ski school. In summer, the resort offers naturalist-led walks, mountain-biking trails accessible by chair lift (bike rentals are available, too), and an indoor recreational climbing wall for people of all ages and abilities (at the end of Ski Park Highway, off Highway 89, 10 miles east of Interstate 5, Mount Shasta, 530/926-8610). About 1.25 miles down the highway is the **Nordic Lodge,** a cross-country-ski center with several miles of groomed tracks (on Ski Park Highway, Mount Shasta, 530/926-8610).

Cheap Eats

The Bagel Café & Bakery

315 N Mount Shasta Boulevard, Mount Shasta ☎ 530/926-1414

As you would expect in a town that caters to climbers, Mount Shasta's restaurants dish out lots of carbohydrates: pizza and pastries are the big sellers here, as well as bagels and strong coffee. Hence, the Bagel Café—the best of the budget-dining options in Mount Shasta and the town's main supplier of fresh-baked bagels, brews, and the most divine coffee in the region. Other crowd pleasers are the fresh vegetarian dishes (try the savory soups or wok-fried veggies and tofu over brown rice), fruit smoothies, organic vegetable juices, pastries, and more. *No credit cards; local checks only; breakfast and lunch daily; no alcohol; www.snowcrest.net/bagel.*

Lily's

1013 S Mount Shasta Boulevard, Mount Shasta ☎ 530/926-3372

Lily's is a popular place that offers very good California cuisine with an ethnic flair. Dinner offerings include spicy Thai noodles, *kung pao* shrimp, and terrific enchiladas *suizas* stuffed with crab, shrimp, and fresh spinach. Lunch dishes are equally varied and imaginative, and if you're looking for something a little different from the usual breakfast fare, try Lily's cheesy polenta fritters. *AE, DIS, MC, V; local checks only; breakfast, lunch Mon—Fri, dinner every day, brunch Sat—Sun and holidays; beer and wine.*

Budget Lunch Tip

In the Rite Aid parking lot at the corner of Lake and Pine Streets in Mount Shasta is a canopied trailer with a sign hanging on it that says Poncho & Lefkowitz. Pull over, queue up with the locals, and chow down on a Pancho Taco, El Supremo Burrito, or other Mexican favorites for less than $5 a plate.

Michael's Restaurant

313 Mount Shasta Boulevard, Mount Shasta ☎ 530/926-5288

Michael and Lynn Kobseff have been running this estimable little restaurant since 1980, which makes them old-timers on the ever-changing Mount Shasta restaurant scene. Some of their best lunchtime offerings are the crisp, greaseless fried zucchini appetizer, the french fries, and a terrific teriyaki turkey sandwich. Their Italian dinners, especially the combination ravioli and linguine plate, satisfy those with lumberjack-size appetites. The small but varied wine list features several bargains. *AE, DIS, MC, V; local checks OK; lunch, dinner Tues–Sat; beer and wine.*

Cheap Sleeps

Stoney Brook Inn

309 W Colombero Street, McCloud, CA 96057-1860 ☎ 530/964-2300

For some serious rest and relaxation, head for the tiny, quiet burg of McCloud, about 10 miles east of Interstate 5 on Highway 89. There you'll find the charming Stoney Brook Inn, one of the few budget bed-and-breakfasts in Northern California. The 18 rooms range in price from around $54 for a room with shared bath to just beyond the Cheap Sleeps limit for their top-of-the-line accommodations. Rates include a vegetarian breakfast. After filling up on the healthy breakfast, kick back with a good book on the pine-shaded wrap-around porch, soak in the hot tub, or steam away your worries in the sauna. Traveling with a group? Sign up for the traditional ceremonial sweat lodge, led by a medicine man from the Karuk tribe. *MC, V; no checks; www.touristguide.com.*

Alpenrose Cottage Hostel

204 E Hinckley Street, Mount Shasta, CA 96067 ☎ 530/926-6724

If you enjoy meeting new people and don't mind sharing a room with strangers, head over to Betty Brown's beautiful Alpenrose Cottage, where you can literally bunk down for a bargain $15 a night (half-price for kids 4–15 with adult). Betty, one of the most easygoing hostel owners you'll ever meet, lives in half the house, leaving the other half open to you (and your roommates). You're welcome to come and go as you like (the door's always open) and to whip up a meal in the fully equipped kitchen. In exchange, you're expected to clean up after yourself—it's that simple. Alpenrose has 12 bunk beds sleeping six women and six men, although on cool summer nights some folks prefer to slumber under the stars on the large deck overlooking a moonlit Mount Shasta. Betty also reserves one room for couples for $30 a night—the best deal in town. *No credit cards; checks OK.*

Evergreen Lodge

1312 S Mount Shasta Boulevard, Mount Shasta, CA 96067 ☎ 530/926-2143
Eenie, meenie, miney, mo. . . . . The number of budget motels lining the streets of Mount Shasta is overwhelming, and while most of them look alike from the outside, they're not all created equal inside. The Evergreen Lodge is one of the better cheap choices. For $55 you can get an air-conditioned room with private bath, cable TV, and telephone. A room with a kitchenette (great for families) is available for an additional $10. There's a tiny pool and hot tub on the premises, though you probably won't even want to dip your big toe into the murky waters. *AE, DIS, MC, V; no checks; www.evergreenlodge.com.*

Mountain Air Lodge

1121 S Mount Shasta Boulevard, Mount Shasta, CA 96067 ☎ 530/926-3411
Set back from the main road in a pleasant pine-shaded area, this 36-room lodge, offering comfort and plenty of conveniences, is often booked far in advance on weekends. The large, contemporary rooms are equipped with private bath, cable TV, air-conditioning, and telephone, and two units have a kitchen. There's also a pool table, Ping-Pong table, and—the pièce de résistance—a huge 8-foot-by-14-foot Jacuzzi that's ideal for soaking your tired dogs after a hard day's hike. For more savings, ask about the weekday ski packages that give a 20 percent discount on room rates and lift tickets. *AE, DIS, MC, V; no checks.*

Shasta Lodge Motel

724 N Mount Shasta Boulevard, Mount Shasta, CA 96067 ☎ 530/926-2815
The Shasta Lodge Motel offers all the standard amenities—private bath, cable TV, telephone, and air-conditioning—although everything is a little frayed around the edges, and things tend to shake a bit when the Southern Pacific comes rolling through (then again, the

entire town shakes a bit when the Southern Pacific passes through). But at $38 a night, who's complaining? The 20-room motel is also just steps away from the downtown shops and restaurants. *AE, DIS, MC, V; no checks.*

Strawberry Valley Inn

1142 S Mount Shasta Boulevard, Mount Shasta, CA 96067 ☎ 530/926-2052

Hosts Chuck and Susie Ryan have incorporated the privacy of a motel and the personal touches of a B&B to create this terrific 14-room inn surrounded by a lush garden and towering oaks. Guest rooms are individually decorated with color-coordinated fabrics, and if you prefer lots of room to romp, ask for a two-room suite. A buffet breakfast featuring fresh fruit, granola, oatmeal, waffles, and pastries is set up next to the inn's stone fireplace (and those who want to dine in private may take a tray to their room). Complimentary wine is poured at the cocktail hour every evening. Sure, it's probably a bit more than you planned on spending, but the Ryans certainly give you your money's worth. *AE, DIS, MC, V; checks OK.*

Lassen Volcanic National Park

Surprisingly, many Californians have never even heard of Lassen Volcanic National Park, much less been there. In fact, it's one of the least crowded national parks in the country, forever destined to play second fiddle to its towering neighbor, Mount Shasta. This is reason enough to go, since the park's 108,000 acres (including 50 beautiful wilderness lakes) are practically deserted, even on weekends.

The heart of the park is 10,457-foot Lassen Peak, the largest plug-dome volcano in the world (its last fiery eruption was in 1915, when it shot debris 7 miles into the stratosphere). The volcano also marks the southernmost end of the Cascade Range, which extends to Canada. A visitors map calls the park "a compact laboratory of volcanic phenomena"—an apt description of this pretty but peculiar place. In addition to wildflower-laced hiking trails and lush forests typical of many national parks, parts of Lassen are covered with steaming thermal vents, boiling mud pots, stinky sulfur springs, and towering lava pinnacles—constant reminders that Mount Lassen is still active. In fact, for decades Lassen held the title of the most recently active volcano in the continental United States, but it lost that distinction in 1980 when Washington's Mount St. Helens blew her top.

Exploring

Lassen Park's premier attractions in the summer and fall are sight-seeing, hiking, backpacking, and camping (sorry, no mountain bikes allowed). The current $5-per-car entrance fee, valid for a week, gets you a copy of the "Lassen Park Guide," a handy little newsletter listing activities, hikes, and points of interest. Free naturalist programs are offered daily in the summer, highlighting everything from flora and fauna to geologic history and volcanic processes. If you have only a day here, spend it huffing up the mountain on the **Lassen Peak Hike,** a spectacular 2.5-mile zigzag to the top. Most hikers can make the steep trek in four to five hours—just don't forget to bring water, sunscreen, and a windbreaker. Another great—and much easier—trail is the 3-mile **Bumpass Hell Hike,** named after a mid-19th-century tour guide. Poor ol' Kendall Bumpass lost a leg on this one, but that was long before park rangers built wooden catwalks to safely guide visitors past the pyrite pools, steam vents, seething mud pots, and noisy fumaroles that line the trail.

Mount Lassen attracts a hardier breed of tourists in the winter, when the park's main thoroughfare is closed and the chief modes of transportation are snowshoes and cross-country skis. Since Lassen Volcanic National Park is more than a mile above sea level, snow accumulates in huge quantities. Though the main road through the park closes around mid-November, the park stays open year-round. Smaller roads are

If the Snowshoe Fits . . .

On Saturday afternoons from January through March, a gregarious naturalist takes anyone who shows up at the Lassen Chalet by 1:30pm on a free, two-hour eco-adventure across the snowy dales of Lassen Volcanic National Park. Here are the rules: you must be at least 8 years old, warmly dressed, and decked out in boots. Snowshoes are provided free (although a $1 donation for shoe upkeep is requested) on a first-come, first-served basis. Pack a picnic lunch. The chalet is at the park's south entrance, 5 miles north of the Highway 36/89 junction. For more details, call park headquarters, 530/595-4444, ext. 3.

A Toy for All Seasons

Come summer or winter, the friendly proprietors of Lassen Mineral Lodge sell just about every outdoor toy you'd ever want to play with in Lassen Park. Fishing and hunting supplies (this is serious deer country) are sold, and they have the only cross-country–ski rentals in the area. You also can get plenty of free advice on where to go and what to do in this neck of the woods. For additional information, see the "Lassen Mineral Lodge" listing under Cheap Sleeps in this chapter (on Highway 36 in Mineral, 530/595-4422).

plowed only from the north and south park entrances up to the ranger stations, and on sunny weekends parking lots are filled with families enjoying every kind of snow toy imaginable.

This is **cross-country skiers'** and **snowshoers'** heaven as well, with uninhibited access to 108,000 acres of mostly untracked snow (snowmobiles are verboten). If you're the adventurous type, consider an overnight **snow-camping trip** cross-country skiing the 30-mile Park Road. If you don't have any snow-camping experience, call **Lassen Ski Touring,** 530/595-3376, and hire a guide.

Ranger stations, located at both entrances to the park, offer interpretive displays and ranger-led walks. The main visitors center is located just inside the northwest entrance station at the Loomis Museum. For additional information, call park headquarters (530/595-4444).

Cheap Eats

It's slim pickin's up here, folks. In fact, Lassen National Park has only one restaurant, the **Summer Chalet Café,** 530/595-3376, which offers inexpensive, basic breakfasts, and sandwiches and burgers for lunch. It's open daily from 8am to 6pm (grill closes at 4pm), May to October (weather permitting), and is located at the park's south entrance.

As such, you might want to consider bringing a couple of coolers of food with you; you can replenish your supplies at **Manzanita Lake Camper Store,** 530/335-7557, at the north end of the park, or at **Lassen Mineral Lodge,** 530/595-4422, on the south side, though both offer slim pickin's at fat prices.

There are, however, a few decent restaurants near the park, but they're not always open when you want them to be, and most everything revolves around a diet of bacon and eggs, sandwiches, steaks, chicken, burgers, pizza, and salads. Essentially there are only two choices outside of the park, and which one you choose depends mostly on which side of the park you're on, north or south. **Uncle Runt's Place,** 530/335-7177, located near the north entrance to the park in the town of Old Station, is a friendly (and a bit funky) little place that serves your standard steaks, chicken, burgers, and sandwiches for lunch and dinner. At the south entrance to the park, the closest restaurant is the **Lassen Mineral Lodge** in the town of Mineral, which serves the usual uninspired American fare (see Cheap Sleeps below).

Cheap Sleeps

Mill Creek Resort

1 Highway 172, Mill Creek, CA 96061 ☎ 530/595-4449

If it's peace and solitude you're after, Mill Creek, 3 miles south of Highway 36, is the place. The resort makes you feel as though you've stepped back in time to a quieter, gentler, and infinitely more affordable era (somewhere around 1925). A quaint general store and coffee shop serve as the resort's center; the nine housekeeping cabins, available daily or weekly, are clean and homey. Seclusion is one of the main charms of the place, but it's also close to cross-country–ski trails and Mount Lassen. Pets are welcome, too. *No credit cards; checks OK.*

Lassen Mineral Lodge

On Highway 36, Mineral, CA 96063 ☎ 530/595-4422

Popular with skiers, hunters, and fishers, Lassen Mineral Lodge offers 20 motel-style accommodations on the doorstep of Lassen National Park. It's set back in the pines 9 miles south of the park's south entrance, so you don't hear the highway noise, but the main lodge is usually bustling with guests. A general store, gift shop, ski shop, and old-fashioned saloon and restaurant are connected to the lodge by a wraparound veranda; there's also a pool and a tennis court. *AE, DIS, MC, V; no checks; www.minerallodge.com.*

Hat Creek Resort

On Highway 89, Old Station, CA 96071 ☎ 530/335-7121

The winter months are spent preparing Hat Creek Resort for the summer onslaught, when hunters and fishers—most of whom have made reservations two years in advance—arrive in droves to occupy these 10 picture-perfect housekeeping cabins and seven motel rooms. What's the attraction? The location. The area around Lassen Volcanic National Park provides some of the best fishing in the world, and fabled Hat Creek runs right through the resort. The cabins, open year-round, come with kitchens where you can cook your catch. Park your RV for less than $30 a night. Uncle Runt's Place, a small saloon and diner, is just down the highway (see Cheap Eats above). The resort is located 11 miles northeast of the park's south entrance. *MC, V; no checks.*

Rim Rock Ranch

13275 Highway 89, Old Station, CA 96071 ☎ 530/335-7114

If having your own rustic cabin for only $40 a day sounds too good to be true, well, that all depends on how you define rustic. Most of Rim Rock's housekeeping cabins were built in the '30s and '40s and don't appear to have been through too many renovations since. But you sure can't beat the price, particularly when it includes a kitchen, utensils, dishes, and a full bath. If the 10 cabins are booked, ask about the two budget-priced motel rooms. The ranch has its own small grocery store, which stocks fishing and hunting gear. Uncle Runt's Place, a small short-order diner and saloon, is across the street (see Cheap Eats above). The ranch is located 14 miles northeast of the park's north entrance. *MC, V; checks OK.*

Sierra Nevada

north lake tahoe
south lake tahoe
yosemite national park
mammoth lakes

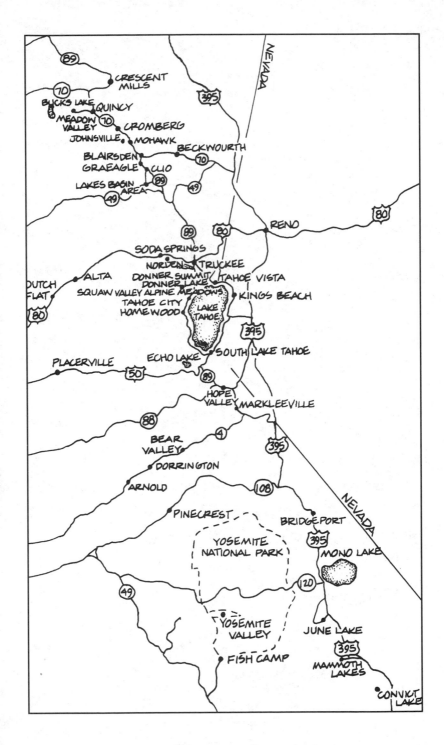

North Lake Tahoe

Frontiersman Kit Carson was guiding General John Frémont's expedition across the Sierra Nevada in 1844 when he stumbled on an immense, deep-blue body of water, a lake so vast the native Washoe Indians were calling it *tahoe* ("big lake"). Carson was the first white man to discover Lake Tahoe, North America's largest alpine lake and the eighth deepest in the world (its deepest point is at 1,645 feet). If completely drained, Tahoe would cover the entire state of California with 14 inches of water.

The California/Nevada border runs straight through the heart of the lake, leaving its west side in California and the east side in Nevada. Despite this east/west state division, the lake is more commonly referred to in terms of its north and south shores. The South Shore area is the most populous and urban, where you'll hear the jingle-jangle of all those slot machines. If you'd rather keep your budget bankroll intact, steer clear of the one-armed bandits and head for the North Shore. There you'll find fewer casinos (and tourists) and more outdoor recreation, including most of Tahoe's best alpine and cross-country ski resorts.

Despite all the great skiing, Tahoe is actually most crowded in summer, when thousands flock here to cool off at the supposedly public shoreline (what constitutes public versus private waterfront is still a matter of heated debate between home owners and county supervisors). Warm-weather activities abound: every water sport imaginable as well as snowmobiling, bicycling, hiking, rock climbing, hot-air ballooning, ice skating, horseback riding . . . you name it. Unfortunately, the area pays dearly for its myriad attractions in the form of tremendous traffic jams, water and air pollution, and a plethora of fast-food joints and condos erected before tough building restrictions were imposed. Despite these glaring scars, Lake Tahoe remains one of the premier outdoor playgrounds of the West, dazzling visitors with its soaring Sierra peaks and twinkling alpine waters.

Access

By car, the main artery to North Lake Tahoe is Interstate 80, which is open year-round, though chains are often required during winter, so don't leave home without 'em. It's a 196-mile, four-hour haul from San Francisco, which many people break up with a pit stop in Sacramento or Auburn. Once you reach the town of Truckee, look for the Highway 89 S turnoff, which leads to North Lake Tahoe (on weekends this stretch can get unbelievably congested, so be prepared). For a quicker route to the casinos, from Interstate 80 exit onto Highway 267, which winds through downtown Truckee, past Northstar-at-Tahoe ski resort, and into the town of Kings Beach.

Although driving here can be more convenient, it is possible to get to Tahoe by public transportation. Greyhound, 800/231-2222, runs several buses a day from San Francisco and Sacramento (and some smaller cities) to Truckee. Amtrak, 800/USA-RAIL, offers a train a day between Oakland and Truckee. Once you're in Truckee, TART (Tahoe Area Regional Transit) shuttles will take you and your mountain bike or skis along the north half of the lake for $1.25 (drivers don't give change) from 6:30am to 6:30pm, seven days a week. For TART schedule information, call 800/736-6365. If you'd rather fly, see "Access" in the South Lake Tahoe section of this chapter.

Exploring

For a grand introduction to the area, take a leisurely 72-mile drive around the lake itself. Highways 50, 89, and 28 hug the shore, providing gorgeous views from the car. Several stellar sights merit pulling over for a closer look, so be prepared to stop and haul out the camera (or camcorder) along the way. Topping the not-to-be-missed list are **Emerald Bay** (off Highway 89 on the West Shore), one of the most photographed sights in the world; **Cave Rock,** the 200-foot-long, drive-through tunnel along Highway 50 on the East Shore; and **Sand Harbor State Park** (off Highway 28 on the East Shore), one of the lake's prettiest—and least visited—beaches. Allow about three hours to loop around the lake, or longer if you're traveling on a summer weekend, on a holiday, or when the road is dusted with snow.

Once you've circled the lake, make a quick stop in **Tahoe City** at the Tahoe North Visitors & Convention Bureau (950 N Lake Boulevard, above McDonald's, Tahoe City, 800/824-6348) and sort through the

Traipsing Through Truckee

For some folks, a vacation isn't really a vacation without a good, long shopping spree. If you live to shop, take the 15-minute drive north from Tahoe City (via Highway 89) to the historic railroad-lumber town of Truckee. Here you'll find dozens of alluring specialty shops and cafes housed in century-old facades along Commercial Row (during the Christmas season, when snow blankets the wooden boardwalks and bright little white lights twinkle in the windows, it all looks like a picture from a fairy tale).

*A couple of other popular shops in town are **Sierra Mountaineer,** which carries everything you'll ever need for exploring the Sierra on foot or on skis (Bridge Street at Jibboom Street, Truckee, 530/587-2025), and the **Bookshelf** at Hooligan Rocks, one of Northern California's best bookstores (11310 Donner Pass Road, at the west end of the Safeway shopping center, Truckee, 800/959-5083 or 530/582-0515). After a long day of browsing, give your feet (and wallet) a break at the budget-priced **Squeeze In,** which offers 57 palate-pleasin' varieties of hefty omelets and 22 versions of a triple-decker sandwich (10060 Donner Pass Road, Truckee, 530/587-9814).*

Sierra Ski Scene

Granted, there's nothing cheap these days about downhill skiing, but a few deals exist, especially if you ski midweek, purchase a multiday pass, or buy a hotel/ski-pass package. Most Tahoe resorts offer super-saver ski packages or discounts each season, so it pays to call your favorite destination and ask about the specials. Here's a roundup of North Lake Tahoe's major downhill ski areas:

Alpine Meadows: A favorite with locals, Alpine's runs are on a par with Squaw Valley's best, but without snowboarders (they're banned from the slopes) and the holier-than-thou attitude of the Squaw staff (off Highway 89, 800/441-4423 or 530/583-4232).

Boreal: Although small and easy, Boreal is a good beginners' resort. It's also the only place in the Tahoe area that offers night skiing (open until 9pm) and, thanks to extensive snowmaking equipment, is usually one of the first ski areas open for business (off Interstate 80, 530/426-3666).

Diamond Peak: Located in Incline Village on the Nevada side of Tahoe's North Shore, this small, family-oriented ski resort guarantees good skiing—if you don't like the conditions, you can turn in your ticket within the first hour for a voucher that's good for another day (from Highway 28, exit on Country Club Drive, turn right on Ski Way, and head to Diamond Peak, 775/831-3249).

Donner Ski Ranch: Just up the road from Sugar Bowl is Donner, where the best feature is the price of the ski passes—you'll pay about half of what neighboring ski areas charge for an all-day ticket. Despite its small size, this unpretentious resort has a lot to offer skiers of all levels: tree skiing, groomed trails, and a few steeps and jumps, not to mention convenient parking and a cozy, rustic lodge (take the Soda Springs exit off Interstate 80, 530/426-3635).

Granlibakken: Tiny and mainly for tots, this is a great place to teach kids the fundamentals. Later, when you'll surely need a libation, you won't have far to go to find the Tahoe City night spots (off Highway 89 at the junction of Highway 28, 800/543-3221 or 530/583-4242).

Northstar-at-Tahoe: Northstar is consistently rated one of the best family ski resorts in the nation, thanks to its numerous amenities. It also has the dubious honor of being called Flatstar by locals because of its frequently groomed trails. This is a completely self-contained resort (you'll find everything from lodgings to stores to a gas station here), so you can park your car and leave it there for the duration of your stay (off Highway 267, 800/GO-NORTH).

Ski Homewood: *This underrated midsize resort has a little of everything for skiers of all levels—along with one of the best views of Lake Tahoe. Midweek specials often knock down the price of a ticket by as much as 50 percent (call ahead for quotes), easily the best ski discount in the area (off Highway 89, 530/525-2992).*

Squaw Valley USA: *Site of the 1960 Winter Olympic Games, Squaw Valley is a resort that people either love (because it has everything a skier could hope for) or hate (because staff members know it has everything and say so with their nose-to-the-sky attitudes). Squaw Valley offers some of the country's most challenging terrain, intensive ski-school programs, top-of-the-line chair lifts, and advanced snowmaking. Unfortunately, it tends to attract the most obnoxious snowboarders and the most egotistical skiers in North America (off Highway 89, 800/545-4350 or 530/583-6985).*

Sugar Bowl: *Here's another good all-around midsize ski resort, with about 60 runs. Sugar Bowl's top attraction is accessibility—it's the closest resort from the valley off Interstate 80, about 30 minutes before Squaw Valley (and several bucks less a pass, thank you). Whether it's worth the drive from the North Shore, however, is questionable (take the Soda Springs exit off Interstate 80, 530/426-3651).*

Tahoe Donner Ski Area: *If you're a beginner or a beginner/intermediate skier and are staying on the North Shore, Tahoe Donner is a viable option, offering short lift lines, few (or no) parking hassles, and relatively low prices (from Interstate 80, take the Donner State Park exit, turn left on Donner Pass Road, then left on Northwoods Boulevard and follow the signs, 530/587-9444).*

mountain of brochures and coupons for good deals on local attractions. If you plan to hike or ride bikes, load up on the free trail maps, too. This is also the place to visit or call if you're having trouble finding a hotel room or campsite (a common problem during peak seasons) or need information on ski packages.

Summer also brings a phenomenal array of lakeside activities, many of which don't cost a dime. **Day hikers** should head for the visitors center on the West Shore (on Highway 89, just north of Fallen Leaf Road and 3 miles north of South Lake Tahoe, 530/573-2674). It's the starting point for several well-marked trails, ranging from an easy half-mile stroll to a 10-mile, leg-burning trek. Serious mountain bikers shouldn't miss huffing up and down the famous 24-mile **Flume Trail,** with its fantastic views of the lake; the trailhead begins at Nevada State Park on the lake's eastern shore. Casual and asphalt-only pedalers can vie with in-line skaters, joggers, and strollers for room on North Tahoe's 15-mile-long, paved trail, beginning at **Sugar Pine Point State Park** on the West Shore and stretching north along the lake to **Dollar Point** on the North Shore. There's also a 3.5-mile paved trail that parallels the **Truckee River** and passes through Tahoe City; the trail starts at the turnoff to Alpine Meadows ski resort on Highway 89. For the truly lazy (or crazy) rider, **Northstar-at-Tahoe** and **Squaw Valley** ski resorts offer miles of pedal-free trails accessible by chair lift or cable car—simply let the lifts tote you and your bike up the slopes, then spend the day cruising (or careening like a deranged daredevil) down the mountains.

If you didn't manage to pack all your recreational toys, **Porter's Ski & Sport** (501 N Lake Boulevard, Tahoe City, 530/583-2314) has the best prices in town for outdoor rental equipment—everything from bikes to skates to tennis rackets, as well as a full line of skis and snowboards. For a dose of aerobics or heavy breathing on the Stairmaster, make a beeline for the **North Tahoe Beach Center** (7860 N Lake Boulevard, across from Safeway, Kings Beach, 530/546-2566). Pay $7, or $12 per couple, and you can jump up and down till you drop. This is also the spot for a good hot soak in a 26-foot-long outdoor Jacuzzi.

Still feeling the urge to try your luck at blackjack or spinning the big wheel? Well, **Nevada** is only a short drive away, and the **casinos** will be delighted to see you. Although the North Shore's casinos are more subdued and less glitzy than the South Shore's high-rolling high-rises, the dealers are still adept at taking your money. If you're a greenhorn, this

Climbing the Walls

Looking for a cheap thrill? Well, for a mere $12 you can climb straight up a wall at Squaw Valley for a full hour (although few folks have the stamina to last that long). Located at the base of Squaw Valley's cable car route, the Headwall is an artificial 30-foot-high cliff dotted with a series of small finger- and toeholds, each more difficult to grasp than the last. Before you begin the challenging ascent, you're hooked up to a harness, which makes it impossible to fall but possible to climb wherever and whenever you choose. For a few more dollars you can rent climbing shoes, though sneakers work almost as well. **Headwall Cafe and Climbing** *is open to people of all ages and abilities, including toddlers, who actually outshine the adults with their nimble moves (off Highway 89 in Squaw Valley, 530/583-ROPE; open daily year-round).*

Nordic Ski Scene

Tahoe's top cross-country–ski center is **Royal Gorge,** *the largest of its kind in the United States, with 200 miles of trails for skiers of all levels, 9,172 acres of skiable terrain, an average annual snowfall of more than 650 inches, 10 warming huts (for defrosting those frozen fingers and toes), and 2 lodges (take the Soda Springs exit off Interstate 80, 530/426-3871). More experienced Nordic skiers should head over to* **Eagle Mountain** *(one of the area's best-kept secrets), which offers 47 miles of challenging trails with fantastic Sierra vistas (from Interstate 80, exit at Yuba Gap, turn right, and follow the signs, 800/391-2254 or 530/389-2254).*

is a good place to learn the ABCs of the games, especially during off-hours. North Shore casinos include the Tahoe Biltmore Hotel, 775/831-0660; Cal-Neva Lodge and Casino, 775/832-4000; Hyatt Regency Lake Tahoe, 702/831-1111; and Crystal Bay Club Casino, 775/831-0512.

North Lake Tahoe also offers a few nocturnal alternatives to the dice and the slots. You can dance any night of the week at **Pierce Street Annex** (850 N Lake Boulevard, behind Safeway, Tahoe City, 916/583-5800), which caters to a thirtysomething crowd but attracts swingers of all ages. **Elevations** (877 N Lake Boulevard, across from Safeway, Tahoe City, 530/583-4867), on the other hand, resembles (and smells like) a college-town hangout, though this is where you'll find the area's top dance bands and the cheapest drinks. During ski season, the lounge of the **River Ranch Lodge** (on Highway 89, at the entrance to Alpine Meadows, about 10 miles north of Tahoe City, 530/583-4264) has a raging après-ski scene, with ski bums from all over kicking back and chowing down on cheap hors d'oeuvres.

Cheap Eats

Log Cabin Café
8692 N Lake Boulevard, Kings Beach ☎ 530/546-7109

Originally a summer home, the funky Log Cabin Café is now *the* place to have breakfast in Lake Tahoe. The owner's penchant for freshness is what makes the Log Cabin such a hit: croissants and muffins are baked every morning, the orange juice is fresh-squeezed, and the fluffy Belgian waffles are topped with fresh fruit and nuts. The large lunch menu features everything from fresh vegetable soup and tofu burgers to pizza, pasta, and sliced-turkey-breast sandwiches filled with cranberries and cream cheese. Behind the restaurant near the lakeshore is a picnic area where you can cool off with ice-cream sundaes and sodas, served throughout the summer. *MC, V; no checks; breakfast, lunch every day; no alcohol.*

Bridgetender Tavern and Grill

30 W Lake Boulevard, Tahoe City ☎ 530/583-3342

Any bar that has Jaegermeister on tap is worth a visit. The fact that the Bridgetender also has 20 beers on tap and great burgers is simply icing on the cake. Tahoe's foremost tavern, a rough-hewn log-and-stone structure built around a trio of healthy ponderosa pines, is frequented by folks who know each other on a first-name basis. The menu is basic—burgers, salads, sandwiches, and various appetizers like pork ribs and deep-fried chicken strips—but the food is filling and cheap. In the summer the outside patio is always packed with giddy tourists unaware of the effects of alcohol at high altitudes. *DIS, MC, V; no checks; lunch, dinner every day; full bar.*

Fire Sign Café

1785 W Lake Boulevard, Tahoe City ☎ 530/583-0871

This converted old Tahoe home has been a favorite breakfast stop for locals since the late '70s. Just about everything here is made from scratch, including the coffee cake and muffins that accompany generous servings of bacon and eggs. Even the savory, thinly sliced salmon used in the cafe's legendary eggs Benedict is smoked on the premises. Popular lunch items include the garden burger, the chicken burrito, the grilled turkey sandwich with green chilis and cheese, and a scrumptious raspberry cobbler. In the summer, dine on the deck under the pines. Expect a long wait on weekends. *MC, V; local checks only; breakfast, lunch every day; beer and wine.*

Rosie's Café

571 N Lake Boulevard, Tahoe City ☎ 530/583-8504

Most folks who spend a few days or more in North Lake Tahoe eventually wind up at Rosie's for breakfast, lunch, dinner, drinks, or all of the above. This humble Tahoe institution serves large portions of traditional American fare—sandwiches, steaks, burgers, salads—but the two dishes that tourists always return for are the hearty Yankee pot roast (the perfect dish for those cold winter nights) and the crisp Southern-fried chicken, both served with mashed potatoes and gravy and a side of sautéed vegetables. Live music is featured every Tuesday night—an event that shouldn't be missed if you care to witness mountain folk at their rowdiest. *AE, DC, DIS, MC, V; no checks; breakfast, lunch, dinner every day; full bar.*

Za's
395 N Lake Boulevard, Tahoe City ☎ 530/583-1812

When the front half of the "PIZZAS" sign fell off this restaurant long ago, the owner decided it was an auspicious omen and renamed the place Za's. Sure enough, Za's turned out to be a hit. In fact, it's one of the most popular restaurants in Tahoe, serving very good Italian food at bargain prices. The herbed bread, baked fresh daily and stacked under hanging braids of garlic, is wonderful, especially when dipped in the accompanying pool of olive oil. Start with the Caesar salad or the baked polenta with wild mushrooms and marsala sauce, and follow that with the golden-brown calzone stuffed with fresh vegetables and mozzarella or the smoked-chicken fettuccine with fresh artichoke hearts and a garlic-cream sauce. Wash it all down with a tumbler of Chianti, but skip the lackluster dessert. There are only a dozen tables, so you'll probably have to join the line of salivating patrons snaking out the door. *MC, V; no checks; dinner every day; beer and wine.*

Cheap Sleeps

North Lake Lodge
8716 N Lake Boulevard, Kings Beach, CA 96143 ☎ 530/546-2731

Although it's far from the action in Tahoe City, the North Lake Lodge is ideal for gamblers (the casinos are less than a mile away) and skiers who prefer the slopes of nearby Northstar. The 21 units range in price from about $65 for a bungalow to $80 for a small cabin to more than $100 for a cabin that sleeps up to six. A few of the rustic buildings, some dating back to the 1920s, have lake views; some units also have a kitchenette or a refrigerator and microwave. The lodge offers a hot tub and picnic area, and there's a public beach nearby. Pets are welcome, too. *AE, DIS, MC, V; no checks; www.tahoe guide.com/go/northlakelodge.*

Lake of the Sky Motor Inn

955 N Lake Boulevard, Tahoe City, CA 96145 ☎ 530/583-3305

This '60s-style A-frame motel, located in the middle of Tahoe City and within walking distance of the restaurants and shops, offers basic no-frills accommodations for budget-minded travelers. Just steps from the ski shuttle stop, it is ideal for skiers (inquire about the ski packages). In the summer guests have access to the inn's heated pool. *AE, DC, DIS, MC, V; no checks.*

Mother Nature's Inn

551 N Lake Boulevard, Tahoe City, CA 96145 ☎ 530/583-0287

You can't beat the Mother Nature's Inn location—right in the middle of Tahoe City, across the street from the lake, and next to the ski shuttle stop. Prices have gone up a bit recently, but it's still one of the best lodgings deal in Tahoe, with weekday rates as low as $55. The guest rooms are located behind an art gallery and gift shop, and each is individually decorated with various wildlife themes (prints of deer, raccoons, bears, and other forest critters) and rustic log furnishings. You have a choice of a queen bed or two doubles, and most rooms have air-conditioning. Be sure to make reservations as early as possible because the inn fills up fast. *DIS, MC, V; no checks.*

Peppertree Inn

645 N Lake Boulevard, Tahoe City, CA 96145 ☎ 530/583-3711

Although a room at the Peppertree is typically priced just out of the Cheap Sleeps range, the inn does offer two-for-one ski lift tickets to its guests. Also, add a whirlpool, cable TV, in-room coffee, and a prime location in downtown Tahoe City, and you've got a deal that's hard to beat. *AE, DC, DIS, MC, V; no checks.*

High-Altitude Hostel

You'll have to book a bunk far in advance if you want to stay at the popular **Squaw Valley Hostel,** *a privately run enterprise near the Squaw ski resort. There are 100 beds packed into nine rooms, which cost about $22 a night on weekdays, $27 on weekends, and even less in the off-season (1900 Squaw Valley Road, off Highway 89 in Squaw Valley, 800/544-4723 or 530/581-3246).*

Tamarack Lodge

2311 N Lake Boulevard, Tahoe City, CA 96145 ☎ 530/583-3350

How often do you have the chance to sleep in the same little cabin that once housed Clark Gable and Gary Cooper? Not very, which is one of the reasons the rustic, secluded Tamarack Lodge should be your first-choice accommodation in Lake Tahoe. It's located a mile east of Tahoe City on busy N Lake Boulevard, yet the 21 wood-paneled rooms and cabins are well hidden behind a grove of pines. Rates range from about $36 for one of the converted old "poker rooms" to $100 for a two-bedroom, two-bath cabin with kitchen and living room (a real deal for two couples). *DIS, MC, V; no checks; www.tamarack attahoe.com.*

Franciscan Lakeside Lodge

6944 N Lake Boulevard, Tahoe Vista, CA 96143 ☎ 800/564-6754, ☎ 530/546-7234, or ☎ 530/546-6300

The best of the area's motel scene, the Franciscan offers access to a private beach and pier, mooring buoys, a heated swimming pool, volleyball nets, a croquet set, horseshoe pits, a children's play area, and is near tennis courts, ski areas, and a golf course. Its 51 plain but adequate units feature one or two bedrooms, full kitchens, private bathrooms, TVs, phones, and daily housekeeping service. The lakeside rooms have large porches overlooking the water (and, of course, they're the first to get booked, so make your reservations early). *AE, MC, V; checks OK.*

South Lake Tahoe

Three premier attractions separate sassy South Lake Tahoe from its sportier northern counterpart: glitzy casinos with celebrity entertainers, several sandy beaches, and the massive Heavenly Ski Resort, the only American ski area that straddles two states. If 24-hour gambling parties or schussing down the slopes of Heavenly is your idea of paradise, then you're in for a treat.

Most of the weekend warriors who flock here on Friday afternoons book their favorite budget lodgings weeks—if not months—in advance. Follow their lead and plan early. For long-term stays, it's often more economical to go in on a condo rental with a group of friends. Then again, many of the casinos offer bargain sleep-and-eat packages (especially during the week) that are the best bets you'll ever make in Tahoe. As long as you don't succumb (too often) to the slot machines, you can pig out at the casino-subsidized restaurants, pass out in the casino-subsidized lodgings, and then hightail it back to the lake without blowing your budget.

Access

The drive from San Francisco to South Lake Tahoe takes about four hours—about the same time it takes to get to North Lake Tahoe, except you have to navigate a few dozen miles of graded S-turns (treacherous S-turns during snowstorms). From San Francisco, take Interstate 80 to Sacramento and follow the signs to Highway 50, which leads to South Lake. Watch out for deer bounding onto the highway, and during winter, carry chains.

Thanks to the many casinos in South Lake, catching a bus from

Sacramento or San Francisco is simple and cheap; call Greyhound, 800/231-2222, for schedule and price information. Once you're in South Lake, the STAGE (South Tahoe Area Ground Express) will shuttle you around town 24 hours a day, year-round, 530/542-6077. South Lake's ski resorts run their own free shuttles daily in winter, and most casinos provide free shuttle service from nearby hotels year-round.

Flying to Lake Tahoe is also an option, albeit an expensive one. Reno Air, 800/736-6247, and TW Express, 800/221-2000, service the South Lake Tahoe Airport, 530/542-6180, but your best budget bet is to fly into Reno-Tahoe International Airport in Nevada, 775/328-6400, and then spend about $17 more for a ride on the Casino Express shuttle bus, 800/446-6128, into South Lake Tahoe.

Exploring

As soon as you roll into town, stop at the **South Lake Tahoe Chamber of Commerce,** where you'll find an entire room filled with free maps, brochures, coupons, and guidebooks to the South Lake region (3066 S Lake Tahoe Boulevard, South Lake Tahoe, 530/541-5255). And if you risked traveling to Tahoe without a hotel reservation, call Lake Tahoe Central Reservation Service, 800/288-2463. You could also contact the casinos for an update on their package deals—sometimes their rates beat out the best budget motels: call Harrah's, 800/648-3773; Caesars

Ski for Free

*Perhaps the best things in life are free. The South Shore's choicest cross-country-ski tracks are at **Sorensen's Resort** in Hope Valley and, yep, they're open to the public at no charge. You'll find more than 60 miles of trails winding through the Toiyabe National Forest—plenty of room for mastering that telemark turn and escaping the Tahoe crowds. Rentals, lessons, tours, and trail maps are available at the Hope Valley Cross-Country Ski Center, located within Sorensen's Resort. From Highway 50 in Myers (the town just before South Lake Tahoe), take Highway 89 S over the Luther Pass to the Highway 88/89 intersection, turn left, and continue a half-mile to Sorensen's. For more details, contact the Ski Center at 916/694-2266 or Sorensen's at 800/423-9949 or 530/694-2203.*

Stellar South Shore Slopes

When the winter months roll around, the tension is almost palpable in South Lake Tahoe as snow-starved locals pray for an early dump. At the first snowstorm, the town springs to life with skiers who make the pilgrimage from Sacramento and the Bay Area to test their prowess on the slopes. Although the South Shore has half as many resorts as the North Shore, they're some of the best: Heavenly, Kirkwood, and Sierra-at-Tahoe. Furthermore, all these resorts run free shuttles from downtown South Lake Tahoe—one heck of a deal that the North Shore resorts have yet to match.

Heavenly Ski Resort: South Lake Tahoe's pride and joy has something for skiers of all levels. And Heavenly is so immense it extends all the way into Nevada; those in the know park on the Nevada side to avoid the crowds, or catch a ride on the free shuttles. Don't look for bargain prices here; Heavenly's all-day lift ticket is one of the costliest in Tahoe (off Highway 50, 800/2-HEAVEN or 775/586-7000).

Kirkwood: When ski conditions just don't get any better, Tahoe locals make the journey over the passes to where the snow is the deepest and the skiing is the sweetest. Kirkwood also offers some tempting ski/lodging packages (off Highway 88 via Highway 89, 209/258-6000).

Sierra-at-Tahoe: Formerly named Sierra Ski Ranch, Tahoe's third-largest ski area is a good all-around resort, offering a slightly better price than most comparable places in Tahoe. It's not worth the drive from the North Shore, but it's a good alternative to Heavenly if you want a change of venue near the South Shore (off Highway 50, 530/659-7453).

Tahoe, 800/648-3353; and Harvey's, 800/427-8397.

In the summer, droves of tourists and locals arrive by bike, car, or boat at **The Beacon** restaurant and bar to scope out the beach, babe, and bar scene—easily the best on the lake. Sit on the Beacon's huge outdoor deck overlooking the beach and order their famous Rum Runner cocktail, a potent blend of rums and juices guaranteed to put a smile on your face (1900 Jamison Beach Road, off Highway 89 at Camp Richardson, 2.5 miles north of the Highway 50 junction, South Lake Tahoe, 530/541-0630. Other popular public beaches include **Nevada Beach,** which has spectacular views of Lake Tahoe and the Sierra Nevada (on Elk Point Road, 1 mile east of Stateline, Nevada), and **El Dorado Beach**—not as pretty, but much closer to town (off Lakeview Avenue, across from Pizza Hut, downtown South Lake Tahoe). In the winter, ski-

Steamboat Skiing

Tahoe's brilliant-blue lake is so deep it never freezes, so it's navigable even in the dead of winter. Capitalizing on that fact, the Tahoe Queen, an authentic Mississippi sternwheeler regularly used for scenic lunch and dinner cruises, doubles as a ferry for South Shore skiers who want to explore the North Shore's resorts. Skiers hop aboard at the base of Ski Run Boulevard in South Lake. The 25-mile ride takes about two hours, disembarking at the West Shore's tiny town of Homewood, where a waiting shuttle transports riders to Squaw Valley ski resort. Passengers return to South Lake the same way they came; however, on the trip back the bar is open, the band is playing, and the boat is rockin'. Round-trip fare (which includes a Squaw Valley lift ticket and dinner) is $105. Reservations are required; call 530/541-3364.

ing is the big sport, and **Heavenly** is the big crowd-pleasin' resort. And no matter what time of year, the scenic three-hour drive around the azure lake provides views of Tahoe you won't soon forget (see the North Lake Tahoe section of this chapter for more information).

The South Lake's number-one nighttime entertainment is—you guessed it—the casino. The three top guns are **Harrah's, Caesars Tahoe,** and **Harvey's,** which are squeezed next to each other on Highway 50 in Nevada and burn enough bulbs to light a small city. Even if you can't take a chance yourself, stroll through to watch the high rollers throw away more bucks than you make in a month or to gawk at those "just-one-more-try" players at the flashy money machines. If you want to try your luck, a mere $10 can keep you entertained for quite a while on the nickel slots. Or spend the night kicking up your heels on the dance floor at **Nero's 2000 Nightclub** in Caesars (55 Highway 50, Stateline, Nevada,

Paddle Pleasures

Care to get a better look at that mysterious stone teahouse in the heart of Emerald Bay? The folks at Kayak Tahoe, located at Camp Richardson on Tahoe's South Shore, can set you up in one of their stable sea kayaks ($14 per hour for a single, $28 per hour for a tandem) and point you in the right direction—then you're on your own to paddle wherever you please. Guided tours and lessons are also available (1900 Jamison Beach Road, off Highway 89 at Camp Richardson, 2.5 miles north of the Highway 50 junction, South Lake Tahoe, 530/544-2011).

775/588-3515) or at **Turtle's Sports Bar and Dance Emporium** in the Embassy Suites (4130 Lake Tahoe Boulevard, South Lake Tahoe, 530/544-5400).

For more than a century, **Walley's Hot Springs Resort** in Nevada has been the place for South Lake residents to unwind after a hard day of skiing or mountain biking, even though it's about an hour-long drive from town (2001 Foothill Boulevard, 2 miles north of the east end of Kingsbury Grade, near Genoa, Nevada, 775/782-8155). For $20, you can jump into their six open-air pools (each is set at a different temperature), utilize the saunas, and watch ducks and geese at the nearby wildlife area. If a good soak or sweat doesn't get all the kinks out, indulge in a rubdown at the resort's massage center (no children under 12 allowed in the resort).

Cheap Eats

Cantina Bar & Grill
765 Emerald Bay Road, South Lake Tahoe ☎ 530/544-1233

The Cantina Bar & Grill (formerly Cantina Los Tres Hombres) is a local favorite not only because it serves the best Mexican food in South Lake; it's also popular because it's inexpensive (nearly everything on the menu is less than $10 and *very* filling), and there always seems to be a daily drink special. The extensive menu offers your tried-and-true Cal-Mex specialties such as tacos, burritos, and enchiladas, but Southwestern dishes are available as well, such as smoked chicken polenta, Texas crab cakes, and grilled pork chops with jalapeño mashed potatoes. The steak fajitas (with shrimp, sweet peppers, and onions) are very good here, as is the chicken smothered in rich mole sauce and served with rice, black beans, and tortillas. The bar stays open till midnight. *MC, V; no checks; lunch, dinner daily; full bar.*

The Red Hut
2723 Highway 50, South Lake Tahoe ☎ 530/541-9024

This all-American coffee shop—complete with an L-shaped Formica counter, booths, and a bubble-gum machine—has become so popular, the owners have added a waiting room. The Red Hut's success is based primarily on its good coffee, hefty omelets with a variety of fillings, friendly waitresses, and, best of all, low prices. Lunch follows the same big-and-cheap all-American formula with a menu of mostly burgers and sandwiches. While the food isn't anything to swoon over, it beats the buns off the fast-food chains down the street. *Cash only; breakfast, lunch every day; no alcohol.*

Sprouts Natural Foods Café

3123 Harrison Street, South Lake Tahoe ☎ 530/541-6969

You don't have to be a granola-loving long-haired type to figure out that Sprouts is among the best places to eat in town. If the line out the door isn't a big enough hint, then perhaps a bite of the marvelous mayo-free tuna sandwich (made with yogurt and lots of fresh veggies) will make you a convert to feel-good food. Owner Tyler Cannon has filled a huge culinary hole in this area with the South Lake's premier vegetarian hangout. Almost everything is made on the premises, including the soups, tempeh burgers, sandwiches (try the Real Tahoe Turkey), huge burritos, muffins, fruit smoothies (a meal in themselves), coffee drinks, and fresh-squeezed juices. Order at the counter, then scramble for a vacant seat (outdoor tables are coveted) and listen for one of the buffed and beautiful servers to call out your name and deliver your tray of earthy delights. This is also an excellent place to pack a picnic lunch for a skiing, hiking, or mountain-biking expedition. *No credit cards; local checks only; breakfast, lunch, dinner every day; beer and wine.*

Yellow Sub

983 Tallac Avenue, South Lake Tahoe ☎ 530/541-8808

Voted Best Deli Sandwich Shop by readers of the *Tahoe Daily Tribune*, the Yellow Sub offers more than 20 versions of overstuffed subs in the 6-inch and 12-inch categories. The deli also offers four kinds of wraps, which are sort of a cross between a burrito and a sandwich. Yellow Sub is a bit hard to find, since it's hidden in a small shopping center across from the El Dorado Campground, but if you want a fat sandwich for a thin price, this is the place. *Cash only; lunch, dinner daily; beer and wine.*

Cheap Sleeps

Chamonix Inn

913 Friday Avenue, South Lake Tahoe, CA 96150 ☎ 800/447-5353
or ☎ 530/544-5274

Chamonix Inn, located near the California-Nevada border, is a haven for skiers and gamblers. The inn offers direct shuttle service to surrounding ski resorts and casinos, and there's a coffee shop (for that quick breakfast before hitting the slopes) and a pool and hot tub (for that long soak afterward). The 32 rooms are basic yet clean, with firm beds, direct-dial phones, and TVs with HBO. Great ski packages are available, too. *AE, DIS, MC, V; no checks; www.chamonixinn.com.*

Emerald Motel

515 Emerald Bay Road/Highway 89, South Lake Tahoe, CA 96150
☎ 530/544-5515

It's hardly the gem its name would suggest, but the Emerald does offer rooms at a jewel of a price. The motel is located on the west end of town, far from the glitzy casinos, so if your goal is to keep your distance from the gambling scene, this may be the place. Most of the nine rooms offer a queen-size bed, a kitchen with microwave oven and coffeemaker, telephone, and cable TV. A few good, reasonably priced restaurants, including Cantina Bar & Grill (see Cheap Eats above), are within walking distance. *AE, MC, V; no checks.*

Lamplighter Motel

4143 Cedar Avenue, South Lake Tahoe, CA 96150 ☎ 530/544-2936

Surrounded by dozens of cheesy hotels and motels catering to low rollers, the Lamplighter is set apart by its meticulously maintained facade. On the inside, the Mr. Clean theme continues, with 28 ultra-tidy (we're talking dust-free) and comfortable rooms. The rates include such standard amenities as direct-dial phone, remote TV, and in-room brewed coffee. There's also a Jacuzzi, the casinos are a mere 50 yards away, and ski packages are available. *AE, DIS, MC, V; checks OK.*

Yosemite National Park

What was once the beloved home of the Ahwahneechee, Miwok, and Paiute Indians is now a spectacular international playground for 4 million annual visitors. Designated a national park in 1890, thanks in part to Sierra Club founder John Muir, the 1,200-square-mile Yosemite National Park is only slightly smaller than the state of Rhode Island. During peak season, however, it seems more like a 1,200-square-foot park. Crowds more typical of Disney World clog the 7-square-mile Yosemite Valley for a glimpse of some of nature's most incredible creations, including El Capitan, the largest piece of exposed granite on earth, and Yosemite Falls, the highest waterfall in North America and the fifth highest in the world.

To avoid most of the crowds, visit in spring or early fall, when the wildflowers are plentiful and the weather is usually mild. You can virtually escape civilization by setting up a tent in Tuolumne Meadows (pronounced too-ALL-um-ee), where numerous trails wind through the densely forested and sparsely populated high country. This grande dame of national parks is most dazzling, and least crowded, in winter, the time of year Ansel Adams shot those world-renowned photographs of the snow-laced valley. Unfortunately, most of the hiking trails are inaccessible at this time of year and the drive may be treacherous; snow and ice limit access to the park, and many of the eastern passes are closed; call 800/427-ROAD for highway conditions. Those who do brave the elements, however, are rewarded a truly unforgettable winter vista.

Exploring

No matter what the time of year, visitors to Yosemite National Park must pay its friendly rangers a $20-per-car entrance fee. In return, you receive a seven-day pass, a detailed park map, and the "Yosemite Guide," a handy tabloid featuring the park's rules, rates, attractions, and current exhibits. One of the best ways to sight-see on the valley floor is by bike. **Curry Village,** 209/372-8319, and **Yosemite Lodge,** 209/372-1208, have bike stands that rent one-speed cruisers (and helmets) daily. More than 8 miles of paved bicycle paths wind through the eastern end of the valley, but bicycles (including mountain bikes) are not allowed on the hiking trails.

Day hikers in the valley have a wide variety of trails to choose from—some boring, some mind-blowing—and all are well-charted on the visitors map. The best easy hike is the **Mirror Lake/Meadow Trail,** a 2-mile round-trip walk (5 miles if you circle the lake) that provides a magnificent view of Half Dome. More strenuous is the popular hike to **Upper Yosemite Falls,** a 7.2-mile round-trip trek with a spectacular overview of the 2,425-foot drop. (Note: Don't wander off the trail or you may join the unlucky souls who have tumbled off the cliffs to their deaths.) The granddaddy of Yosemite hikes is the very steep ascent to the top of 8,840-foot-tall **Half Dome,** a 17-mile, round-trip, 10- to 12-hour-long thigh-burner that requires Schwarzenegger-like gusto and the nerve to hang onto climbing cables anchored in granite—clearly not a jaunt for

Yosemite by the Numbers

General Park Information:	*209/372-0200 (recorded)*
Road and Weather Conditions:	*209/372-0200 (recorded)*
Lodging Reservations:	*559/252-4848*
Campground Information:	*209/372-0265 or 209/372-0200 (recorded)*
Campground Reservations:	*800/436-7275*
Wilderness (Backpacking) Permits:	*209/372-0310*

Off-Season Savings

From late October through late March (excluding holidays), you can save up to 30 percent on room rates and quadruple your chances of getting a preferred reservation date. Bring lots of warm clothing; Yosemite is usually covered with more than a foot of snow in winter.

everyone. But those who reach the top are rewarded with stunning valley views. When the snowstorm season hits, most hiking trails are closed, and many people haul out their snowshoes or cross-county skis for valley excursions, or snap on their alpine skis and schuss down the groomed beginner/intermediate hills of **Badger Pass Ski Area** (on Glacier Point Road, 6 miles east of Highway 41, Yosemite, 209/372-1330).

If you'd rather keep your feet firmly planted on lower ground, tour the **Yosemite Valley Visitors Center,** 209/372-0200, which houses some mildly interesting galleries and museums. The center's **Indian Cultural Museum** hosts live demonstrations of the native Miwok and Paiute methods of basket weaving, jewelry making, and other crafts. Nearby are a reconstructed Miwok-Paiute village, a self-guided nature trail, and an art gallery showcasing the master photographer whose name is almost synonymous with this place: Ansel Adams.

Unless bumper-to-bumper traffic is your idea of a vacation in the woods, skip Yosemite Valley during summer weekends and join the rebel minority who know there's more than one way to view the area. **Glacier Point,** a rocky ledge 3,215 feet above the valley floor, has what many consider one of the best vistas on the continent: a bird's-eye view of the entire valley and a panoramic expanse of the High Sierra. The view is particularly striking at sunset and under a full moon. The point is located at the end of Glacier Point Road, open only in the summer.

At the southern entrance to the park, 35 miles south of the valley, lies **Mariposa Grove,** home to some of the planet's largest and most ancient living things. The most popular attraction is the 2,700-year-old **Grizzly Giant,** the world's oldest sequoia. Pick up a self-guided trail map in the box at the grove trailhead or attend one of the free ranger-led walks, offered regularly; check the "Yosemite Guide" for current schedules.

Due north of Yosemite Valley is the famous **Tioga Pass** (Highway 120), the highest automobile pass in California, which crests at 9,945 feet (and is closed in the winter). The ideal time to tour the 60-mile-long east-west stretch is in early summer, when the meadows are dotted with wildflowers and you can occasionally spot some wildlife lingering near the lakes and exposed granite slopes. Numerous turnouts offer prime photo opportunities, and roadside picnic areas are located at **Lembert Dome** and **Tenaya Lake.** This is also the route to **Tuolumne Meadows,** the gorgeous subalpine meadows along the Tuolumne River. The meadows are a popular camping area (half the campsites are available on a first-come, first-served basis and half require reservations) and the base for backpackers heading into Yosemite's beautiful high country.

Backpackers are required to obtain a wilderness permit in person. The permits are free, but only a limited number are distributed; call 209/372-0740 for more information. The 3.5-mile hike to **May Lake** is a favorite route for backpackers, and the 6-mile hike to the **Glen Aulin High Sierra Backpacker's Camp** offers a spectacular spot for pitching a tent. Five clusters of canvas cabins (for four to six occupants) are available to backpackers in the High Sierra region; prices average $150 for two per night and include breakfast, dinner, and a shower. These cabins are booked through an annual lottery each fall; call 559/454-2002 for details.

If you've always wanted to backpack in Yosemite but don't have the equipment or experience, here's your chance. Call **Southern Yosemite Mountain Guides,** 559/658-TREK, and ask for a free brochure of their guided and catered backpacking adventures, which range from leisurely weekend family outings to challenging two-week treks. Guided mountain-bike tours, fly-fishing excursions, and rock-climbing clinics are also available. If you're partial to viewing Yosemite by car, pick up a copy of the **Yosemite Road Guide** or the **Yosemite Valley Tour** cassette tape at the Yosemite Valley Visitors Center. It's almost as good as having Ranger Rick in the backseat of your car. City slickers might also want to consider seeing the park on **horseback.** The thrill (and ease) of riding a horse into Yosemite's beautiful backcountry just might make it worth the splurge. Select a stable in Yosemite Valley, Wawona, or Tuolumne Meadows, then call 209/372-8348 or 209/372-8427 to make a reservation.

Additional information on Yosemite National Park is available on the Internet at www.nps.gov/yose and www.yosemitepark.com.

Cheap Eats

While the sight-seeing in Yosemite is unparalleled, the dining is not. Why? Because all of the inexpensive places to eat are run by concessionaires that cater to a captive audience and must appeal to everyone's taste (read: pizza, burgers, salads, etc.). Your best bet is to bring as much of your own food as possible, because most of the park's restaurants offer mediocre (or worse) cafeteria-style food (the only exception is the lofty Ahwahnee Restaurant, but you'll have to fork over a bundle to eat there). Here's a rundown on the better budget-oriented places to eat in Yosemite Village; for a full list of all the cafes, cafeterias, and restaurants in the park, check out the park's Web site at www.yosemitepark.com.

Degnan's Pasta Place

Yosemite Village ☎ 209/372-8437

Located within the Village Mall, Degnan's Pasta Place has a pseudo-rustic ambience with its high-beamed ceiling and central fireplace. The menu features a variety of pasta dishes with an array of various sauces. You can also get freshly made hot breadsticks, salads, and desserts. *No credit cards; local checks only; lunch, dinner every day (Apr–Oct 30); no alcohol.*

Garden Terrace

Yosemite Village ☎ 209/372-1269

Located at Yosemite Lodge, the Garden Terrace is popular with families for its moderately priced, all-you-can-eat, serve-yourself buffet, which offers the usual array of soups, pasta, salads, and carved meats. *Lunch, dinner every day (May–Dec); no alcohol.*

Tuolumne Meadows Lodge

Yosemite Village ☎ 209/372-8413

Perhaps it's the fact that you're eating under a tent set up beside the Tuolumne River that makes breakfast and dinner a charmingly rustic affair despite the standard American fare that's served. Dinner reservations are required. *AE, DC, DIS, MC, V; checks OK; breakfast, lunch, dinner every day (mid-June–mid-Sept, depending on snowfall); no alcohol.*

Wawona Lawn Barbecue

Yosemite Village ☎ 209/375-6556

Each Saturday evening in the summer, the Wawona Hotel hosts a big old-fashioned barbecue dinner on the lush green lawns outside the hotel (the aroma alone will lead you here). It's truly worth the trip to feast on American classics—steaks, hamburgers, and corn on the cob—in the grandest national park in the United States. *Dinner Sat (Memorial Day–Labor Day); no alcohol.*

Cheap Sleeps

Reservations for all Yosemite National Park accommodations may be—and usually are—made up to a year in advance, so try to plan your trip as early as possible. Rates are subject to change daily for all lodgings; the fees listed here are averages. For more information on Yosemite lodgings and to make reservations, write to Yosemite National Park, Yosemite, CA 95389, call 559/252-4848, or visit the park's Web site at www.nps.gov/yose. Most Yosemite campsites may be booked up to eight weeks in advance; for camping reservations, contact Reserve America, 800/436-7275, www.reservations.nps.gov.

Curry Village

Yosemite Valley, southeast of Yosemite Village ☎ 559/252-4848

The cheapest sleeps in Curry Village are the 427 canvas tent cabins (about $44 a night) that sleep up to five people. Bathroom facilities are shared and, to avoid tempting the always-hungry bears, no food or cooking is allowed. The 80 small wood cabins sleep up to five people and are costlier, but some have private bathrooms. Unfortunately, both the tent cabins and the wood cabins have sagging, uncomfortable beds, and only the wood cabins are heated. These lodgings are actually just a step up from camping, but if you adopt the right "roughing-it" attitude, they can be a lot of fun. Open year-round. *AE, DC, DIS, MC, V; checks OK; www.yosemitepark.com.*

Housekeeping Camp

Yosemite Village, west of Curry Village ☎ 559/252-4848

The emphasis here in Yosemite Village, west of Curry Village, is on "camp," which is more or less what you'll be doing if you're lucky enough to get a reservation for one of the 282 identical concrete-

and-canvas structures (two walls and the roof are made of cloth). The good news is that regardless of whether you're a party of one or four (the maximum allowed), the price is the same: $47 a night (may change seasonally). The bad news is that the units are cramped and uncomfortable and serve as sacred feeding ground for the voracious alpine mosquito (bring repellent). Each unit is equipped with one double bed and two fold-down cots (attached by one end to the wall), and outside are a picnic table, shelves, and an outlet for a hot plate and other appliances. Shared bathroom, shower, and laundry facilities and a grocery store are nearby. Open from mid-April to early October, weather permitting. *AE, DC, DIS, MC, V; checks OK; www. yosemitepark.com.*

Tuolumne Meadows Lodge and White Wolf Lodge

Off Tioga Road, north of Yosemite Valley ☎ 559/252-4848

Tuolumne Meadows Lodge and White Wolf Lodge are the park's only inexpensive accommodations located outside of Yosemite Valley. They offer the same type of lodgings as their cousins in the valley—small wood cabins and canvas tent cabins—yet they're far from the maddening crowds. White Wolf has 24 tent cabins (shared bath only) and 4 wood cabins (private bath optional) that are always booked a full year in advance. Tuolumne Meadows Lodge has 69 tent cabins (shared bath only). Open from mid-April to early October, weather permitting. *AE, DC, DIS, MC, V; checks OK; www.yosemite park.com.*

Yosemite Lodge

Yosemite Valley, west of Yosemite Village ☎ 559/252-4848

If camping or sleeping in a canvas tent cabin sounds more like something out of Dante's *Inferno* than a stay in paradise, your only inexpensive alternative in the park is the 495-room Yosemite Lodge, which has standard motel-style rooms and a smattering of small wood cabins (private bath optional for both). On summer weekends, the area around the lodge is a zoo, with parades of tour buses roaring through. Fortunately, a short walk in any direction gets you away from the masses. Lodge reservations are definitely needed far in advance. Open year-round. *AE, DC, DIS, MC, V; checks OK; www. yosemitepark.com.*

Mammoth Lakes

At the base of 11,053-foot Mammoth Mountain are nearly a dozen alpine lakes and the sprawling town of Mammoth Lakes—a mishmash of inns, motels, and restaurants built primarily to serve patrons of the popular Mammoth Mountain Ski Area. Ever since resort founder Dave McCoy mortgaged his motorcycle for $85 in 1938 to buy his first ski lift, folks have been coming here in droves (particularly from Southern California) to carve turns and navigate the moguls at one of the best downhill areas in the United States. In addition to skiing, this section of the eastern Sierra Nevada has been famous for decades for its fantastic fishing holes. In fact, here the trout is king, and several fishing derbies celebrate its royal status. This natural kingdom is no longer the exclusive domain of fishers and skiers, however. Word has gotten out about Mammoth's charms, attracting every kind of outdoor enthusiast and adventurer to this spectacular region in the heart of the High Sierra.

Exploring

Whether you've migrated to the Mammoth area to ski, fish, play, or simply rest your weary bones, stop by the **Mammoth Lakes Visitors Bureau** (in the Village Shopping Center, on Main Street, Mammoth Lakes, 800/367-6572 or 760/934-2712, www.visitmammoth.com). You'll find wall-to-wall maps, coupons, brochures, and day planners, as well as copies of the Forest Service's excellent (and free) "Winter Recreation Map" and "Summer Recreation Map," which show the area's best routes for hiking, biking, sledding, snowmobiling, and cross-country skiing. The friendly bureau staff will even help you find an affordable place

MAS Transit Ski Shuttle

If you've ever seen the several-mile-long traffic jams converging on Mammoth Mountain Ski Area's parking lot, then you know why veteran Mammoth skiers always park their wheels in town and take the shuttle to the resort. These shuttles are not only convenient, they're free. And no matter where you're staying, a Mammoth Area Shuttle (MAS) stop is most likely nearby. The ubiquitous buses run from 7am to 5:30pm daily during ski season, and swing by their stops every 15 minutes to shuttle skiers to one of the resort's three entrances. For more information, call 760/934-0687.

to stay in Mammoth. If you need to rent ski gear or practically any other athletic and outdoor equipment, visit the bustling **Kittredge Sports** (on Main Street, next to the Chevron gas station, Mammoth Lakes, 760/934-7566).

Once you've unpacked your bags, it's time to lace up your hiking boots and explore. A top attraction is **Devil's Postpile National Monument,** one of the world's premier examples of basalt columns. The tall, slender rock columns were formed nearly 100,000 years ago when lava from the erupting Mammoth Mountain cooled and fractured into multisided forms. They've become such a popular attraction that between June 15 and September 15 (the road is closed in winter), rangers close the access road to daytime traffic and require visitors without a special permit to travel by shuttle (fee is about $9 round-trip). Shuttles pick up riders every 15 minutes at the Mammoth Mountain Ski Area parking lot (on Minaret Road, off Highway 203 W, 760/934-2505) and drop them off at a riverside trail for the less-than-half-mile walk to the monument. After you've seen the Postpile, follow the trail for another 2 miles to the beautiful **Rainbow Falls,** where the San Joaquin River plunges 101 feet over an ancient lava flow into a deep pool, often creating rainbows in the mist. If you follow the trail to Red's Meadow, you'll be at one of the entrance points to the 228,500-acre **Ansel Adams Wilderness,** a popular backpacking destination highlighted by the jagged **Minarets,** a series of steep, narrow volcanic ridges just south of massive Mount Ritter.

True to its name, the Mammoth Lakes area boasts 10 lakes (none of which, oddly enough, are named Mammoth). The largest and one of the most striking is **Lake Mary,** and even though it's set high in the mountains, it's easy to get to: head west on Main Street, which turns into Lake Mary Road; drive past Twin Lakes; and continue on till you see it. Numerous hiking trails at Lake Mary lead to nearby smaller, less crowded lakes, including **Horseshoe Lake,** a great place for swimming (the water is slightly warmer than in neighboring lakes). Trout fishers frequently try their luck at Lake Mary, although most anglers prefer to cast their lines in **Convict Lake,** where you can rent a boat and stock up at the Convict Lake Resort's tackle shop (from Highway 395 a few miles south of town, take the Convict Lake Road exit, just south of Mammoth Lakes Airport, 760/934-3800). Another hot spot for snagging some meaty trout is **Hot Creek,** the most popular catch-and-release fishery in California (on average, each trout is caught and released five to six times a month). Only a few miles of the creek are accessible to the public; the rest is private property (on Hot Creek Hatchery Road, just off Highway 395 at the north end of Mammoth Lakes Airport, 800/367-6572 or 760/934-2712).

Mountain biking is another hugely popular sport here in the summer, when the entire Mammoth Mountain Ski Area is transformed into one of the top bike parks in the country, and a national mountain-bike championship race takes place (on Minaret Road, off Highway 203 W, Mammoth Lakes, 800/367-6572 or 760/934-0606). Thirty-four dollars (less for kids) buys you an all-day pass to 60 miles of single-track trails and a gondola that zips you and your bike up to the top of the mountain. From there it's downhill all the way (be sure to wear a helmet), with trails ranging in difficulty from the mellow "Paper Route" ride to the infamous "Kamikaze" wheel-spinner. If you don't want to pay to ride a bike, there are dozens of great trails where mountain bikes are permitted.

A Kick in the Brass

*Granted, life is often one big outdoor party in Mammoth Lakes, but when the annual **Mammoth Lakes Jazz Jubilee** swings into gear in July, hold on to your Tevas—nearly everyone in this toe-tapping town starts kicking up their heels when a dozen world-class bands start tootin' their horns. This three-day jazz extravaganza usually happens the first weekend after the Fourth of July, and opening day is free. A much more sedate but definitely worthwhile musical event is the annual **Sierra Summer Festival Concert,** a tribute to everything from chamber to classical that begins in late July and winds down in early August. For more information about either event, contact the Mammoth Lakes Visitors Bureau, 800/367-6572 or 760/934-2712, www.visitmammoth.com.*

Mammoth's Hot Springs

*Dozens of natural hot springs dot the Mammoth area, although most of the remote ones are kept secret by tourist-weary locals who probably wouldn't make you feel very welcome even if you discovered one. The more accessible springs, however, definitely welcome visitors, including the free **Hot Creek Geologic Site**, where the narrow creek feeds into a series of artificial pools—some only big enough for two, others family-size. These pools are equipped with cold-water pipes that usually keep the water temperature toasty yet not unbearably hot. Although the Forest Service discourages soaking in the pools because of sporadic spurts of scalding water—yes, there is a small risk of getting your buns poached—most people are more concerned about whether or not to show off their birthday suit (swimsuits are optional). Take the Hot Creek Hatchery Road exit off Highway 395 (at the north end of Mammoth Lakes Airport) and follow the signs. Call the Mammoth Lakes Visitors Bureau for more details at 800/367-6572 or 760/934-7566. Open daily from sunrise to sunset.*

With winter comes an onslaught of downhill skiers, who journey here to schuss the slopes of **Mammoth Mountain Ski Area,** 800/686-6624. With 3,500 skiable acres, 150 runs, 30 chair lifts, and a 70 percent chance of sunny skies, Mammoth is lauded as one of the nation's top downhill resorts. Unfortunately, it can also be one of the country's most crowded ski areas, particularly on weekends, when more than 10,000 Los Angelenos make the lengthy commute. (Tip: About 90 percent of the skiers arrive on Friday night and leave Sunday afternoon, so come on a weekday.) A Mammoth lift ticket costs at least $60 for an adult, but you can shave about $10 off the price by purchasing a half-day pass, and a multiple-day ticket will reap even greater savings. Discounts are available for children, teens, and senior citizens.

Mammoth Lakes also has mile upon mile of perfectly groomed **cross-country ski** trails, winding through gorgeous stretches of national forest and immense meadows. Nordic skiers of all levels favor the **Tamarack Cross-Country Ski Center** at Tamarack Lodge on Twin Lakes, which offers 25 miles of groomed trails, extensive backcountry trails, lessons, rentals, and tours (on Lake Mary Road, 2.5 miles southwest of town, Mammoth Lakes, 760/934-2442).

MAMMOTH LAKES

181

Cheap Eats

The Breakfast Club

Corner of Old Mammoth Road and Highway 203, Mammoth Lakes

☎ 760/934-6944

The best place to start your day in Mammoth Lakes is the Breakfast Club, a favorite with both the locals and the hoards of weekend skiers that drive up from L.A. It takes a big appetite to finish their huge omelets, pancakes, and various other classic American morning fare, all served with house-made muffins and pastries. *Cash only; breakfast every day; beer and wine.*

Giovanni's

437 Old Mammoth Road, Mammoth Lakes ☎ 760/934-7563

If you've been to Mammoth before, then you've probably been to Giovanni's, which has long been considered the best pizzeria in Mammoth Lakes. The vast menu offers a wide array of choices besides pizza, such as lasagne, chicken parmigiana, and portobello mushroom ravioli, but it's the pie that draws the crowds. You're offered a choice of thin, regular, or whole-wheat crust and three kinds of sauces: Italian (spicy tomato sauce and mozzarella), New York (olive oil, herbs, and mozzarella), or pesto (basil, garlic, pine nuts, olive oil, and mozzarella). There are also 12 beers on tap and a decent selection of reasonably priced wines. A lunch special—small pizza with your choice of two toppings and choice of soup or salad for only $5.50—is available Monday through Saturday until 4pm, and the sports bar features happy hour from 4pm to 6pm Monday through Thursday. *AE, MC, V; local checks only; lunch Mon–Sat, dinner every day; beer and wine.*

Grumpy's Saloon & Eatery

361 Old Mammoth Road, Mammoth Lakes ☎ 760/934-8587

If it moos, oinks, or clucks it's on the menu at Grumpy's Saloon & Eatery, one of the most lively restaurants in Mammoth. In fact, it's so popular that the owners closed the old location and built a new, larger restaurant up the street (and the rustic log-cabin theme is a definite improvement). Hefty Grumpy Burgers (made from certified Angus ground beef and served with choice of fries, coleslaw, or barbecued beans) and baby back pork ribs are the big sellers here, along with hot "doggers," Mexican food, sandwiches, salads, house-made chili, and 20 different beers on tap. To keep everyone entertained, Grumpy's has 20 big-screen TVs, two pool tables, an array of video games, and even an outdoor sand volleyball court. Be sure to stop by during happy hour—Monday through Thursday from 4pm to 6pm—for free popcorn, ribs, chicken wings, and other snacks. *AE, MC, V; no checks; lunch, dinner every day; full bar (open until 2am).*

Roberto's Café

271 Old Mammoth Road, Mammoth Lakes ☎ 760/934-3667

For the town's top tamales, tortillas, and fajitas, go to Roberto's Café, a local favorite. While you're waiting for a table, order a pitcher of "Horny Bob" cocktails from the small bar at the entrance and throw a little après-ski party. The menu offers all the classic Mexican dishes, piled to the rim with lusciously gooey cheese, beans, rice, and chopped lettuce. Trust us, you finish one of these plates and you won't be hungry the entire next day. *DC, DIS, MC, V; no checks; lunch, dinner every day; full bar.*

Cheap Sleeps

Davison Street Guest House

19 Davison Street, Mammoth Lakes, CA 93546 ☎ 760/924-2188
or ☎ 619/544-9093

For as little as $15 a night in summer, you can slumber on a bunk bed at this classy, five-bedroom A-frame lodge, which once served as a private residence. Although the Guest House is cramped and you have to share the bathrooms and kitchen with other visitors, it is clean, cute, comfortable, and warm—and, a plus for sun worshipers, there's a large deck in back. In the winter, its location near the slopes makes this a skier's paradise. Inexpensive private rooms (without baths) are also available. Rates increase slightly in winter. *No credit cards; checks OK.*

Executive Inn

54 Sierra Boulevard, Mammoth Lakes, CA 93546 ☎ 760/934-8892

Recently renovated inside and out, the Executive Inn's new owner does a commendable job of providing the basic creature comforts— queen-size bed, coffeemaker, telephone, TV, heater, and private bath with tub—at reasonable rates. Located just off Main Street, the 40-room inn is within walking distance of several restaurants and ski-shuttle stops. *AE, DIS, MC, V; no checks.*

Motel 6

3372 Main Street, Mammoth Lakes ☎ 800/4-MOTEL-6

Okay, so it's a Motel 6, but it's still one of the best budget hotels in Mammoth. A $1.5-million renovation in 1997 really spruced up the 151 accommodations, but don't expect a lot of elbow room. Perks include air-conditioning, TVs, and telephones in all the rooms; a ski-shuttle stop right out front; a heated pool (summer only); free coffee in the lobby; and a convenient location on Main Street that's within walking distance of the shops and restaurants. *AE, DC, DIS, MC, V; no checks.*

Ullr Lodge

5920 Minaret Road, Mammoth Lakes, CA 93546 ☎ 760/934-2454

Let's face it: the Ullr (pronounced YOU-ler) Lodge's 19 spartan, garish rooms look best with the lights off (everything—from the carpets to the bedcovers—reeks of cheapness), but the prices make it worth considering. You can choose from the dorm rooms (about $15 a night in summer and $20 in winter), a room with shared bath (from $30 to $50), or a room with private bath and TV (in the $40 to $60 range). There's also a community kitchen, sauna, lounge with fireplace, and easy access to a ski-shuttle stop. *MC, V; no checks.*

Gold Country

sacramento
north gold country
south gold country

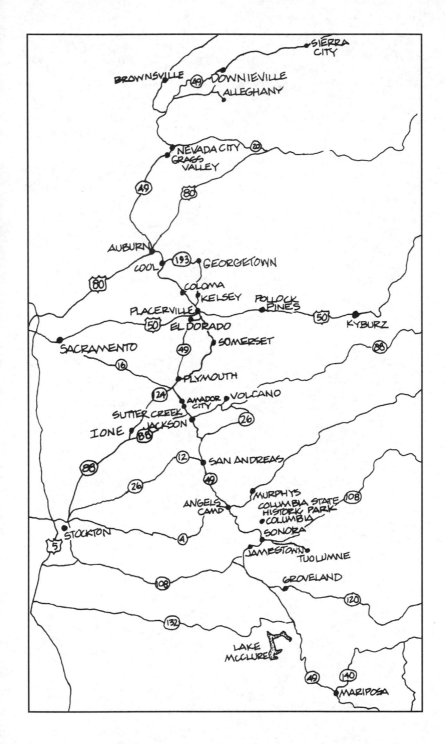

Sacramento

Sacramento has long been regarded as San Francisco's second-class stepsister, but with its increasing number of skyscrapers, trendy restaurants, and swanky hotels (not to mention the NBA's Sacramento Kings), California's capital city is no longer the sleepy little valley town folks used to whiz through on their way to Lake Tahoe. Located 90 miles northeast of the Bay Area, the city is best known for its dual status as the seat of state government and the epicenter of California's biggest industry: agriculture (locals affectionately call it the Big Tomato and Sacratomato). But disregard any disparaging words you may have heard about this agricultural hot spot: there are no cows (or even cowboy hats) within city limits, and most of the city slickers do not pick tomatoes for a living.

This former Gold Rush boomtown sprang up where the American and Sacramento Rivers meet—an area now known as Old Sac. In 1839 Swiss immigrant John Sutter traversed both rivers, built his famous fort, and established New Helvetia, his "New Switzerland" colony. But his hopes that the thriving colony would evolve into his own vast empire were dashed when gold was discovered near Sutter's sawmill in 1848. Sutter's colonists deserted New Helvetia to search for the precious nuggets, and as word of the gold discovery spread, thousands more wound their way to the hills above Sacramento to seek their fortune. Sutter himself never prospered from the Gold Rush and died a bitter, penniless man.

Today, Sacramento is home to more than a million people,

many of whom play politics with the capital crowd or practice law. They dote on their spectacular Victorian homes and fine Craftsman-style bungalows, and are justly proud of the tree-lined streets and thick carpets of grass that surround their homes and parks.

In the scorching summer months, when thermometers often soar into the three-digit range, many folks beat the heat by diving into swimming pools, chugging around the delta in a houseboat with a fishing pole in hand, or floating down the American River. Once the sun sets, however, things cool off dramatically, and Sacramentans often enjoy their evening meals alfresco. Winters are punctuated by the famous tule fog—so thick it blocks the sun for weeks at a time—and cooler temperatures than in San Francisco. And as all ski buffs know, locals always get the jump on their Bay Area neighbors racing to the snowy slopes of Lake Tahoe, thanks to the city's proximity to the Sierra Nevada.

Access

In Italy all roads lead to Rome, and in California all highways lead to Sacramento. If you're coming by car, Highways 99, 16, 50, and 160 and Interstates 80 and 5 lead to the capital—in fact, it's hard not to pass through Sacramento. Barring rush-hour traffic jams, it's about a 90-minute drive from San Francisco, and approximately seven or eight hours from Los Angeles. Amtrak, stationed at 4th and I Streets, has several trains serving the city daily; call 800/USA-RAIL for reservations and schedules. Sacramento is the hub for Greyhound buses traveling throughout the state (715 L Street at 7th Street, 800/231-2222). The Sacramento International Airport, 12 miles north of town off Interstate 5, has daily flights to most major U.S. cities, including San Francisco and Los Angeles, as well as to Canada, 916/929-5411. For shuttle service to and from the airport, call Super Shuttle, 800/258-3826.

Transit Tips

Exploring

To best appreciate the Big Tomato, start your tour of the town in **Old Sacramento,** the city's historic district. Perched along the Sacramento River, the 4-block-long stretch is filled with dozens of restaurants, gift shops, and saloons, worth a once-over on your way toward the **California State Railroad Museum.** This grand monument to the glory days of locomotion and the Big Four is the largest museum of its kind in the nation and a must-see for locomotive lovers of all ages (111 I Street at 2nd Street, 916/445-6645). The granddaddy of Old Sac attractions is the **Sacramento Dixieland Jubilee,** 916/372-5277, the world's largest Dixieland jazz festival, which attracts thousands of toe tappers and bands from around the world each Memorial Day weekend.

One mile south of Old Sac is the **California Towe Ford Museum of Automotive History,** a giant warehouse containing the largest antique Ford collection in the country; nearly every model ever manufactured by the Ford Motor Company is parked here (2200 Front Street,

A River Runs Through It

River City Bicycle Route

The American River Parkway, a 5,000-acre nature preserve that runs along the river from Discovery Park to Folsom Lake, is a great spot for two-wheeling. On sunny Sunday afternoons, even the locals spend a few hours pedaling their bikes along the mostly flat 22-mile-long bike trail that parallels the river. You can rent a bike for about $15 a day at City Bicycle Works (2419 K Street at 24th Street, Sacramento, 916/447-2453).

916/442-6802). Nearby is the **Crocker Art Museum,** home of the largest art collection in the region, including contemporary California art by such talents as Wayne Thiebaud and Robert Arneson. The museum is housed in one of the city's most elaborate Victorian structures (216 O Street, between 2nd and 3rd Streets, 916/264-5423).

A few blocks northeast of the Crocker Art Museum is the awe-inspiring **state capitol building,** restored in the 1970s to its original magnificence with $67.8 million in taxpayers' dollars (so come see what you paid for). You may wander around the building on your own, but you really shouldn't miss the free tours given daily every hour between 9am and 4pm, which include an overview of the legislative process and, if you're lucky, a chance to see the political hotshots in action. Tickets are handed out a half hour before the tour on a first-come, first-served basis in the basement of room B-27 in the capitol (10th Street, between L and N Streets, 916/324-0333). After you've marveled at the capitol's interior, spend some time feeding the brazen squirrels scampering around the beautifully landscaped 40-acre **Capitol Park.** Stop by the poignant Vietnam Veterans' Memorial in the park's northeast corner. Etched into panels of India black granite are the names of 5,615 Californians who died in the war. For a step back in time, take a stroll through pioneer **John Sutter's fort,** built in 1839 (27th and L Streets, 916/445-4422).

Thanks to a recent influx of Generation X-ers, a cadre of cheap cafes, coffee shops, and breweries now proliferates in the downtown area. East of the capitol you'll find the original (ergo the coolest) coffee hangout, **Java City** (1800 Capitol Avenue at 18th Street, 916/444-5282), and next door, be sure to check out **Paesano's,** a trendy haunt serving gourmet pizza and pasta at most reasonable prices (1806 Capitol Avenue between 18th and 19th Streets, 916/447-8646).

For great shopping and people-watching downtown, visit the **Tower** triangle, home of the original **Tower Records,** opened in 1941 (Broadway and 16th Street, 916/444-3000); **Tower Books,** 916/444-6688, which attracts as many browsers as buyers; **Tower Pipes and Cigars,** 916/443-8466, a heady-scented shop where a dexterous Cuban hand rolls fresh cigars in the window; the **Tower Theater,** 916/443-1982, one of Sacramento's last bastions of foreign, art, and cult flicks; and the **Tower Cafe,** 916/441-0222, where on balmy summer nights, locals lounge on the patio with their tall glasses of premium brewskis.

For some hip SacTown nightlife, be sure to check out **Harlows Night Club** (2708 J Street, 916/441-4693), which features live local and Bay Area bands most evenings. A more subdued crowd throws darts, sips English ales on tap, and munches quality pub grub at the **Fox and Goose** (1001 R Street at 10th Street, 916/443-8825), where live music ranging from jazz to bluegrass and folk can be heard every night except Sunday. If it's cheap beer, free popcorn, loud jukebox music, and heavy scamming you're after, the legendary **Pine Cove** (502 29th Street at E Street, 916/446-3624) is the place, serving 75-cent glasses of premium Pabst Blue Ribbon—this ain't no sippin' beer—guaranteed to bring on a buzz.

Those of you cruising through the city during the last two weeks of August should set aside a hot day or night to visit the **California State Fair,** Sacramento's grandest party. While the carnival rides and games are predictably head spinning and zany, even snobby locals who abhor the annual event admit the livestock exhibits alone are worth the admission price. Other fair highlights include daily horse races, nightly rodeos, and live concerts in the beer garden (Cal Expo, off Interstate 80 Business Loop, 916/263-3000).

Those Lion Eyes

Have you mingled with the monkeys or marveled at the mighty roar of a lion lately? Well, here's your chance. Take a gander at these amazing critters and their friends at the Sacramento Zoo, which boasts more than 150 species of exotic animals housed in 15 acres of elaborate zoological gardens. Afterward, picnic at the duck pond across the street, and if you have tots in tow (and some energy left), take them to Humpty Dumpty's Fairytale Town, a giant kid-pleasin' playground full of slides, swings, and tunnels graced by fairy-tale characters (both attractions are in William Land Park, corner of Land Park Drive and Sutterville Road, Sacramento, 916/264-5885 for zoo, 916/264-5233 for Fairytale Town).

Cheap Eats

Cornerstone Restaurant

2330 J Street, Sacramento ☎ 916/441-0948

There are dozens of breakfast cafes in Sacramento, and the best of the lot is the Cornerstone Restaurant (which explains the wait on the weekends). It's not that the food is anything special (the menu offers all the standard American breakfast fare), but the servings are huge, the service is fast and friendly, and the price is right. For example, a four-egg omelet with home fries, toast, and fruit costs under $6. *Cash only; breakfast every day; no alcohol.*

The Fox and Goose

1001 R Street, Sacramento ☎ 916/443-8825

You'll see chaps chugging down pints of bitter and having a jolly good time over a game of darts at this bustling British pub, almost as genuine as any neighborhood spot you're likely to find in the United Kingdom. This River City institution offers a wee bit of everything—beer, breakfast, lunch, and live music—at very reasonable prices. There are 18 beers on tap, including brews from England, Ireland, and Scotland. For breakfast choose from a variety of omelets (you may order eggs from free-range chickens for a small additional price) as well as kippers (Atlantic herring), grilled tomatoes, crumpets, and such authentic English treats as bangers and mash. The lunch menu features a wide array of sandwiches and salads as well as a daily soup. At night the place swings to folk, jazz, Celtic, alternative, and blues tunes. *AE, MC, V; local checks only; breakfast every day, lunch Mon–Fri; beer and wine; www.infovillage.com/fox&goose.*

Rubicon Brewing Company

2004 Capitol Avenue, Sacramento ☎ 916/448-7032

If you're in the mood for a good beer and a great burger, head over to the Rubicon Brewing Company in downtown Sacramento. Besides handcrafting the city's best beers—try a pitcher of the award-winning India Pale Ale—the brewery also offers tasty pub food: sandwiches, salads, chicken wings, french fries, and such at down-to-earth prices.

AE, DC, DIS, MC, V; checks OK; breakfast Sat–Sun, lunch, dinner every day; beer and wine.

Siam Restaurant

5100 Franklin Boulevard, Sacramento ☎ 916/452-8382

This admirable tiny Thai restaurant located just outside the downtown area turns out delicious soups, unusual salads, fiery-hot curry dishes, and seafood entrees such as garlic prawns, sautéed mussels, steamed clams cooked with fresh ginger, and calamari laced with garlic, onion, and chili paste. Other favorites include the drunken noodles (pan-fried noodles mixed with green peppers, vegetables, garlic, mint, and your choice of pork, chicken, or beef) and deep-fried pompano with a sweet and sour sauce. Cool your fevered mouth with a tasty Thai iced tea, a Thai beer, or a sweet scoop of coconut ice cream. The Siam is always hopping, so reservations are recommended. *AE, MC, V; no checks; lunch, dinner Tues–Sun; beer and wine.*

Taco Loco Taqueria

2326 J Street, Sacramento ☎ 916/447-0711

1122 11th Street at L Street, Sacramento ☎ 916/447-TACO

Adjacent to the Cornerstone Restaurant (our top breakfast pick) is one of SacTown's best Mexican restaurants: Taco Loco Taqueria. What makes this place special are the unique and imaginative ingredients that they use to spice up south-of-the-border standards. Examples? Try the charbroiled black-tip shark taco, *gordo* shrimp burrito, or snapper ceviche tostada—all so fresh that Taco Loco Taqueria doesn't even own a freezer. Wash it all down with a Los Cabos margarita while soaking up the sun on the front patio, and it's easy to see why this is one of our favorite lunch spots. *MC, V; no checks; lunch, dinner every day; beer and wine.*

Willie's Burgers

2415 16th Street, Sacramento ☎ 916/444-2006

And for all you pro-grease, anti-health nuts, there's Willie's Burgers, Sacramento's version of Tommy's Burgers in L.A., complete with paper-towel dispensers mounted on the walls (regular napkins just won't do) to sop up the mess from your artery-clogging double-chili-cheeseburger-with-extra-onions-and-bacon, large fries, and a large chocolate shake to wash it all down, thank-you-very-much. It's absurdly cheap and always open late to satisfy your drunken urges for sinfully delicious, greasy grub. *Cash only; lunch, dinner every day; no alcohol.*

Cheap Sleeps

Capitol Park Hotel

1125 9th Street, Sacramento, CA 95814 ☎ 916/441-5361

Although the Capitol Park Hotel houses primarily elderly folk on a long-term basis, the friendly proprietor keeps about 15 rooms available for overnighters of any age. Even though there is no parking lot (a public parking garage is down the street), this is one of the best deals in town. For less than $40 you get a worn yet comfy room with air-conditioning, cable TV, and large windows. But the best part is the location—just steps away from the state capitol; only a room at the pricey Hyatt Regency could get you closer. *Cash only;.*

Capitol Travel Inn

817 W Capitol Avenue, Sacramento, CA 95691 ☎ 916/371-6983

If you have wheels and don't mind the short drive into West Sacramento (where there are no tourist—or even resident—attractions), this 38-room inn might be worth your while. A room costs about $35 a night, which pays for a large color TV, a direct-dial phone, air-conditioning, and a free place to park the car. Note: The inn isn't within walking distance of Sacramento's star attractions, so some sort of transport is essential for sight-seeing. *AE, MC, V; no checks.*

Quality Inn

818 15th Street, Sacramento, CA 95814 ☎ 916/444-3980

Budget lodgers might feel compelled to kneel and shout "hallelujah" on the steps of the Quality Inn—the best cheap sleep in Sacramento. A mere $59 buys you a night in a remodeled, sparkling-clean room with air-conditioning (a godsend during Sacramento's hellaciously hot summers), TV (with HBO, no less), direct-dial phones, and a swimming pool. The 40-room Quality Inn is also in a great location— just blocks from the state capitol, the Governor's Mansion, and the

Sacramento Convention Center—and there's even plenty of free parking. *AE, DC, DIS, MC, V; no checks.*

Sacramento Econo Lodge

711 16th Street, Sacramento, CA 95814 ☎ 916/443-6631

Only a handful of cheap hotels in downtown Sacramento make you feel safe. This is one of them. Located opposite the Governor's Mansion, the Sacramento Econo Lodge has 41 no-nonsense rooms with telephones, TVs, and firm beds. In the morning, warm up with a free cup of coffee and donuts, grab a free map of Sacramento's downtown attractions, and hit the road. *AE, DC, DIS, MC, V; no checks.*

Sacramento International Hostel

900 H Street, Sacramento, CA 95814 ☎ 916/443-1691

First, the NBA's Sacramento Kings bounced into town, then an official AYH-affiliated youth hostel opened its doors—Sacramento, you've hit the big time at last! In 1995, at a cost of more than $2 million, the Llewellyn Williams Mansion, a 12,000-square-foot Victorian beauty, was transformed into one of the finest youth hostels in the country. It offers 60 bunk beds as well as bedrooms for families, and takes all members at $15 a head and nonmembers at $18 (family rates are available). Located just behind City Hall in the heart of downtown, the hostel is within walking distance of Sacramento's major sights, including the capitol and Old Sac. *MC, V; no checks.*

North Gold Country

By 1849, word had spread throughout the United States, Europe, and other corners of the globe that gold miners were becoming millionaires overnight in California. In just one year, more than 80,000 eager souls stampeded their way across water and land to reach the hilly terrain now known as the Gold Country and the Mother Lode. Many of the '49ers had to fight for their claims to the land, claims that left the average miner with little more than dirt and grime in his pocket. Crime and starvation were rampant, and when the exhausted miners put away their picks and pans for the night, most sought comfort in drinking, gambling, and prostitutes. It was a wild and heady time that brought riches to relatively few, but changed the Golden State forever.

You can follow in the miners' footsteps (geographically, at least) by cruising along the aptly numbered Highway 49, the zigzagging, 321-mile road that links many of the mining towns. You'll find some of the most authentically preserved towns in the northern Gold Country, including Grass Valley, where more than a billion dollars in gold was extracted, and Nevada City, former home of one of the region's more famous gold miners, President Herbert Hoover.

Exploring

Unlike the southern Gold Country, which has towns and attractions extending southward for more than 100 miles, the places worth visiting in the northern Gold Country are all within a 13-mile radius (something to consider if you prefer walking to driving). Although **Auburn** is the largest town in the area and has been the seat of Placer County since 1850, nowadays it serves mainly as a pit stop for vacationers headed for Lake Tahoe. Its few noteworthy sights, including the many shops and restaurants of Old Town and the impressively domed **Placer County Courthouse,** are best seen out the car window as you head toward the far more congenial towns of Grass Valley and Nevada City.

Only 4 miles apart, **Grass Valley** and its smaller, cuter cousin, **Nevada City,** share many Gold Rush–town characteristics: historic landmarks, a restored "old town," Victorian-era architecture, hard-rock–mining museums, and hard-to-find parking. Unfortunately, neither town offers an abundance of inexpensive lodgings—this is fancy B&B country—so vacation here in the off-season and make reservations far in advance, or be prepared to shell out a little more hotel money than you bargained for.

Grass Valley, once known for rich quartz mines and Gold Rush entertainers like Lola Montez and Lotta Crabtree, has a historic and slightly scruffy downtown that's a pleasure to explore. Stop first at the Chamber of Commerce (248 Mill Street, Grass Valley, 800/655-4667 or 530/273-4667) for a free walking-tour map of the town and two terrific brochures listing more than two dozen scenic walking, hiking, and

Try a Shuttler Approach

If you've ever visited downtown Nevada City or Grass Valley on a weekend, you know how hard it is to find a parking spot (and to think you came here to get away from it all). This time, why not leave the car at the hotel and let Gold Country Stage's shuttles do all the driving? A measly $2 buys you an all-day pass good for both towns as well as rides to major attractions in outlying areas. Call 530/477-0103 for a free map and riders' guide.

mountain-biking trails. Don't miss the 10-ton Pelton Waterwheel (at 30 feet in diameter, it's the world's largest) on display at the exemplary **North Star Mining Museum** (south end of Mill Street, Grass Valley, 916/273-4255; closed in winter) housed in what was once the power-house for the North Star Mine. Just outside town is the 800-acre **Empire Mine State Historic Park** (10791 E Empire Street, Grass Valley, 530/273-8522), the oldest, largest, and richest gold mine in California; its underground passages once extended for 367 miles and descended 11,007 feet into the ground.

Nevada City, established in 1849 when miners found gold in Deer Creek, occupies one of the most picturesque sites in the Sierra foothills. When the sugar maples blaze in autumn, the town resembles a small New England village, making it hard to believe this was once the third-largest city in California. Pick up a free walking-tour map at the Cham-ber of Commerce (132 Main Street at Coyote Street, Nevada City, 530/265-2692) and put on your walking shoes. Town highlights include the **National Hotel** (211 Broad Street at Pine Street, Nevada City, 530/265-4551), the state's oldest continuously operating hotel, where the cozy Gold Rush–era bar is ideal for a cocktail or two, and the **Fire-house No. 1 Museum** (214 Main Street at Commercial Street, Nevada City, 530/265-5468), where the Gold Rush memorabilia includes relics from the infamous and ill-fated Donner Party.

Sixteen miles north of Nevada City, up the steep and winding N Bloom-field Road, is the 3,000-acre **Malakoff Diggins State Historic Park,** where you'll find the world's largest hydraulic gold mine, as well as a monument to the devastating results of hydraulic mining. Nearly half a mountain was washed away, leaving behind a 600-foot-deep canyon of exposed, minaret-shaped, rust-colored rock—an eerily beautiful sight to some, but an eyesore to most. The mining didn't stop until a court order was issued in 1884, by which time the runoff had turned the San Francisco Bay a murky brown. Overlooking the park is the semirestored mining town of **North Bloom-field,** where a visitors center displays—what else?—hydraulic-mining mem-orabilia (23579 N Bloomfield Road, Nevada City, 530/265-2740).

If you plan to stay in the area for more than a day or two, devote a half day to the scenic little mountain town of **Downieville.** Located an hour's drive up Highway 49 at the junction of the Yuba and Downie Rivers, the town hasn't changed much since the 1850s, with venerable buildings lining boardwalks along crooked Main Street and trim homes cut into the canyon walls above. Downieville's population hovers around 300 now, though during its heyday more than 5,000 prospectors panned the streams and worked the mines. Sights to see include the **Downieville Museum,** housed in a former Gold Rush–era Chinese store, and the **Sierra County Courthouse,** 530/289-3215, where you can admire gold dug out of the rich Ruby Mine.

Cheap Eats

Main Street Cafe & Bar

213 W Main Street, Grass Valley ☎ 530/477-6000

Contemporary, casual, and colorful, the Main Street Cafe is popular among locals and tourists for its standard but accomplished American lunch menu featuring a variety of burgers, salads, and sandwiches for under $10. Dinner's probably out of your price range, but if you feel like splurging on fresh seafood—steamed mussels, swordfish, salmon—or thick-cut steaks, this is the place to do it. *AE, MC, V; local checks only; lunch, dinner every day; full bar.*

Tofanelli's

302 W Main Street, Grass Valley ☎ 530/272-1468

Tofanelli's is one of Grass Valley's cultural and culinary meeting places that is famous for its veggie burger. The tostadas also make a very good lunch, including the version topped with marinated chicken breast (or marinated tofu), brown rice, the house pinto beans, greens, carrots, and tomatoes. Tofanelli's whips up several vegetarian dishes, but the kitchen can also turn out a mean hamburger and Reuben sandwich. Each week the chefs prepare a new dinner menu, which might feature charbroiled chicken breast with sun-dried tomatoes and a balsamic cream sauce, spring vegetables with orange chipotle (smoked jalapeño chili) sauce, as well as the favored vegetarian lasagne with three cheeses, fresh spinach, and house-made marinara. Be sure to save room for Katherine's Chocolate Cake, complemented perfectly by one of Tofanelli's dozen coffee or espresso drinks. On the weekend, indulge in the bounteous brunch served in the garden room and courtyard. *AE, MC, V; checks OK; lunch Mon–Fri, dinner Mon–Sat, brunch Sat–Sun; beer and wine.*

Cirino's

309 Broad Street, Nevada City ☎ 530/265-2246

Nevada City folk come to ever-popular Cirino's for its large, family-style Italian dishes, including the veal piccata prepared with a tangy lemon caper sauce and the penne pasta with salmon, leeks, and dill. Each belly-packing dinner comes with garlic focaccia, soup (a thick Boston clam chowder is served on Friday) or salad, and a choice of spaghetti with a marinara sauce, spaghetti aglio e olio (with garlic and olive oil—simple, but delicious), or fettuccine alfredo. Expect a large, loud, bustling environment that's kid friendly and full of the wonderful aroma of roasted garlic. *AE, DIS, MC, V; local checks only; lunch Fri–Sun, dinner every day; full bar.*

Cowboy Pizza

315 Spring Street, Nevada City ☎ 530/265-2334

Cowboy Wallie, the founder of this pizza joint, gussied up the place with cowpoke kitsch—you'll see everything from a Gene Autry Singing Cowboy poster to the official emblem of the Manure Movers of America. But before you even walk through the door of this wacky place, you'll smell the garlic loaded onto the Gilroy Pizza, cooked in an old stone-floor oven. If you prefer the stinking rose in moderation, bite into the Greek vegetarian version (artichoke hearts, feta, black olives, fresh tomatoes, garlic, and oregano) and you'll soon be bucking for more. You can wash down your slices with a pint or two of an all-natural microbrew. Tip: Locals know it's best to place an order in advance—otherwise, you'll have to wait a bit. For some peculiar reason, Chinese fortune cookies are served at the end of every Cowboy Pizza meal. *No credit cards; checks OK; dinner Wed–Sun; beer and wine.*

Cheap Sleeps

Coach & Four Motel

628 S Auburn Street, Grass Valley, CA 95945 ☎ 530/273-8009

If all you're looking for is a clean room with a comfortable bed and the standard amenities—phone, TV, air-conditioning, refrigerator, and private bath—the Coach & Four might fill the bill. The aging 17-room motel offers a complimentary continental breakfast and is within walking distance of Grass Valley's Old Town (okay, so perhaps it's a long walk), and it's right next to a shuttle stop that takes you to Nevada City for a buck. Your pooch is welcome here, too. *AE, DIS, MC, V; no checks.*

Gold Country Inn

11972 Sutton Way, Grass Valley, CA 95945 ☎ 800/247-6590 or ☎ 530/273-1393

If neither the Coach & Four nor the Holiday Lodge (see below) has panned out, this 84-room Best Western-owned inn on the outskirts of town may have a room in your price range. The Gold Country offers several price breaks, including a 10 percent AAA discount, a 10 percent senior discount, and a children-under-12-sleep-free deal. Other perks include an outdoor spa, pool, and free in-room coffee. *DIS, MC, V; checks OK.*

Holiday Lodge

1221 E Main Street, Grass Valley, CA 95945 ☎ 800/742-7125 or ☎ 530/273-4406

Located just outside downtown Grass Valley, this 36-room pet-friendly motel is a short drive from the Old Towns of both Grass Valley and Nevada City. It's slightly more upscale than the Coach & Four, offering all the same perks—TV, air-conditioning, phone, and private bath—plus a few bonuses, such as a sauna and swimming pool. A 9-hole golf course beckons from across the street, and for you gold diggers who want to splurge, there's the Holiday Lodge Goldpanning Vacation package, where an "expert guide leads the way through the wilds of the Sierra to the most promising gold-panning location." And we've got some real estate in Florida . . . . *AE, DC, DIS, MC, V; no checks.*

Miner's Inn

760 Zion Street, Nevada City, CA 95959 ☎ 530/265-2253

If you can get a room at the Miner's Inn, you've struck it rich. Nevada City's premier cheap sleep offers 20 remodeled cabinlike motel rooms surrounded by a small, shady park. The plain-Jane digs are clean, comfy, and equipped with air-conditioning, color TV, and phones (nonsmoking units are available). And it's a pleasant 1-mile stroll down S Pine Street to Nevada City's historic downtown. A nearby restaurant and lounge round out the amenities. *AE, MC, V; checks OK.*

Northern Queen Inn

400 Railroad Avenue, Nevada City, CA 95959 ☎ 530/265-5824

More upscale and expensive than the Miner's Inn, this is still a good deal for the dollar if you're traveling in the "low season" and want a spacious room with a queen-size bed (a second bed is only a few bucks more). The attractive, modern, 86-room inn, in a wooded setting at the edge of town, offers all the standard perks: cable TV, in-room coffee, private baths, small refrigerators, and a heated pool and spa. There's a restaurant and bar on the premises, and Nevada City's historic district is just a short walk away. The inn fills quickly, so reserve far in advance. *AE, DC, MC, V; checks OK; www.northernqueen inn.com.*

South Gold Country

The rolling hills of the southern Gold Country are honey-combed with mysterious caverns and abandoned mines, including the deepest gold mines on the continent. Most of the Gold Rush towns were abandoned by the 1870s, although some have survived by mining for tourist dollars instead. As a result, it's not always easy to steer clear of the tourist trappings. Most journey to this area for the fishing, camping, hiking, rafting, and mountain biking—and some come to pan for gold. Yep, there still are some precious nuggets in those hills and mountain streams, and you can even hire a prospector to show you how and where to try your luck. But bear in mind that all that glitters is not gold (there's plenty of fool's gold in these parts), and your chances of hitting the jackpot are probably much better in Reno.

Exploring

This tour of the southern half of the Gold Country kicks off, aptly, where it all began: **Coloma,** where carpenter James Marshall discovered gold at John Sutter's mill in 1849. A working replica of the famous sawmill, a small museum, and other gold-related exhibits are on display at **Marshall Gold Discovery State Historic Park,** a 280-acre expanse of shaded lawns and picnic tables that extends through three-quarters of the town (on Highway 49, Coloma, 530/622-3470). Coloma is silly with tourists and rafters on summer weekends, so plan your visit during the week, when you can picnic in peace and float down the American River without fear of colliding into wayward rafts.

An 8-mile drive south on Highway 49 leads to **Placerville,** doomed by its crossroads location at Highway 50 to serve mainly as a pit stop for Tahoe-bound travelers. One of the first camps settled by miners who branched out from Coloma, Placerville was originally dubbed Dry Diggins because of a lack of water. The moniker became Hangtown after a series of grisly lynchings in the mid-1800s (which, for some perverse reason, the town still takes a kind of pride in); eventually, pressure from "respectable" townsfolk resulted in its current name. Home to an uninspiring array of gas stations, budget chain hotels, and 24-hour coffee shops, Placerville doesn't have much to offer visitors except some Old Town gift shops and its famous "Hangtown fry"—a concoction of bacon, eggs, and oysters popular with early miners—which nowadays is dished out at the **Bell Tower Cafe** (423 Main Street in Old Town, Placerville, 530/626-3483). If spelunking sets your heart aflutter, a mile north of downtown in Bedford Park is the **Gold Bug Mine,** a city-owned hard-rock gold mine. Tours of the mine lead you deep into the lighted shafts (on Bedford Avenue 1 mile north of town, Placerville, 530/642-5238). **El Dorado County Museum,** adjacent to the county fairgrounds, showcases such Gold Rush–era relics as Pony Express paraphernalia, an original Studebaker wheelbarrow, and a restored Concord stagecoach (100 Placerville Drive, Placerville, 530/621-5865).

Three miles south of Placerville on Highway 49 sits the small town of **El Dorado,** whose denizens tolerate but in no way cultivate tourism. In fact, most travelers pass right on through—except for those who know about **Poor Red's.** It may not look like much from the outside (or the inside, for that matter), but this bar and restaurant is known throughout the Gold Country for serving great barbecued chicken, steak, and

There's Gold in Them Thar Hills

For a true taste of the Gold Country, hire a prospecting company to teach you the art of panning. Prices range from $10 for a half-hour excursion to $600 for a six-day gold-digger's-delight helicopter trip. Learn how to pan, sluice, and snipe (that is, find gold in crevices) just like the '49ers did nearly 150 years ago. And, yes, you get to pocket whatever gold nuggets (or, more likely, gold dust) you find. Panning outfits include Jensen's Pick & Shovel Ranch in Angels Camp, 209/736-0287; Roaring Camp Mining Company in Pine Grove, 209/296-4100; and Gold Prospecting Expeditions in Jamestown, 209/984-4653.

Rapid Transit

Whitewater rafting is big business in the Mother Lode, particularly during summer, when thousands of rafters converge on the weekend to brave the American River's brutal Class IV rapids. Although a full-day trip down the river will cost you a cool $90 or more on weekends, O.A.R.S. (Outdoor Adventure River Specialists), California's leading river outfitter, offers half-day trips for only $59 during the week, as well as one- to three-day trips down the less-congested Merced, Tuolumne, and Stanislaus Rivers. For more information, call 800/346-6277.

pork ribs at unbeatable prices. Furthermore, it has an international claim to fame as the birthplace of the Golden Cadillac cocktail. So many Golden Cadillacs have been poured here that Red's is now the largest user of Galliano liqueur in North America, as a gilded plaque from Italy, on prominent display, proudly attests (6221 Pleasant Valley Road, downtown El Dorado, 530/622-2901).

To the south on Highway 49 are the blink-and-you'll-miss-'em towns of **Nashville,** site of the first stamp mill in the Mother Lode (now occupied by a trailer park); **Plymouth,** host of the popular Amador County Fair and Rodeo during the first weekend of August; and **Drytown,** named for its lack of gold but known (ironically) by '49ers for the 27-or-so saloons that used to profit here. A few miles past Drytown is **Amador City,** the smallest incorporated city in California. Lined with false-fronted antique and specialty shops, this blocklong nonmetropolis is a good place to stop, stretch your legs, and window-shop.

You'll find a better array of shops, however, about 2 miles south in **Sutter Creek.** This self-proclaimed "nicest little town in the Mother Lode" boasts some beautiful buildings from the 1800s, including the landmark **Knight's Foundry,** the last water-powered foundry and machine shop in the nation; self-guided tours are offered daily (81 Eureka Street off Main Street, Sutter Creek). Also of interest: the multicultural artwork and handmade willow furniture at the Cobweb Collection (83 Main Street, Sutter Creek, 209/267-0690); the contemporary and American arts at Fine Eye Gallery (71 Main Street, Sutter Creek, 209/267-0571); and the regional prints, watercolors, and stone carvings at Sutter Creek Gallery (35 Main Street, Sutter Creek, 209/267-0228).

A 4-mile drive to the south, just past the enormous Georgia Pacific lumber mill, is **Jackson,** the seat of Amador County and the last place in California to outlaw prostitution. Two sights Gold Rush buffs shouldn't

Grape Expectations

*Between the towns of Placerville and Murphys lie several first-rate wineries pro-
ducing everything from rich, spicy zinfandels to full-bodied chardonnays and
fruity rieslings. Most are small, family-owned establishments offering free public
tours, tastings, and picnic sites. Here's a north-to-south roundup of some of the
area's best:*

*Placerville's **Boeger Winery** offers a tasting room in its early 19th-century building plus picnic tables in the shade (530/622-8094, www.boegerwinery.com); and
Sierra Vista Winery features picnic areas with great views of the Crystal Range
(530/622-7221, www.sierravistawinery.com).*

*In Camino, **Madrona Vineyards** is perched at a 3,000-foot elevation (530/644-
5948); and in Somerset, **Granite Springs Winery** boasts a barn-style building,
a separate tasting room, and a pondside picnic area (530/620-6395).*

*Nestled in the Shenandoah Valley are **Amador Foothill Winery,** where you
can sample wines in a state-of-the-art complex (209/245-6307, www.amador
foothill.com); **Charles Spinetta Winery and Gallery,** which has a nature gallery
in its beautiful tasting room and a picnic ground overlooking a pond (209/245-
3384, www.cswinery.com); **Montevina Wines,** with an impressive tasting area
and arbor-covered patio (209/245-6942, www.montevina.com); **Shenandoah
Vineyards,** which offers tasting in an old cellar, along with an art gallery and
grand views (209/245-4455); and tiny **Story Winery,** where the tasting room
overlooks the scenic Consumnes River (209/245-6208, www.zin.com).*

*The town of Murphys offers the small tasting room of **Black Sheep Vintners**
(209/728-2157, www.blacksheepwinery.com); and the beautiful setting of
Stevenot Winery (209/728-3436).*

*At **Chatom Vineyards,** located in an attractive building in the town of Douglas
Flat, visitors may picnic on the patio (209/736-6500).*

miss are the **Amador County Museum** (225 Church Street, Jackson,
209/223-6386), if only for the scale models of the local hard-rock
mines, and **Kennedy Tailing Wheels Park,** site of the Kennedy and the
Argonaut, the Mother Lode's deepest mines. Though the mines have
been closed for decades, their head frames and some huge tailing
wheels remain to give an idea of how waste from the mines was conveyed over the hills to a settling pond (from Main Street, turn up onto
Jackson Gate Road, Jackson). If all this touring has given you a '49er-size

appetite, indulge in a messy Moo-Burger and shake at **Mel and Faye's Diner,** a local landmark since 1956 (see Cheap Eats below).

For a great side trip from Jackson, take a spin through the town of **Volcano,** so wonderfully authentic that it borders on decrepit (it doesn't get more Gold Rush than this, folks). After the winding drive down Ram's Horn Grade, cool off in the funky, friendly bar at the **St. George Hotel** (16104 Pine Grove–Volcano Road, Volcano, 209/296-4458). Or in early spring, picnic amid the nearly half million daffodils (in 100 different varieties) in bloom along Daffodil Hill, a 4-acre ranch just above town (3 miles north of Volcano on Ram's Horn Grade, follow the signs). An outdoor amphitheater, hidden behind stone facades along Main Street, is the site of popular summer theatricals performed by the Volcano Theatre Company (1 block north of the St. George Hotel, Volcano, 209/296-2525). At nearby **Indian Grinding Rock State Historic Park,** you'll find an enormous limestone outcropping—the largest of its kind in America—dotted with thousands of holes created by native Miwoks from years of grinding their acorn meal on the rock. The park also has an Indian artifacts museum (off Pine Grove–Volcano Road, 1.5 miles north of Highway 88, Pine Grove, 209/296-7488).

Back on Highway 49, a few miles south of Jackson, is the "Historic 49" turnoff to **Mokelumne Hill** (pronounced moh-KAHL-uhm-nee), once so rich with gold that claims were limited in size to 16 square feet. Although there's little going on these days in this sleepy blocklong town, it's still a pleasant 15-minute drive through Mokelumne's green pastures, along its historic but minuscule Main Street, and back onto the highway.

Cruise right on through the overcommercialized and truly uninspiring town of San Andreas, and you'll eventually pull into **Angels Camp,** made famous by Mark Twain's short story "The Celebrated Jumping Frog of Calaveras County." Every year, on the third Saturday in May, thousands of frog fans flock to the Calaveras County Fair to witness the **Jumping Frog Jubilee,** 209/736-2561, one of the premier frog-jumping contests in the world. The festival takes place at the Frogtown Fairgrounds 2 miles south of town, and features a rodeo, carnival rides, live music, and—for those of you who forgot to bring one—frogs for rent. Ribbit.

A winding 9-mile drive east of Angels Camp along Highway 4 leads to picturesque **Murphys,** a former trading post set up by brothers Dan and John Murphy in cooperation with local Indians (John married the chief's daughter). Though you won't find cheap sleeps here, it's still

Where Skiers Grin and Bear Valley It

If you're touring the Gold Country in winter, don't forget your downhill or cross-country skis, because right off Highway 4 is the eighth-largest ski area in the state—the Bear Valley Ski Company. Downhillers can schuss down more than 60 trails (serviced by 11 lifts that can accommodate 12,000 skiers per hour), while cross-country fans can explore one of the largest trail systems in the country. Bear Valley also has a full line of rental equipment (including snowboards), great ski-school packages, and special weekday discounts that often cut the cost of a ticket in half; call ahead for price quotes (located off Highway 4, about 50 miles east of the Highway 49 intersection in Angels Camp, 209/753-2301).

worth the detour off Highway 49 just to stroll down Murphys' tree-lined Main Street or, better yet, to sample a pint of Murphys Brewing Company's outstanding Murphys Red, served on tap at the **Murphys Historic Hotel and Lodge** (457 Main Street, Murphys, 209/728-3444).

Eighteen miles northeast on Highway 4 is **Calaveras Big Trees State Park,** 209/795-2334, a popular summer retreat that offers camping, swimming, hiking, and fishing among towering sequoias. Many of the **numerous caverns** in the area (discovered by prospectors) can be toured, including Mercer Caverns, 209/728-2101, which has crystalline stalactites and stalagmites in a series of descending chambers; Moaning Cavern, 209/736-2708, where a 100-foot stairway spirals down into a chamber so huge it could house the Statue of Liberty; and California Caverns, 209/736-2708, the West's first commercially developed cave and the largest single cave system in Northern California (it has yet to be fully explored).

The next major stop to the south is **Columbia,** where some mighty fortunate '49ers unearthed a staggering $87 million in gold over a 20-year period. This former boisterous mining town also came within two votes of beating out Sacramento in the race to be named state capital. Once the gold-mining business dwindled, however, Columbia's population of 15,000 nearly vanished. You can view the city's well-preserved facades and mining artifacts in **Columbia State Historic Park,** a true Gold Country treasure. This is the Mother Lode's best-preserved park, so if you haven't had your fill of Gold Rush nostalgia, follow the free, short, self-guided tour. For more history on the area, pick up a walking-tour booklet for $1 at the visitors center or sign up for a guided tour of

Sonora Money-Saver

*At the **Diamond Back Grill** you can fill up on a bowl of black-eyed-pea-and-ham soup for $3.75 or, for less than $10, splurge on such daily specials as grilled venison or salmon (110 S Washington Street, downtown Sonora, 209/532-6661).*

a mine. For a more leisurely view of the park, hop aboard one of the horse-drawn stagecoaches. And to learn how to pan for gold, ask about the Matelot Gulch Mining Company's free lessons or call park information, 209/532-0150.

When the traffic starts to crawl along Highway 49, you're probably closing in on **Sonora,** which in '49er days continuously competed with Columbia for the title of wealthiest city in the southern Mother Lode. Today, Sonora is the Gold Country's largest and most crowded town. Search for a parking space along Washington Street (no easy feat on weekends), feed the meter, do a little window shopping, and take a peek at the **Tuolumne County Museum,** located in the century-old jail (158 W Bradford Street, Sonora, 209/532-1317).

A couple of miles southwest of Sonora on Highway 49 is **Jamestown.** For decades this 2-block-long town has been Hollywood's favorite western movie set: scenes from famous flicks like *Butch Cassidy and the Sundance Kid* were shot here, and vintage railway cars and steam locomotives used in such TV classics as "Little House on the Prairie," "Bonanza," and "High Noon" are on display at the **Railtown 1897 State Historic Park** (on 5th Avenue at Reservoir Road, near the center of town, Jamestown, 209/984-3953). You can view the vehicles at the roundhouse daily, or, if it's a weekend and you're traveling with young kids, take them for a ride on the rails.

Cheap Eats

B of A Cafe
1262 S Main Street, Angels Camp ☎ 209/736-0765

This bright, lively cafe, housed in a converted 1936 Bank of America building, attracts crowds of tourists and locals alike. Lunch items range from gourmet baby greens salads and a country-style quiche of

Just One Bite, Snow White . . .

*Every autumn, droves of people—about a half million each year—come to a small ridge just east of Placerville dubbed **Apple Hill Orchards**. What's the attraction? Why, apples, of course—baked, fried, buttered, canned, candied, and caramelized, to name just a few variations. Dozens of apple vendors sell their special apple concoctions, and on weekends the atmosphere is positively festive, with everyone basking in the mountain sunshine while feasting on such treats as hot apple pie à la mode. In September and October (peak apple-harvest season), it's definitely worth a stop. From Highway 50, take the Carson Road exit and follow the signs.*

the day to roasted eggplant sandwiches with herbed mayonnaise on multigrain bread. Dinner's more pricey, but it's worth the extra few dollars for the juicy lemon-rosemary chicken, marinated baby back ribs, and sliced pork loin marinated with an Australian maple-syrup-based sauce. All entrees are served with fresh bread, soup or salad, and herb-roasted red potatoes. B of A also offers ginger-glazed duck, salmon, steak, and a great pasta of the day, but be sure to make a reservation because the seats get booked up fast. *MC, V; local checks only; lunch daily, dinner Thurs–Sun; beer and wine.*

Mel and Faye's Diner

205 Highway 49, Jackson ☎ 209/223-0853

Mel and Faye have been churning out good eats at their highway-side diner since 1956, and the place is still a favorite, primarily because you pay small prices for big burgers. Mel chops the onions himself for his special Moo-Burger, a sloppy double cheeseburger smothered in onions and a special sauce that will stick with you for the rest of the day. The shakes are thick enough to properly clog your straw, but skip the pies. *No credit cards; local checks only; breakfast, lunch, dinner every day; beer and wine.*

Smoke Cafe

18191 Main Street, Jamestown ☎ 209/984-3733

One of Jamestown's liveliest restaurants, the Smoke Cafe is named after a 1920s baseball pitcher from the Cleveland Indians who, after a career of smoking fast balls down the pipe, opened this ex-slot-machine saloon. Creative Mexican fare dominates the menu, and favored dishes include the black bean burritos, flautas, fajitas, spicy corn chowder, and a powerful garlic soup made with beef broth and sprinkled with croutons and Jack cheese. For a nightcap, ask bartender John Aldabe to make you the Smoke's award-winning After Burner, a potent concoction of Kahlúa, cinnamon, schnapps, and Absolut Peppar. *DIS, MC, V; checks OK; dinner Tues–Sun; full bar.*

Sweetie Pies

577 Main Street, Placerville ☎ 530/642-0128

Stop for lunch at this cute little house on Main Street and order one of the freshly made soups served with house-baked sourdough bread. Or you might fancy a slice of the vegetable quiche and a freshly tossed garden salad. Whatever you choose, save room for the pie. Better yet, eat dessert first—it's that good. Don't miss the knockout thick, rich olallieberry pie or the rhubarb pie filled with tart chunks of the real thing. Other sweet-tooth delights include cream pies, poppyseed cake, lemon tea cake, and cinnamon and pecan rolls. Should you need more than a sugar rush to get you pumped, various coffee drinks ought to do the trick. Breakfast at Sweetie Pies is sweet and simple: coffee, tea, pastries, muffins, and, of course, pies. *MC, V; checks OK; breakfast every day, lunch Mon–Sat; beer and wine.*

Good Heavens: A Restaurant

49 N Washington Street, Sonora ☎ 209/532-3663

According to local lore, this historic building lined with old-fashioned paintings once housed a coffin-maker downstairs and a bordello upstairs. For the past dozen years, however, it's been the setting for a delightful boutique cafe noted for its very good daily lunch specials, including a divine mushroom, spinach, Monterey Jack, and turkey sausage crepe topped with a creamy lemon sauce and served with a Parmesan-pasta flan and fresh steamed vegetables. Standard menu items include house-made soups and salads and a creative

Cheap Jamestown Eats

*Always a popular afternoon stop is **Jim Town Frosty,** your basic low-budget burger hut that serves above-average shakes, fries, and stuffed jalapeños (north end of Main Street at Humbug Street and Highway 49, Jamestown, 209/984-3444).*

selection of sandwiches and hamburgers. Each meal starts with fresh herb-and-cheese biscuits and a choice of wonderful freshly made jams. *No credit cards; checks OK; lunch Wed–Mon, dinner Fri–Sat; beer and wine.*

North Beach Cafe

14317 Mono Way, Sonora ☎ 209/536-1852

Grab a seat at the counter to sample chef Terry La Torre's flair with both Italian food and the theater (he's quite the performer). The simple lunch menu features chicken and steak sandwiches, burgers, soups, and salads, while the predominantly Italian dinner menu offers a dozen or so pastas, fresh fish, veal, chicken, and steak—and reasonable prices. His best dishes are the pork tenderloin and the triangle tip in mushroom sauce. The pasta and fish plates, such as the petrale sole in lemon butter, tend to get drowned with La Torre's sauces, but prices are so low—and his histrionics so entertaining—that it's hard to complain. *AE, MC, V; checks OK; lunch Mon–Sat, dinner every day, brunch Sun; beer and wine.*

Cheap Sleeps

Gold Country Inn Motel

720 S Main Street, Angels Camp, CA 95222 ☎ 800/851-4944
or ☎ 209/736-4611

If you can get past the garish facade—gold was never a color meant for buildings—you'll find 40 clean, modern rooms equipped with color TVs, direct-dial phones, air-conditioning, and queen-size beds. The motel makes a good base for visiting some of the Gold Country's best attractions—caverns, state parks, museums—and the rates won't make a huge dent in your wallet. *AE, DIS, MC, V; no checks; info@goldcountryinn.com.*

Ebbetts Pass Lodge

1173 Highway 4, Arnold, CA 95223 ☎ 209/795-1563

Although it's definitely off the Gold Country circuit, Ebbetts Pass Lodge has its strong points. Each of the 15 rooms includes a color TV (with HBO), kitchenette, queen-size bed, and barbecue area. The lodge is set high among cool, sweet-smelling pines directly down the highway from Calaveras Big Trees State Park, Moaning and Mercer Caverns, and Bear Valley Resort, among other attractions. If you don't mind the extra drive to get here, and could care less about sleeping in a historic mining town, this place might be for you. Pets okay with $5 fee. *AE, MC, V; no checks.*

Columbia Gem Motel

22131 Parrotts Ferry Road, Columbia, CA 95310 ☎ 209/532-4508

Small, weathered, and just a little on the dilapidated side, the 12 rooms and cabins of the secluded "Gem" are a great bargain if a spot of rust or mildew here and there doesn't get your dander up. Located a mile from Columbia State Park, the Columbia's freestanding cabins (be sure to request the cabins, not the rooms) come with cable TV, air-conditioning, in-room coffee, and, best of all, little furnished front porches that overlook the pines. *AE, DIS, MC, V; no checks; www.columbiagem.com.*

Old Well Motel

15947 Highway 49, Drytown, CA 95699 ☎ 209/245-6467

Drytown is so small that if all 11 rooms at this roadside motel were filled, the town's population would probably double. But it's still a great place to stay, primarily because of the $42-every-day price and its prime location in the heart of the Mother Lode. The rooms are a bit cramped and there's not much to feast your eyes on, but should you get hungry and restless, a small cafe on the premises serves breakfast, lunch, and dinner, and a nearby creek helps lull you to sleep. *AE, MC, V; checks OK.*

Jackson Gold Lodge

850 N Highway 49, Jackson, CA 95642 ☎ 209/223-0486

Although they won't give you much of a feel for Gold Rush times, the 36 modern rooms at the Jackson Gold Lodge are comfortable and tidy. The price includes a continental breakfast served in the lobby, local calls, remote cable TV, and use of the heated pool in summer. Considering the location and amenities, the Jackson Gold is probably the best deal for your dollar in the Mother Lode. *AE, DC, DIS, MC, V; no checks; www.jacksongoldlodge.com.*

Cary House Hotel

300 Main Street, Placerville, CA 95667 ☎ 530/622-4271

For a bit more than you'd pay at one of Placerville's many budget chains, you can get a clean, comfy Gold Rush–era room with private bath at Cary House. Although the 34 rooms have that eau-de-Grandma's-house smell, the Old Town location can't be beat (for Placerville, that is). *AE, DIS, MC, V; no checks.*

Gunn House Hotel

286 S Washington Street, Sonora, CA 95370 ☎ 209/532-3421

The first two-story adobe structure in Sonora, built by Dr. Lewis C. Gunn in 1850, is now the best low-priced hotel in town (though rates lift it out of the Cheap Sleeps category during the high season). Each of the 20 rooms is filled with period antiques to create a Victorian atmosphere, yet none of the modern comforts—TV, phone, air-conditioning, private bath—have been left out. A swimming pool and patio, shaded balconies, and Italian restaurant with a cocktail lounge are also on the property. Room rates include continental breakfast. *AE, DIS, MC, V; checks OK.*

Rail Fence Motel

19950 Highway 108, Sonora, CA 95370 ☎ 209/532-9191

Although bland and uninspiring compared to the Gunn House, this motel just east of Sonora on Highway 108 offers eight small, tidy rooms with TVs, private baths, and air-conditioning for about $35 per night. There's also a small pool and patio on the 11-acre property, and dogs are welcome if you make arrangements in advance. *MC, V; no checks.*

Gables Cedar Creek Inn

22564 Twain Harte Drive, Twain Harte, CA 95383 ☎ 209/586-3008

You may have to dig a little deeper into your pocket (particularly during the high season) to pay for a room, but if you're looking for a romantic, secluded Gold Country getaway that won't cost a bundle, bunk down here. Located a half mile from the tiny town of Twain Harte, the Gables is literally hidden among hundreds of pines and cedars, surrounded by flowers in spring, and blanketed with colorful leaves in fall. The seven units range from a creekside loft with wood-burning fireplace (the most popular room) to a surprisingly affordable four-bedroom house that faces the Twain Harte golf course. All units come with attractive country furnishings, kitchen area, cable TV, telephone, and bathroom with shower. *AE, DIS, MC, V; no checks; www.yosemitegold.com/cedarcreek/index.html.*

Central Coast

santa cruz area
monterey
pacific grove
carmel-by-the-sea
big sur

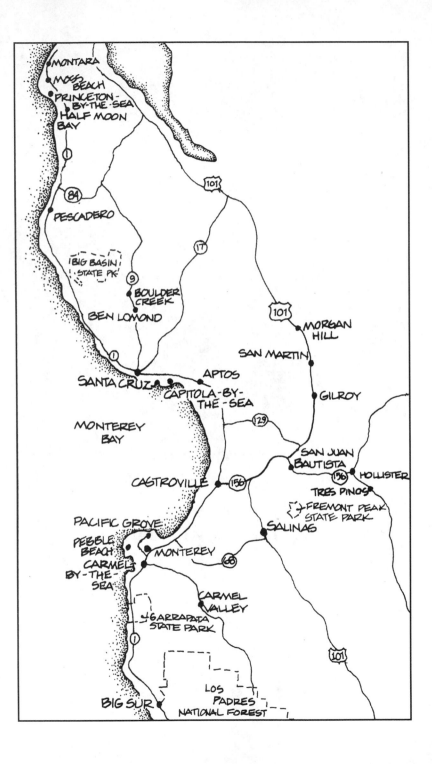

MONTARA
MOSS BEACH
PRINCETON-BY-THE-SEA
HALF MOON BAY
1
84
PESCADERO
101
17
BIG BASIN STATE PK
9
BOULDER CREEK
BEN LOMOND
101
MORGAN HILL
SAN MARTIN
1
APTOS
SANTA CRUZ
CAPITOLA-BY-THE-SEA
GILROY
MONTEREY BAY
129
SAN JUAN BAUTISTA
156
HOLLISTER
CASTROVILLE
156
TRES PINOS
FREMONT PEAK STATE PARK
PACIFIC GROVE
SALINAS
PEBBLE BEACH
MONTEREY
CARMEL-BY-THE-SEA
68
CARMEL VALLEY
GARRAPATA STATE PARK
1
101
LOS PADRES NATIONAL FOREST
BIG SUR

Santa Cruz Area

Santa Cruz is a chimerical place, skittering from diamond-bright beach to swampy slough to moody redwood grove to cafe society to rustic farm, in just about the time it takes to say "Surf's up!" The city rings the north end of **Monterey Bay** and is bisected by the **San Lorenzo River,** which spills into the sea. Santa Cruz (Spanish for "holy cross") was founded by the ubiquitous Father Junípero Serra when he built the Mission of the Holy Cross here in 1791 (the mission was destroyed in the mid–19th century by earthquakes). Despite its holy beginnings, Santa Cruz is now a devil-may-care, saltwater-taffy seaside resort, embodied by both the wet suit–clad surfer set and the roller-coaster world of the famous Boardwalk, where the roar of revelers mingles with the plaintive bark of sea lions. But peer a little closer and you'll see the city's intellectual side, bolstered by the presence of a University of California campus and the town's well-known (and occasionally controversial) ultraliberal politics.

Exploring

Santa Cruz attracts more than 3 million visitors each year, and most of them flock to the half-mile-long, nearly 100-year-old **Santa Cruz Beach Boardwalk** (400 Beach Street, Santa Cruz, 831/423-5590), the last remaining beachfront amusement park on the West Coast. Take a spin on the famous **Giant Dipper,** one of the best and oldest wooden roller coasters in the country (with a great view at the top), then grab a seat on one of the intricately hand-carved horses on the 1911 **Looff Carousel** (both rides are listed on the National Register of Historic Places). Of course, the Boardwalk also caters to the hard-core thrill seekers who yearn for those state-of-the-art, whirl-and-twirl rides that do their best to make you lose your lunch. Buy a day pass for less than $20 and stand in line for rides like the **Riptide** and the **Bermuda Triangle,** and you won't be disappointed. If you're here with the crowds on a Friday night in the summer, don't miss the Boardwalk's free concerts, featuring the likes of the Shirelles, Chubby Checker, and Sha Na Na.

Beaches are Santa Cruz's other crowning glory. At the western edge of the city, on the north end of West Cliff Drive, is **Natural Bridges State Beach,** named after the surrounding water-sculpted, bridgelike rock formations. The beach is popular with surfers, windsurfers, tide-pool trekkers, and sunbathers, as well as fans of the monarch butterflies that roost in the nearby eucalyptus grove from late October through February. On the south end of West Cliff Drive is **Lighthouse Field State Beach,** the birthplace of American surfing. This beach has several benches for sitting and gazing, a jogging and bicycling path, and a park with picnic tables, showers, and even plastic-bag dispensers for cleaning up after your dog (one of the few public places in town where canines are allowed). The nearby brick lighthouse is now home to the **Santa Cruz Surfing Museum** (at Lighthouse Point, Santa Cruz, 831/420-6289), the first of its kind in the world, which is chock-full of hang-ten memorabilia; admission is free.

Between the lighthouse and the Boardwalk is that famous strip of the sea known as **Steamers Lane,** the summa cum laude of California surfing spots (savvy surfers say *this*—not Southern California—is the place to catch the best breaks in the state). Watch the dudes ride the gnarly waves, then head over to the marvelous (but often crowded) white-sand **Santa Cruz Beach** fronting the Boardwalk. The breakers are

Scenic Train Trips

Locomotive lovers, kids, and fans of Mother Nature should hop aboard the historic narrow-gauge Roaring Camp Train for a 6-mile round-trip excursion up the steepest grades in North America. The steam-powered train winds through stately redwood groves to the summit of Bear Mountain. Another train, called the Big Trees Narrow Gauge Railroad, offers an 18-mile round-trip ride through mountain tunnels and along ridges with spectacular views of the San Lorenzo River before stopping at the Santa Cruz Beach Boardwalk (on Graham Hill Road, off Highway 17, Felton, 831/335-4400, www.roaringcamprr.com).

Boardwalk Bargains

Save a bundle at the Boardwalk by visiting on "1907 Nights." Every summer from July to September, after 5pm on Monday and Tuesday, the Santa Cruz Beach Boardwalk celebrates the year it opened by reducing its prices to 50 cents a ride (it's normally $1.50 to $3), and two bits also buys a hot dog, soft drink, or cotton candy. Call 831/423-5590 for more Boardwalk details.

tamer here, making this a favorite spot for sunbathing, swimming, picnicking, and sailing. In the center of the action is the 85-year-old **Municipal Wharf,** where you can drive your car out to the shops, fish markets, and seafood restaurants.

The **Pacific Garden Mall** (a.k.a. **Pacific Avenue**) is Santa Cruz's main shopping district, and until the Loma Prieta earthquake hit in 1989, it was a charming amalgam of Victorian houses, street musicians, bag ladies and gentlemen, inexpensive restaurants, bookstores, antique shops, and New Age head shops. It has substantially recuperated from the apocalypse (the earthquake's epicenter was only 10 miles away), and in many ways is better than ever, with interesting new shops and new places to eat. As you make your way down the mall, look for the **Octagon Building,** an ornate, eight-sided Victorian brick edifice built in 1882 that has survived numerous quakes. The building once served as the city's Hall of Records, and now it's part of the **McPherson Center for Art and History** (705 Front Street, Santa Cruz, 831/429-1964), where museums showcase 10,000 years of the area's past as well as contemporary art of the Pacific Rim. Next door is the excellent **Santa Cruz County Conference and Visitors Council** (701 Front Street, Santa Cruz, 800/833-3494).

The Pacific Avenue area is a good place to get some cheap eats, too. The nearby **Bookshop Santa Cruz** (1520 Pacific Avenue, Santa Cruz, 831/423-0900) has an inventory worthy of any university town, with a particularly good children's section, an adjacent coffeehouse, and plenty of places to sit, sip, and read a bit of your prospective purchase. Across the street is the ever-present but fast-moving line of people waiting to buy a freshly baked bagel at **Noah's Bagels** (1411 Pacific Avenue, Santa Cruz, 831/454-9555). For great organically grown produce and other picnic-basket goodies, shop at the **Farmers Market,** held Wednesdays from 2:30pm to 6:30pm on Lincoln Street, between Pacific Avenue and Cedar Street. For some serious hiking and mountain biking, drive

Northern Elephant Seal Mating Season

*You're not the only one having fun in the sun: drive 22 miles north of Santa Cruz, and you'll come upon **Año Nuevo State Reserve**, a unique and fascinating breeding ground for northern elephant seals. A close encounter with a 2½-ton male elephant seal waving his humongous schnozz is an unforgettable event. Even more memorable is the sight of two males fighting and snorting (they can be heard for miles) over a harem of a few dozen females. The mating season starts in December and continues through March. Reservations are required for the 2½-hour naturalist-led tours (held rain or shine from December 15 through March 31). Tickets are quite cheap, but they sell out fast, so plan about two months ahead; call 800/444-7275 for more information, or log onto www.cal-parks.ca.gov (click on "Visit the Parks: San Francisco–Bay Area," then "San Mateo County: Año Nuevo State Reserve").*

about 23 miles north to the 18,000-acre **Big Basin Redwoods State Park,** California's first state park and its second-largest redwood preserve. Eighty miles of trails wind past 300-foot-high redwoods and waterfalls, and there's even access to **Waddell Beach** (21600 Big Basin Way, off Highway 236, 9 miles north of Boulder Creek, 831/338-8860).

Just east of Santa Cruz sits **Capitola-by-the-Sea,** a tiny, very popular resort town nestled around a small bay. The whole downtown is only a few blocks long, but the quaint, jumbled mix of restaurants, gift shops, and beachwear boutiques and the city's intimate scale are reminiscent of resort towns of yesteryear. Capitola's broad, sandy beach attracts lots of sun worshipers, primarily because it's sheltered from the wind; the city is also bordered by a charming promenade. At the west end of town is the bustling 867-foot-long **Capitola Pier**—the place to hang out, admire the view of the town, and, on weekends, listen to live music. Many anglers come here to try their luck at reeling in the big one (you don't need a license to fish from a pier in California).

Cheap Eats

Caffe Lido

111 Monterey Avenue, Capitola ☎ 831/475-6544

Located right on the beach at Capitola, you would expect Caffe Lido to be a high-priced tourist trap serving uninspired food, but that's far from the reality. At dinner you can get good pasta dishes for about $10 and various grilled chicken and seafood plates for about $15. Lunchtime offerings include soups, salads, pastas, and *panini* (hot sandwiches such as the three cheeses with sun-dried tomatoes and the grilled chicken breast with roasted red peppers and fontina cheese). If you're traveling with your dog, you can sit outside and leash him to your table and they'll even bring Fido a doggy bowl. Reservations are recommended at peak times. *AE, MC, V; checks OK; lunch, dinner every day; full bar.*

Dharma's Restaurant

4250 Capitola Road, Capitola ☎ 831/462-1717

Hidden inside a small shopping center is Dharma's Restaurant, where folks have been dining for years on the great vegetarian food served for breakfast, lunch, and dinner. The menu features American and Mexican fare, including a variety of veggie burgers, quesadillas, burritos, and nachos, plus house specialties such as steamed veggies, international sautés, and the ever-popular chili. This may be the only place on the coast where you can order a vegetarian chili dog. *No credit cards; checks OK; breakfast, lunch, dinner every day; beer and wine; www.infopoint.com.*

Gayle's Bakery and Rosticceria

504 Bay Avenue, Capitola ☎ 831/462-1200

Home of the best breads and pastries in town, Gayle's also dishes up a wonderful array of soups, salads, pastas, casseroles, and meats hot off the rotisserie for lunch and dinner. Gayle, her husband, Jo Ortiz, and their partner, Louisa Beers, are the authors of *The Village Baker's Wife,* a cookbook on classic regional pastries from Europe and America. Their restaurant is frequently crowded so take a number, make your choices from the deli counters, and then find a table, inside or out. *MC, V; checks OK; breakfast, lunch, dinner every day; beer and wine.*

The Crepe Place

1134 Soquel Avenue, Santa Cruz ☎ 831/429-6994

The Crepe Place is a Santa Cruz institution that has whipped up delicious crepes for more than 25 years. It has been honored on numerous occasions as the "Best After-Hours Eatery" by its fans. The menu lists 15 crepes—the Spinach Supreme is particularly good—or you can choose your own combination of ingredients. Soups, salads, dessert crepes, and the popular Tunisian doughnut (a large, hot, yeasty doughnut cooked to order with your choice of a dessert topping) round out the menu. Eat in the wood-paneled dining room or outside in the garden. The restaurant is located in a business/shopping area less than 1 mile east of downtown. *AE, MC, V; local checks only; lunch, dinner every day, brunch Sat–Sun; full bar.*

El Palomar

1336 Pacific Garden Mall, Santa Cruz ☎ 831/425-7575

El Palomar offers fine Mexican food in a beautiful 1930s hotel with dramatic high cathedral ceilings, a lovely mural, and a large fireplace. In addition to all of the traditional standbys there are pleasant surprises such as the burritos *de camarones* (flour tortillas stuffed with prawns, cheese, whole beans, and salsa) and the tasty *posole* (hominy simmered with pork in a rich, mild, chili-flavored broth). The taco bar in the courtyard serves quick meals in generous portions from an inexpensive à la carte menu. *AE, DC, DIS, MC, V; local checks only; lunch, dinner every day; full bar.*

India Joze Restaurant

1001 Center Street (at Cedar Street), Santa Cruz ☎ 831/427-3554

A favorite for many years, this airy, casual restaurant serves creative and healthy East Indian and other world cuisines with a California twist. Some dishes are expensive, but many won't blow your budget and are quite good, such as the Nasi Goreng made of fried rice, chicken, calamari, and fresh vegetables served with a peanut–coconut milk sauce. India Joze hosts a squid festival in August featuring squid tastings, squid drawing competitions, squid cooking classes, and other events celebrating the 10-armed cephalopod. *AE, DC, DIS, MC, V; no checks; lunch, dinner every day, brunch Sun; beer and wine.*

O'mei Restaurant

2316 Mission Street, Santa Cruz ☎ 831/425-8458

Named after a mountain in the Sichuan province of China, this acclaimed Chinese restaurant is a wondrous little paradox tucked into one of Santa Cruz's many strip malls. Owner/chef Roger Grisby is not Chinese, nor are any of his cooks, but his food caters more to the Chinese palate than do most Chinese restaurants in California. Predictable northern Chinese offerings such as Mongolian beef and moo-shu pork are on the menu, but your best bet is to forgo the old standbys. Pushing the envelope of Chinese cuisine, O'mei offers tasty provincial curiosities such as litchi chicken, leg of lamb sautéed with hot-and-sour cabbage, and an enchanting black-sesame ice cream. Another plus: O'mei boasts a limited but well-chosen wine list, with all wines available by the glass. *AE, MC, V; no checks; lunch Mon–Fri, dinner every day; beer and wine.*

Zoccoli's Italian Delicatessen

1534 Pacific Avenue, Santa Cruz ☎ 831/423-1711

A survivor of the 1989 Loma Prieta earthquake, this 50-year-old local favorite escaped the major devastation to downtown Santa Cruz. They continue to make excellent sandwiches—both hot and cold varieties—for less than $5. The menu also features lasagne, spaghetti, ravioli, vegetarian minestrone, and daily specials such as stuffed peppers, baked chicken, and linguine with pesto. Near this deli is Zoccoli's Restaurant, which serves very good, reasonably priced pasta dishes for lunch Monday through Friday and dinner every day (431 Front Street at Cathcart Street, Santa Cruz). *MC, V; local checks only; breakfast, lunch Mon–Sat (9am-6pm), lunch Sun (11am–5pm); beer and wine.*

Carpo's

2400 Porter Street (Porter Street exit off Highway 1), Soquel ☎ 831/476-6260

What a find! Carpo's is conveniently located right off Highway 1, where the village of Soquel meets Capitola. Carpo's essentially serves fast food, but it's good, cheap fast food: burgers and hot dogs, broiled and fried seafood, soups, salads, chili, and house-made desserts. Sample the skewered broiled prawns served with pasta and vegetables or the fish-and-chips. Order at the counter and seat yourself in one of the attractive booths or hunker down outside on the patio. Expect to mingle with the locals here—they love Carpo's. *MC, V; checks OK; lunch, dinner every day except holidays; beer and wine.*

Cheap Sleeps

Jaye's Timberlane Resort

8705 Highway 9, Ben Lomand, CA 95005 ☎ 831/336-5479

The town of Ben Lomand is just up the road from Felton, and from there it's an easy drive to Santa Cruz. Jaye's offers 10 small, rustic, freestanding one- and two-bedroom cabins with kitchens. They're quite tidy and some have fireplaces. Cabins 1 through 6 are set just off the highway, and cabins 7 through 10 are tucked farther back in the redwoods. A swimming pool, barbecue, and picnic table are also available. *AE, MC, V; no checks.*

Big Basin Redwoods State Park Tent Cabins

21600 Big Basin Way, Boulder Creek, CA 95006 ☎ 800/874-8368

Big Basin has one of the area's best bargains: 36 highly sought-after tent cabins nestled next to a creek in a grove of redwood trees and huckleberry bushes. You can rent one of these cabins (which sleep up to four comfortably) for about $49 a night depending on the season, and four friends may camp out on the ground in front at no extra cost. Each cabin has wood floors and walls, a canvas roof, screened doors and windows, a wood-burning fireplace, and two double beds. A picnic table, storage cabinet, and grill are set up outside the door. There's no electricity in these units, so bring a propane lantern along with your sleeping bag, or rent bed linens ($10 for the duration of your stay) at the tent-cabin host site. Bathroom facilities (with coin-operated hot showers) and a laundry are in nearby buildings. Although Big Basin is 23 miles north of Santa Cruz, many people make the trek here and the cabins fill up fast. Reservations are required year-round and are taken by phone and on-site (try to reserve a cabin at least two months in advance). *MC, V; no checks.*

Davenport Bed & Breakfast Inn

1 Davenport Avenue, Davenport, CA 95017 ☎ 831/425-1818

The rooms at this cheery inn, 9 miles up the coast from Santa Cruz, are decorated with a mixture of antiques, ethnic treasures, and local arts and crafts. Eight of the guest rooms are located on the second floor of the New Davenport Cash Store Restaurant, and four more are in the adjacent historic house. Each room has a private bath, telephone, radio, and vase of fresh flowers. The units above the store share a large balcony with a great ocean view. Guests are treated to a complimentary drink at the bar and a continental breakfast. The inn's moderately priced restaurant serves some of the best food in the area for breakfast, lunch, and dinner. *AE, DIS, MC, V; checks OK; www.swanton.com.*

Fern River Resort Motel

5250 Highway 9, Felton, CA 95018 ☎ 831/335-4412

Located 4 miles up a curvy, redwood-lined road from Santa Cruz, Fern River is a simple but pleasant mountain/river resort with 14 cabins set on 4 acres. In the summer you can bask in the sun on the San Lorenzo River beach or go for a dip. And 20 miles of hiking trails in Henry Cowell Park are accessible just across the river. Fern River also offers Ping-Pong tables, badminton, tetherball, horseshoes, board games, toys, and books. The studio cabins qualify as a cheap sleep (even during the peak-season summer months), but you'll pay more for the cabins that sleep two to six people, although these larger units have fully equipped kitchens, making them a pretty good deal, too. *AE, MC, V; checks OK; www.quick-link.net/fernriver.html.*

Pigeon Point Light House Hostel

210 Pigeon Point Road, Pescadero, CA 94060 ☎ 650/879-0633

The Pigeon Point hostel is set at the base of one of the tallest lighthouses on the Pacific Coast, halfway between San Francisco and Santa Cruz. The beautiful windswept grounds are landscaped with native plants, and the 270-degree view of the ocean can't be matched anywhere in the region. The hostel's four houses were residences for the Coast Guard lighthouse staff until high-tech lighthouse electronics gave them the boot. But the Coast Guard's loss is your gain. Separate men's and women's bunk rooms and four rooms for couples (which cost an extra $12 per night) accommodate a total of 52. The facilities are clean and comfortable, and the price can't be beat—at the time this book went to press, the most expensive nightly rate was $16 for a nonmember adult, and the lowest was $6.50 per child. Be sure to spend some time in the hostel's legendary hot tub overlooking the ocean, well worth the $3-per-half-hour fee (only guests are permitted). Reservations are strongly recommended, although some bunk beds are held for walk-ins starting at 4:30pm. The reception desk is open from 7:30am to 9:30am and 4:30pm to 9:30pm daily. *MC, V; checks OK; www.norcalhostels.org.*

Blackburn House Motel

10 Cedar Street, Santa Cruz, CA 95060 ☎ 831/423-1804

The Blackburn is a two-story Greek Revival house built in 1856 for Judge Blackburn, the first mayor of Santa Cruz. Within the house are three basic one-person rooms (guests share one bathroom), and scattered among the pretty flower-trimmed property is a cluster of 31 cabins. Each cabin has a kitchenette and some of the units are suites. The Boardwalk and downtown Santa Cruz are just a few blocks away. *AE, DIS, MC, V; no checks.*

Continental Inn

414 Ocean Street (near Broadway), Santa Cruz, CA 95060
☎ 831/429-1221

The Continental is typical of the pre-1960 motels just north of the Boardwalk: small, clean rooms with thin walls, comfortable beds, and cheap decor. This 37-room inn sits on a street littered with fast-food chains and small businesses, but it's only about a 15-minute walk to the beach. In exchange for the dull surroundings, you get bargain rates year-round. Besides, this is one of the few inns in Santa Cruz that lets you bring your pooch. *AE, DIS, MC, V; no checks.*

Guest House Pacific Inn

330 Ocean Street, Santa Cruz, CA 95060 ☎ 831/425-3722

The relatively new Guest House is a cut above most of the other motels north of the Boardwalk. The 36 rooms are pleasant and comfortable, furnished with a queen- or king-size bed, couch, dresser, and table, along with cable TV, mini-refrigerator, and coffeemaker; some even have hot tubs. If you don't have a private hot tub, you can unwind in the hotel's indoor or outdoor tub, or take a dip in the pool, which is sheltered from the wind. The beach and Boardwalk are only 4 blocks away. *AE, DIS, MC, V; no checks; www.guesthouse.net.*

Harbor Inn

645 7th Avenue, Santa Cruz, CA 95062 ☎ 831/479-9731

Tucked away on the eastern end of town, only 2 blocks from Twin Lakes State Beach, is the homey, funky Harbor Inn. It's managed by a friendly staff, and the inn's 19 guest rooms have open-beam ceilings, queen-size beds, cable TV, microwave ovens, hot plates, fridges, and phones. The decor is 1940s antique. The least expensive rooms (some have shared baths) range from about $45 a night in the winter to $65 on a summer weekend. The two-room suites have two double beds, and although these units cost more, they're well priced for this part of the California coast. *AE, DIS, MC, V; no checks.*

Santa Cruz Hostel and Carmelita Cottages

321 Main Street, Santa Cruz, CA 95061 ☎ 831/423-8304

The popular Santa Cruz Hostel is spread out among six attractive Victorian cottages that were donated to the establishment and recently renovated. Each sleeps 8 to 13 people in bunk beds and has a shared bathroom with showers. The units are comfortably but not lavishly furnished, and are only 2 blocks from the beach and Boardwalk. The place is a steal at $16 per person per night, or $13 per night if you're a hostel member (an annual membership, which costs $25, is worth considering, since the place is open only to members in the summer). Reservations are accepted by mail and telephone (if you reserve by mail, allow at least two weeks prior to your desired arrival), and half of the beds are held for walk-ins starting at 5pm. The reception desk is open from 8am to 10am and 5pm to 10pm daily. *MC, V; no checks; info@hi-santacruz.org; www.hi-santacruz.org.*

Santa Cruz KOA Kampground

1186 San Andreas Road, Watsonville, CA 95076 ☎ 800/562-7701 or ☎ 831/722-0551

KOA Kampgrounds are typically for motor homes, but this one also has 50 "Kamping Kabins." This is a family-oriented establishment, with a large heated swimming pool, hot tub, game room, mini-golf course, and bicycles for rent. The one- and two-room log cabins are quite small with no furnishings except a double bed and bunk beds with plastic-covered mattresses. You have to bring your own linens or sleeping bags. The cabins each sport a swing on the porch, a picnic table and benches in front, and a barbecue. Clean, modern shower facilities are in separate buildings. A one-room cabin costs about $55 and a two-room cabin, which sleeps up to six with its double bed and two sets of bunkbeds, is approximately $65. The campground is set in a rural area 10 miles down the highway from Santa Cruz and 1 mile from Manressa Beach. *AE, DIS, MC,V; no checks; www.koakampgrounds.com.*

Monterey

If you're looking for the romantically gritty, working-class fishing village of John Steinbeck's *Cannery Row*, you won't find it here. Even though Monterey was the sardine capital of the western hemisphere during World War II, overfishing forced most of the canneries to close in the early '50s, and Monterey began trawling for tourist dollars instead. The low-slung factories of Cannery Row and Fisherman's Wharf have been turned into tacky clothing boutiques, knickknack stores, and yogurt shops. But the town itself, set on the south end of Monterey Bay, still has more than its fair share of breathtaking seacoast vistas, pretty Victorians, historic adobes, and secret gardens full of succulents, herbs, and native plants. It's also the home of a world-famous aquarium. To catch the town at its best, come in the spring or during the sunny Indian-summer months; other times, expect it to be foggy and slightly cool—and expect hotel rates to drop accordingly.

Exploring

The glory of the town is the amazing, high-tech 322,000-square-foot **Monterey Bay Aquarium** (886 Cannery Row, 831/648-4888 for general information, 800/756-3737 for advanced tickets), which features more than 300,000 fascinating fish and other denizens of the (local) deep—not to mention the world's largest indoor, glass-walled aquarium (it's three stories high and holds 1 million gallons of seawater!). The bat ray–petting pool (not to worry, their stingers have been removed) and the two-story sea-otter tank thrill kids and adults alike, particularly when the sea otters get to scarf down a mixture of clams, rock cod, and shrimp at 10:30am, 1:30pm, and 3:30pm every day. Try to visit midweek to

Family Attractions

Your kids will love the Dennis the Menace Playground, designed by cartoonist Hank Ketcham himself. He created enough climbing apparatuses to please a monkey (Camino El Estero and Del Monte Boulevard, near Lake El Estero). For fun on the water, take your Curious Georges on a paddleboat—only $7 per half hour—and pedal around Lake El Estero, 831/375-1484. Families with older kids can rent bicycles and in-line skates at the Monterey Bay Recreation Trail, which runs along the Monterey shore for 18 miles to Lover's Point in Pacific Grove. More adventurous sorts should get a sea kayak at one of the rental outlets along Del Monte Boulevard and explore the coast. And what could be more thrilling to a little Free Willy fan than embarking on one of the whale-watching trips that sail from Fisherman's Wharf in the winter and spring?

escape the crowds that consistently flock to this beloved institution; advance tickets are recommended in the summer and on holidays.

To capture the flavor of Monterey's heritage, follow the 2-mile "Path of History," a walking tour of the town's most important historic sites and splendidly preserved old buildings—remember, this city was thriving under Spanish and Mexican flags when San Francisco was still a crude village. Free tour maps are available at various locations, including the **Custom House** (at the foot of Alvarado Street, near Fisherman's Wharf, 831/649-7118), California's oldest public building, and **Colton Hall** (on Pacific Street, between Madison and Jefferson Streets, 831/649-7118), where the California State Constitution was written and signed in 1849. Nautical history buffs should visit the **Maritime Museum of Monterey** (5 Custom House Plaza, in Stanton Center, near Fisherman's Wharf, 831/373-2469), which houses ship models, whaling relics, and the two-story-high,

The World's Oldest Jazz Festival

*For a terrific, toe-tappin' time in Monterey, visit on the third weekend in September, when top talents like Wynton Marsalis, Etta James, and Ornette Coleman strut their stuff at the **Monterey Jazz Festival**, one of the country's best jazz jubilees and the oldest continuous jazz celebration in the world. Tickets and hotel rooms sell out fast—so plan early (diehard jazz fans make reservations at least six months before showtime); call 925/275-9255 for more festival facts.*

10,000-pound Fresnel lens used for nearly 80 years at the Point Sur lighthouse to warn mariners away from the treacherous Big Sur coast.

The landmark **Fisherman's Wharf,** the center of Monterey's cargo and whaling industry until the early 1900s, is awash today in mediocre (or worse) restaurants and equally tasteless souvenir shops. Serious shoppers are better off strolling **Alvarado Street,** a pleasantly low-key, attractive downtown area with a much less touristy mix of art galleries, bookstores, and restaurants. Alvarado Street is also the site of the popular **Old Monterey Farmers Market and Marketplace,** a good spot for free family entertainment and picnic-basket treats; it's held on Tuesday year-round from 4pm to 7pm in the winter and 4pm to 8pm in the summer.

Cheap Eats

Bagel Bakery

201 Lighthouse Avenue, Monterey ☎ 831/649-1714

452 Alvarado Street, Monterey ☎ 831/372-5242

There are two Bagel Bakeries in Monterey, and two more in Carmel and Pacific Grove, because folks around here love noshing on these doughy treats. Baked throughout the day, these bagels are good with the bakery's other specialty, the breakfast omelets, or as a base for creative sandwiches with fillings ranging from pastrami to freshly ground peanut butter. The New Yorker bagel, layered with lox, cream cheese, tomato, and onion, is delicious and costs half as much as what you'd pay in most restaurants. Bagels are the perfect fast food . . . and a great cheap eat. *Cash only; breakfast, lunch every day; no alcohol.*

Epsilon

422 Tyler Street, Monterey ☎ 831/655-8108

This pretty little Greek restaurant in downtown Monterey serves all the classical Greek dishes such as moussaka and spanakopitta, plus some lesser-known items like *taskebob,* a delicacy from Asia Minor made with tender, browned pork pieces sautéed in a spicy tomato sauce. If that isn't Greek enough for you, there are Greek desserts, Greek wines, and Greek coffee. Eureka! *Cash only; lunch Tues–Fri, dinner Tues–Sun; beer and wine.*

The First Awakening

125 Ocean View Avenue (in the American Tin Cannery Outlet Center),
Monterey ☎ 831/372-1125

Just a hop, skip, and jump away from the popular Monterey Bay Aquarium, the high-ceilinged, light-filled First Awakening is considered by many locals to have the best breakfasts in town. Even the finickiest eater is likely to find something to order off the large menu. Every dish is made with fresh ingredients, and you can't go wrong with the gourmet pancakes or any of the nearly dozen types of omelets. Lunch offerings include a huge variety of good sandwiches and salads. *AE, DIS, MC, V; checks OK; breakfast, lunch every day; beer and wine.*

India's Clay Oven

150 Del Monte Avenue, Monterey ☎ 831/373-2529

The most popular Indian restaurant in town, India's Clay Oven's extensive menu has all the traditional favorites such as tandoori chicken and *rogan josh*. South Indian dishes also make an appearance, such as *idli* (steam-cooked rice-and-lentil cakes) and *masala dosa* (pancakes stuffed with mashed, spiced potatoes). If you're really hungry, try to eat your way through the 18-course buffet lunch—it's an all-you-can-eat meal offered Monday through Friday for less than $10. There's a children's menu, too. *AE, DC, DIS, MC, V; local checks only; lunch, dinner every day; beer and wine.*

Jugen

409 Alvarado Street, Monterey ☎ 831/373-6463

Conveniently located on downtown Monterey's main street, this Japanese restaurant has 40 kinds of sushi as well as all the traditional teriyaki and tempura entrees. The menu also includes six types of noodles—always a comfort food and always inexpensive. Have a cold Japanese beer or some hot sake, and rest those travel-weary tootsies. *AE, MC, V; no checks; lunch Mon–Fri, dinner every day; beer and wine.*

Old Monterey Café

489 Monterey Street, Monterey ☎ 831/646-1021

The Old Monterey Café is one of those warm and welcoming places full of good food, and with a helpful staff and charm to spare. The extensive breakfast menu has everything you could hope for, and lunch is almost as good. Wander in and you'll probably make this a home base for at least one cheap eat for every day you're visiting Monterey. *MC, V; local checks only; breakfast, lunch every day; no alcohol; www.cafemonterey.com.*

Papa Chanos

462 Alvarado Street, Monterey ☎ 831/646-9587

If all your sight-seeing has left you a mite peckish, pull up a chair at Papa Chanos, beloved by locals for its big, fresh tacos, quesadillas, enchiladas, and, best of all, delicious burritos. Wash all this filling fare down with an imported or domestic beer and you'll be ready to tour again, with barely a dent in your wallet. *Cash only; lunch every day; beer only.*

Cheap Sleeps

Casa Verde Inn

2113 N Fremont Street, Monterey, CA 93940 ☎ 831/375-5407

Monterey's budget motel row is on Fremont Street, where the basic, clean, no-frills motel rooms start as low as $42 on weekdays from October to April. Alas, the rest of the year the $42 rooms often jump up in price to $120. With these caveats in mind, try the Casa Verde Inn, which offers some of the most competitive rates on Fremont Street. The inn's comfortable, newly wallpapered rooms are equipped with cable TVs (with HBO), VCRs, and phones. Vibrant flower beds give the grounds a cheery feeling, and a little restaurant on the property serves Italian dinners. Guests are also treated to free maps of Monterey. *AE, DC, DIS, MC, V; no checks.*

Comfort Inn

1252 Munras Avenue, Monterey, CA 93940 ☎ 800/228-5150 or 408/372-2708

1262 Munras Avenue, Monterey, CA 93940 ☎ 800/228-5150 or 408/372-8088

These side-by-side properties offer simple, tidy motel rooms decorated with some of the ugliest art you're bound to see in this town. All of the rooms have a TV with HBO and a VCR, and a continental breakfast is included in the rate. Some units come with a refrigerator and microwave oven, too. Each of these two motels has a small swimming pool surrounded by concrete and located just off busy Munras Avenue—the kind of pools only a child could get excited about. Pools like these always seem to be uninhabited in Monterey, surely because everyone's at the beautiful beach nearby. *AE, DC, DIS, MC, V; no checks; www.hotelchoice.com.*

Cypress Tree Inn

2227 N Fremont Street, Monterey, CA 93940 ☎ 831/372-7586

The Cypress Tree is one of the more pleasant motels on bustling Fremont Street. The tidy inn offers 55 rooms with queen-size beds, telephones, TVs, and tiny desks. The Cypress Bakeshop serves coffee, juice, and muffins until noon, and box lunches are sold on weekdays. Other on-site amenities include a tourist-information and referral center, a sauna and hot tub, and a coin-operated laundry. *AE, DC, DIS, MC, V; no checks.*

Del Monte Pines

1298 Munras Avenue, Monterey, CA 93940 ☎ 800/633-6454 or ☎ 831/375-2323

The attractive Del Monte Pines motel has 19 large, pleasant rooms with color cable TVs (with HBO), VCRs (movie rentals are available), and coffeemakers. Some rooms have fireplaces and hot tubs. Room

---

Finding a Bargain Bed

Ask a Monterey innkeeper what his or her nightly rates are, and you'll likely get six or more quotes for the same room—depending on a variety of factors. Most Monterey hotels have room rates for winter weekdays, winter weekends, summer weekdays, summer weekends, bad-weather days, post-earthquake weeks, and those we-know-you're-desperate-for-a-room periods when the Monterey Jazz Festival, Laguna Seca race days, and other popular events come to town. The bottom line is that the price of a room can triple during peak periods.

For the best bargains, travel on weekdays and always ask about special rates (such as AAA, student, government employee, and senior-citizen discounts) and package deals, which may include dinner or tickets to the Monterey Bay Aquarium. Also look for hotel-discount coupons at the Monterey Peninsula Visitors and Convention Bureau's Center (Stanton Center at the Custom House Plaza, across from Fisherman's Wharf, Monterey, 831/649-1770).

rates include a continental breakfast and, in the summer, use of the heated swimming pool. In the off-season the midweek rates are low, but they skyrocket when the weather heats up and on weekends and holidays, just as they do at the other lodgings on Munras Avenue. The Del Monte Shopping Center is across the street, and Monterey's major attractions are just a 10-minute drive away. You can even buy tickets to the Monterey Bay Aquarium here, which can save you a long wait in line. *AE, DC, DIS, MC, V; no checks.*

The Westwind Lodge

1046 Munras Avenue, Monterey, CA 93940 ☎ 800/821-0805
or ☎ 831/373-1337

This 52-room motel has a wide variety of rooms and suites with amenities such as fireplaces and kitchens, and one has a private patio and spa. The least expensive rooms are equipped with a queen-size bed—and they barely qualify as a cheap sleep during the winter months, October through April (the rest of the year, the prices are not for bargain hunters). Westwind has an indoor heated pool, a spa and private sauna, in-room coffee, an expanded continental break-fast, and cable TV. *AE, DC, DIS, MC, V; no checks.*

Pacific Grove

Established more than a century ago as a retreat for pious Methodists, this beautiful Victorian seacoast village retains its decorous old-town character, though it's loosened its collar a bit since the early days. Less tourist-oriented than Carmel, less commercial than Monterey, P.G. (as locals call it) is a place to settle down, buy a home, and raise 2.5 obedient children. There's no graffiti, no raucous revelers, and not an unleashed dog in sight. The area exudes peace and tranquility—a city of gorgeous beaches, impressive architecture, and even reasonably priced accommodations just a jog from the sea.

Exploring

Introduce yourself to the town by strolling the 4 miles of trails that meander between the white-sand beaches and rocky, tide-pool-dotted coves at **Lover's Point Beach** (off Ocean View Boulevard on the east side of Point Pinos) and **Asilomar State Beach** (off Sunset Drive on the west side of Point Pinos). You can sit and enjoy the view from the landmark Lover's Point (which, by the way, was named for lovers of Jesus Christ, not the more carnal kind).

At the tip of **Point Pinos** (Spanish for "Point of the Pines") stands the Cape Cod–style **Point Pinos Lighthouse** (Asilomar Boulevard at Lighthouse Avenue, 831/648-3116), the oldest continuously operating lighthouse on the West Coast, built in February 1855. This National Historic Landmark is open to the public Thursday through Sunday, from 1pm to 4pm, and admission is free.

Pacific Grove bills itself as "Butterfly Town, U.S.A." in honor of the thousands of monarchs that migrate here from late October to mid-March. Two popular places to view the butterflies are the **Monarch Grove Sanctuary** (at Lighthouse Avenue and Ridge Road) and **George**

The 17-Mile Drive

If you want to cruise in your car through the privately owned Pebble Beach and 17-Mile Drive enclave of mansions and manicured golf courses, it will cost you $7.50, but it's almost worth it just to contemplate the lifestyles of the very rich. You'll see everything from a spectacular Byzantine castle with a private beach (the Crocker Mansion near the Carmel gate) to several tastefully bland California nouvelle country-club structures. The sea and forest setting is as beautiful and perfectly maintained as you would expect in this gated community. In addition to such often-photographed landmarks as the gnarled Lone Cypress clinging to its rocky precipice, there are miles of hiking and equestrian trails winding through groves of native pines and wildflowers that provide glorious views of Monterey Bay. Self-guided nature tours are outlined in a variety of brochures, available for free at the gate entrances and at the Inn at Spanish Bay (on the 17-Mile Drive, near the Pacific Grove gate, 831/647-7500) and the Lodge at Pebble Beach (near the Carmel gate, 831/624-3811).

There are five entrance gates to this province for the very rich. The most famous stretch is along the coast between Pacific Grove and Carmel. Visitors may enter the 17-Mile Drive for free on foot or bike, although cyclists are required to use the Pacific Grove gate—and must dust off the wheels of their bikes, of course.

Washington Park (at Sinex Avenue and Alder Street). To learn more about the monarchs, visit the charmingly informal and kid-friendly **Pacific Grove Museum of Natural History** (at the intersection of Forest and Central Avenues, 831/648-3116), which has a video and display on the butterfly's life cycle, as well as exhibits of other insects, local birds, mammals, and reptiles; admission is free.

For good books (particularly local guidebooks) and coffee, amble over to the nearby **Bookworks** (667 Lighthouse Avenue, 831/372-2242), which also has an extensive array of magazines and newspapers. You can nibble on snacks here, too, but if all your hiking, biking, and browsing has given you a big appetite, Pacific Grove has plenty of good, inexpensive restaurants.

Cheap Eats

Allegro Gourmet Pizzeria

1184 Forest Avenue, Suite E (in the Forest Hills Shopping Center),
Pacific Grove ☎ 831/373-5656

This is the Pacific Grove pizza joint favored most by the locals. You can even buy your pizza by the slice if you prefer. Allegro is also known for tossing a tasty Caesar salad. Dine in the informal, friendly restaurant and listen to the Italian tunes, or take your pizza out to the glorious beach. A branch of Allegro has opened in the Barnyard Shopping Mall, too. *AE, DIS, MC, V; checks OK; lunch Fri–Sun, dinner every day; beer and wine.*

Brazilian Café & Restaurant

1180 Forest Avenue, Suite F, Pacific Grove ☎ 831/373-2272

Family owned and operated, this cafe has an interesting selection of Brazilian dishes, including *moquecas*—fish, shrimp, or prawns in a sauce of simmered vegetables, herbs, lime-coconut milk, and *dendê* (a Brazilian palm oil), served with rice. Everything is fresh and delicious, and you can broaden your horizons by washing it all down with some Brazilian Xingu, the black beer of the Amazon, or perhaps a nonalcoholic Guarana, an energy drink made from powdered nuts. *DIS, MC, V; no checks; dinner Mon–Sat; beer and wine.*

Fishwife Restaurant

1996½ Sunset Drive (at Asilomar Boulevard in the Beachcomber Inn),
Pacific Grove ☎ 831/375-7107

The Fishwife is famous for its impeccably fresh fish and good service. The long roster of seafood dishes includes fried calamari, grilled cajun snapper, fillet of sole *doré*, and prawns Belize, as well as the daily specials. It's a family-friendly restaurant with a kids menu and a casual, cheerful atmosphere. If you're not a big fan of fish, there are also steak and pasta options. The Boston clam chowder and Key Lime pie are divine. *AE, DIS, MV, V; no checks; lunch, dinner Wed–Mon, brunch Sun; beer and wine; www.critics-choice.com/restaurants/fishwife.*

Michael's Grill & Taqueria

197 Country Club Gate Center, Pacific Grove ☎ 831/647-8654

You're not likely to stumble across the town's most popular fast-food place, because it's tucked away in a corner of a shopping mall. Michael's prepares all of its Mexican and Cajun specialties on the premises, using original recipes and no animal fat. Choose from blackened-chicken burritos, veggie quesadillas, charbroiled shrimp, burgers, and chicken sandwiches. This is a place-your-order-and-sit-down kind of taqueria—nothing fancy but, given the low prices, the food can't be beat. *No credit cards; checks OK; lunch, dinner Mon–Sat; beer and wine.*

Pepper's Mexicali Café

170 Forest Avenue, Pacific Grove ☎ 831/373-6892

Another local favorite, the popular, often crowded Pepper's specializes in Mexican seafood dishes such as tacos stuffed with mahimahi, swordfish, or salmon. It's also noted for the house-made tamales, chiles rellenos, and fajitas, and there's a good selection of wine and beer. The chips and salsa are dynamite, and the staff is friendly. *AE, DIS, MC, V; local checks only; lunch Mon, Wed–Sat, dinner Wed–Mon; beer and wine.*

Red House Café

662 Lighthouse Avenue (at 19th Street), Pacific Grove ☎ 831/643-1060

Open for breakfast and lunch, this small cafe in a pretty, century-old house on a corner in downtown Pacific Grove usually has a line of folks waiting patiently to sample the fine fare. Order at the counter, then hope for a free table. The menu is simple but everything is deli-

Pacific Grove Victorian Homes

Pacific Grove is famous for its Victorian houses, inns, and churches, and hundreds of them have been declared historically significant by the Pacific Grove Heritage Society. Every October, some of the most beautiful and artfully restored are opened to the public on the Victorian Home Tour ($12 per person); call 800/656-6650 for more information. If you can't make the tour, at least admire many of the faces of these lavish lovelies clustered along Lighthouse Avenue, Central Avenue, and Ocean View Boulevard.

cious: Irish oatmeal, Belgian waffles, fresh pastries, and scrambled eggs for breakfast; tangy, fresh lemonade with refills and all kinds of sandwiches, soups, salads, and pizzas for lunch. While you're waiting for your food, stroll through the garden shop next door. *No credit cards; checks OK; breakfast, lunch Tues–Sat; beer and wine.*

Tillie Gort's Café
111 Central Avenue, Pacific Grove ☎ 831/373-0335

Tillie Gort's serves tasty, predominantly vegetarian food for reasonable prices. Homemade soup, stuffed baked potatoes, hot and cold sandwiches, all kinds of burgers (the saintly and the sinful), veggie stir-fry, pastas, and Mexican food make up much of the menu. It's a good bet that there's something here for everyone in your group. Just be sure to top off your meal with a homemade black-bottom cupcake stuffed with cream cheese and chocolate chips—ooh la la! *AE, DIS, MC, V; local checks OK; lunch, dinner every day; beer and wine.*

Vivolo's Chowder House
127 Central Avenue, Pacific Grove ☎ 831/372-5414

Vivolo's is reminiscent of a college hangout, with large, colorful avant-garde works of art on the walls. The clam chowder is the dish of choice here, served in edible sourdough "bowls," and for dinner there are all kinds of seafood dishes, pasta, chicken, and steak. The lunch menu offers burgers, sandwiches, pasta, and fish-and-chips. Paper and crayons are on the tables to help keep the fidgety young ones (and old ones) entertained before their soup arrives. *MC, V; local checks only; lunch, dinner every day; beer and wine.*

Cheap Sleeps

Andril Fireplace Cottages
569 Asilomar Boulevard, Pacific Grove, CA 93950 ☎ 831/375-0994

Andril's 13 cottages are scattered among the pines on spacious grounds just a short walk from the sea—and they're one of the best bargains in the area. Each cottage has a wood-burning fireplace, two beds (a double and a queen), cable TV and a VCR, a phone, and a kitchen. Though the sign out front says Andril is a motel, it's really more like a little resort. There are barbecues, a spa, and a Ping-Pong table, and well-behaved pets are welcome for an extra charge. The cottages are so popular that they're booked primarily by the week in the summer. *AE, MC, V; checks OK; andrilman@aol.com; www.andrilcottage.com.*

Asilomar Conference Center

800 Asilomar Boulevard, Pacific Grove, CA 93950 ☎ 831/372-8016

Located on 105 choice acres next to a wide, gorgeous beach, the state-owned Asilomar is a peaceful, nonprofit retreat frequently used for conferences, although many of its 315 units are rented to visitors, too. The rustic but pleasant Historic Buildings offer less expensive rooms than what you'd find in the newer, larger Deluxe Buildings; expect to pay about $77 a night for two people, which includes a full breakfast. Or bring family and friends and share the low cost of an apartment-style Guest Inn Cottage that sleeps up to seven. Architect Julia Morgan, of Hearst Castle fame, designed the center's master plan as well as some of the original buildings. Designated a National Historic Landmark, the resort has a large heated swimming pool and a beach popular with surfers. *MC, V; checks OK; www.asilomarcenter.com.*

The Beachcomber

1996 Sunset Drive, Pacific Grove, CA 93950 ☎ 800/634-4769
or ☎ 831/373-4769

This modern, comfortable motel offers 26 rooms in a variety of sizes, and some units have patios overlooking Spanish Bay. When the weather heats up, you can jump into the swimming pool, which is sheltered from the sea breezes by a glass wall, or dive into the ocean at nearby Asilomar State Beach (it's within walking distance). Seafood fans appreciate having the Fishwife Restaurant right next door. If you're a member of AARP or AAA, ask about room discounts. Unfortunately, the Beachcomber's rates jump way out of the Cheap Sleeps price range on summer weekends. *AE, DC, DIS, MC, V; no checks.*

Bide-A-Wee

221 Asilomar Boulevard, Pacific Grove, CA 93950 ☎ 831/372-2330

The genteelly shabby Bide-A-Wee has no doubt seen better days, but it's still a pleasant place to stay, and if you're willing to spend a little more money, you can get a room with a kitchenette and fireplace. Set on a quiet, wooded street just 1 long block from the beach, the 17 fairly large, comfortable rooms are a cut above the motel-row-like accommodations so plentiful nearby. This is the kind of place where you could hole up and write your novel—and you can even bring your dog to keep you company. Although the rates here are some of the most reasonable in the area, the Bide-A-Wee is slated for a renovation so the prices may increase once that's completed. *AE, DC, DIS, MC, V; no checks; dkim@aol.com; www.hotel.worldres.com.*

Borg's Motel

635 Ocean View Boulevard, Pacific Grove, CA 93950 ☎ 831/375-2406

Borg's would be just another bland, large complex with perfunctory motel rooms except for two sterling advantages: location and price. This 60-room motel is situated directly across the street from Monterey Bay and Lover's Point—an ideal spot even if you don't get a room with a view. There's cable TV, too, but why would you stare at the tube when you can admire some of the most beautiful scenery in the world? *AE, MC, V; no checks.*

The Larchwood Inn

740 Crocker Avenue, Pacific Grove, CA 93950 ☎ 831/373-1114

The 27 rooms at the Larchwood are larger, newer, and more tastefully furnished than many others in its price range, which is probably why you can get a room at budget rates here only during the off-season. But this is a great place to stay even in the winter, especially if you book a room with a fireplace. And you certainly can't complain about the location: an attractive, quiet neighborhood 2 blocks from Asilomar State Beach. Continental breakfast is included. *AE, DIS, MC, V; checks OK; www.montereyinns.com.*

Olympia Motor Lodge

1140 Lighthouse Avenue, Pacific Grove, CA 93950 ☎ 831/373-2777

Many of the 38 rooms in this modern two-story motel have large sliding-glass doors that open onto the outside walkway, meaning you'll need to keep the curtains shut for privacy. Still, some rooms have balconies and ocean views, and there's a heated pool and a free continental breakfast. Like most places in the area, its rates on summer weekends virtually double, even for a budget motel room. *AE, DC, MC, V; checks OK.*

Pacific Grove Motel

Lighthouse Avenue at Grove Acre Avenue, Pacific Grove, CA 93950
☎ 831/372-3218

A family kind of place, this 30-room motel has a little bit of everything: a playground and barbecue area with picnic tables, a pool and a hot tub, and even water bottles conveniently set outside for cleaning the salt spray off your car windows. Scuba divers often stay here, and an area for rinsing off wet suits has thoughtfully been provided. Each room is equipped with a refrigerator, and moderately priced two-bedroom units are available. *AE, DIS, MC, V; no checks; www.pacificgrovemotel.com.*

The Wilkie's Inn

1038 Lighthouse Avenue, Pacific Grove, CA 93950 ☎ 831/372-5960

This 24-room motel in a quiet neighborhood offers tidy, cheery accommodations, pretty landscaping, and a helpful staff. Its prices are among the lowest in town for comparable digs. All rooms have cable TV with HBO. Some rooms have kitchens, microwaves, and partial ocean views; all units have coffeemakers and for a few bucks more you can get a fridge. The location—next door to the Butterfly Grove, 1 block off the 17-Mile Drive, and 2 blocks from the beach—can't be beat. *AE, DC, DIS, MC, V; no checks.*

Carmel-by-the-Sea

About 35 years ago, Carmel was a quaint little seaside town with a relaxed Mediterranean atmosphere conducive to such artistic pursuits as photography, painting, and writing. Luminaries like Robert Louis Stevenson, Robinson Jeffers, Mary Austin, Sinclair Lewis, Edward Weston, Upton Sinclair, and Ansel Adams at one time or another have called Carmel home. Today, though, the very name of this city has become synonymous with a spectacular fall from grace, and antidevelopment folks up and down the coast use the term "Carmelization" with their lips curled in disgust. The charmingly ragtag bohemian village (which once banned skateboards, high heels, and ice-cream cones) has long since given way to a cute but uptight, conservative, and very wealthy coastal tourist village filled with frozen-yogurt stands, T-shirt stores, and shops hawking outrageously overpriced paintings of waves breaking on sandy shores.

As a result, many turn up their nose at the town, irritated by the relentless traffic—both vehicular and pedestrian—and the too-darling doodads sold at exorbitant prices. But come to Carmel on the right day—preferably midweek in the off-season, when the sun is shining and a good, stiff breeze is blowing in from the sea—and you'll discover all the charm that made this burg so famous. Stroll the streets in the early morning or early evening to avoid the crowds and admire the varied, eccentric architecture: Hansel-and-Gretel cottages abut Italian villas, and Spanish haciendas nudge tiny Tudor-style houses. Flowers abound in every place and in every season—in window boxes, on traffic islands, in pretty little courtyards furnished with benches for weary wanderers. And then there's the setting: even the city's firmest detractors have to admit that Carmel boasts one of the most beautiful beaches on the Central Coast.

Part of Carmel's charm lies in the unusual city ordinances that ban sidewalks, streetlights, franchises, billboards, and even residential addresses. That's right, no one living within the city limits has a numerical street address. Instead, people have homes with names like Periwinkle and Mouse House, and residents go to the post office to pick up their letters and magazines, gossiping all the while about local celebrity citizens such as former mayor Clint Eastwood, Kim Novak, and Doris Day.

Exploring

Carmel is a little bit o' heaven for shoppers with hefty disposable incomes. But even if you can't afford a lizard-skin gym bag or a Waterford crystal birdbath, it's still fun—and free—to window-shop (and people watch) among Carmel's oh-so-chic boutiques. Some of the more interesting downtown spots are the **Carmel Bay Company** (Ocean

Park Your Car, Ride a Bike

*Parking in Carmel can be as tricky as cornering Clint "Make My Day" Eastwood for an autograph—and the parking tickets are priced high enough to keep the city's coffers overflowing. Avoid the "Carmel crunch" by finding a motel where you can stash your car; then walk, ride a bus, or, better yet, bike through the tiny town. If you didn't pack your two-wheeler, you can rent a bike for about $24 a day, including a lock and helmet (cheaper than a parking ticket!), from **Adventures by the Sea** (299 Cannery Row, Monterey, 831/372-1807). If you rent two or more bikes, they will deliver them to Carmel.*

Carmel Bach Festival

The annual three-week-long **Carmel Bach Festival,** *led by internationally famous conductor Bruno Weil, offers numerous concerts, recitals, lectures, master classes, open rehearsals, and parties—and more than half of them are free. In addition to Bach masterpieces, you'll hear scores by Vivaldi, Scarlatti, and other baroque composers. The classical music celebration starts in mid-July; series tickets are sold starting in January, and single-event tickets (ranging from about $12 to $50) go on sale in April. Call 831/624-2046 for a list of free events and additional festival facts.*

Avenue at Lincoln Street, 831/624-3868), purveyors of a large, classy collection of California-style gardening tools and household furnishings; **GJ's Wild West** (San Carlos Street, between 5th and 6th Avenues, 831/625-9453), which sells Western-style clothes and accessories; **Dansk Designs** (Ocean Avenue at San Carlos Street, 831/625-1600), a housewares outlet store; and the **Secret Garden** (Dolores Street, between 5th and 6th Avenues, 831/625-1131), which offers unique gardening gadgets. Just outside of town are two luxe suburban malls also worth a stroll: the **Barnyard** (Highway 1 at Carmel Ranch Lane, 831/624-8886) and the **Carmel Rancho Shopping Center** (next door to the Barnyard, 831/624-4670).

If your sprees have left you shopped out, visit one of the town's two great beaches. **Carmel Beach City Park,** at the foot of Ocean Avenue, tends to be overcrowded in the summer (even though its chilly aquamarine water is unsafe for swimming), but the beautiful white sand and towering cypresses are worth the price of sunbathing among the hordes. Or head a mile south on Scenic Drive (the street running alongside the beach) to spectacular **Carmel River State Beach,** where the locals go to hide from the tourists. The Carmel River enters the Pacific here, and you'll see a bird sanctuary frequented by pelicans, hawks, sandpipers, kingfishers, willets, and the occasional goose. There's also a fantastic view of Point Lobos (for more information on this popular spot, see the Big Sur section of this chapter). But beware: swimming at the Carmel River Beach is dangerous when the surf is high.

A half mile up the river is the restored **Mission San Carlos Borromeo del Río Carmelo,** better known as the **Carmel Mission** (3080 Rio Road at Lasuen Drive, several blocks west of Highway 1, 831/624-3600).

Established in 1770, this was the headquarters of Father Junípero Serra's famous chain of California missions, and it was his favorite (Serra is buried in front of the altar in the sanctuary). The vine-covered baroque church with its 11-bell Moorish tower, completed in 1797, is one of California's architectural treasures. The mission houses three extensive museums, and its surrounding 14 acres are planted with native flowers and trees. The cemetery has more than 3,000 graves of Native Americans who worked and lived in the mission; in place of a gravestone, many plots are marked by a solitary abalone shell.

Other interesting structural landmarks include the storybook cottages that Hugh Comstock constructed in 1924 and 1925 to indulge his wife's love of dollhouses and fairy tales. For a free list of the cottages, stop by or call the **Carmel Visitor Information Center** (on San Carlos Street, second floor, between 5th and 6th Avenues, 831/624-2522). **Tor House,** the former home of poet **Robinson Jeffers,** is a rustic granite building that looks as though it were transplanted from the British Isles. Constructed over several years beginning in 1914, today it's the residence of one of Jeffers's descendants. Even more intriguing is the nearby four-story **Hawk Tower,** which Jeffers built for his wife, Una, with huge rocks he hauled up from the beach below. Guided tours of the house and tower (26304 Ocean View Avenue at Stewart Way, 831/624-1813) are available for a fee on Friday and Saturday by reservation only; no children under 12 admitted.

Carmel has an active theater scene, perhaps best represented by the **Pacific Repertory Theatre** company, which puts on an outdoor Shakespeare festival each summer and performs other classics such as *The Madness of George III* and *Death of a Salesman* in its indoor theater from March through October. Tickets are reasonably priced; call for details, 831/622-0100. A number of quality art galleries are located between Lincoln and San Carlos Streets and 5th and 6th Avenues. Particularly noteworthy is the **Weston Gallery** (6th Avenue at Dolores Street, 831/624-4453), which showcases 19th- and 20th-century photographers' works, including a permanent display featuring such famous Carmelites as Edward Weston, Ansel Adams, and Imogen Cunningham.

Cheap Eats

Allegro Gourmet Pizzeria

3770 The Barnyard (Highway 1 and Carmel Valley Road), Carmel
☎ 831/626-5454

See the Pacific Grove review in this chapter.

Bagel Bakery

26539 Carmel Rancho Boulevard (in the shopping center at Highway 1 and Carmel Valley Road), Carmel ☎ 831/625-5180

See the Monterey review in this chapter.

Caffé Napoli

Corner of Ocean Avenue and Lincoln Street, Carmel ☎ 831/625-4033

Little Napoli

Dolores Street between Ocean Avenue and Lincoln Street, Carmel
☎ 831/626-6335

What a treat to find these two very Italian restaurants serving good food for reasonable prices in the midst of Carmel village. Charmingly decorated with Italian flags and gingham tablecloths, Caffé Napoli is the flagship of the two, but Little Napoli, located around the corner, has virtually the same menu. Both serve great soups, salads, pasta, and pizza, and have an extensive wine list. These are popular places, so reservations are advised. *MC, V; local checks only; lunch, dinner every day; beer and wine; www.littlenapoli.com.*

Katy's Place

Mission Street, between 5th and 6th Avenues, Carmel ☎ 831/624-0199

There are always lines of people waiting to dive into hearty portions of Katy's comfort food. Famous for breakfast, Katy's offers numerous variations of pancakes, waffles, and eggs, including a dynamite eggs Benedict. Breakfast and lunch are served in the pretty, bustling dining room or on the patio under the redwoods. The price of dining at Katy's has grown with the place's reputation, so you may want to eat later in the morning and call it brunch. *No credit cards; local checks only; breakfast, lunch every day; beer and wine.*

Mediterranean Market

Ocean Avenue at Mission Street, Carmel ☎ 831/624-2022

For the perfect picnic-basket ingredients, go to this wonderful-smelling market that stocks a large selection of meat, cheese, salad, bread, and wine. Take your picnic to beautiful Carmel Beach or, if you want to eat right away, park yourself on a bench at pretty Devendorf Park across the street from the market. *AE, DIS, MC, V; checks OK; 9am–6pm every day; full bar.*

Paolina's

San Carlos Street, between Ocean Avenue and 7th Avenue (in the David Croft Studios), Carmel ☎ 831/624-5599

Tucked inside a small mall between studios and shops, Paolina's has been serving reasonably priced Italian fast food for nearly a half century. If you've just a spent a long day at the beach and don't feel like getting dressed up to dine, this is a great casual little place to stop for lunch or dinner. And it's a kid-friendly restaurant, so don't hesitate to bring the brood. The menu features an array of panini (sandwiches), soup, pizza, salad, pasta, chicken, and dessert. For kids who like plain pizza with cheese, a huge slice will only set you back $2.50. Espresso, wine by the glass, and beer on tap (Moretti, Gordon Biersch, and Anchor Steam) are also available. *MC, V; local checks only; lunch, dinner every day; beer and wine.*

Thunderbird Bookshop Café

3000 The Barnyard (Highway 1 and Carmel Valley Road), Carmel ☎ 831/624-9414

Here's the kind of bookstore and cafe that every American town should have. In addition to books, you'll find an interesting though familiar mix of goodies to eat such as big, puffy popovers, homemade turkey pot pie, macaroni and cheese, veggie lasagne, four soups-of-the-day, and apple and berry pies. The Thunderbird also boasts a big central fireplace in the dining area, classical music playing in the background, and a friendly staff. Book lovers will think they've died and gone to heaven. *AE, DIS, MC, V; local checks only; lunch, dinner every day; beer and wine.*

Cheap Sleeps

Carmel Oaks Inn

5th Avenue and Mission Street, Carmel, CA 93921 ☎ 831/624-5547

If you have your heart set on staying in a charming old Carmel inn and money is a consideration, be prepared to hunt for a deal. They do exist during the off-season, but usually only after innkeepers have decided that they'd rather take you in at a lower room rate than not have any guests at all. The 17-room Carmel Oaks Inn, set in the heart of Carmel, has in the past advertised rooms for $59 "subject to availability." So you might try your luck. Designed in a California-country style, the inn is charming and in the morning the staff brings a picnic basket filled with breakfast goodies to your room or the sunny deck. *AE, MC, V; no checks.*

Carmel River Inn

Highway 1 at the Carmel River Bridge, Carmel, CA 93922
☎ 800/882-8142 or ☎ 831/624-1575

The Carmel River Inn is set along the banks of the Carmel River on the southern edge of town, about 1.5 miles from the heart of the city. Brilliant flower gardens and cypress and pine trees dot the 7-acre property, and there's a heated swimming pool. The main building's 19 guest rooms are priced out of the budget traveler's reach, but 3 of the 24 cottages come close to qualifying as a cheap sleep. Each of the three cottages sleeps two people and has log cabin–style furnishings as well as a refrigerator, coffeemaker, cable TV, and phone. The popular Barnyard and Carmel Rancho Shopping Centers are nearby. *MC, V; no checks; www.carmelriverinn.com.*

Carmel Village Inn and Annex

Ocean Avenue and Junípero Street, Carmel, CA 93921 ☎ 800/346-3864 or ☎ 831/624-3864

Although nicely landscaped and well run, this inn is essentially a basic 58-room motor lodge, but its central Carmel location makes it worth checking out. Unfortunately, rates only fall within the Cheap Sleeps range during the winter months (November through January).

Finding a Cheap Sleep in Carmel

What? All the budget beds are booked? Well, maybe not all. At no cost to you, the staff at A Place to Stay will help you find an affordable lodging in this tony town— if one exists. You'll find the office on Mission Street between 5th and 6th Avenues in Carmel, or call 800/847-8066 or 831/624-1711 for more information.

If you're traveling with another couple, the two-bedroom units may be a better deal. There's a complimentary continental breakfast served in the lounge, plus free parking. *AE, MC, V; no checks; info@ carmelvillageinn.com; www.carmelvillageinn.com.*

Colonial Terrace Inn

San Antonio Avenue, between 12th and 13th Avenues, Carmel, CA 93921 ☎ 800/345-8220 or ☎ 831/624-2741

The Colonial Terrace is located in a peaceful residential neighborhood, just a block from the southern (and less populated) end of Carmel Beach. The inn has seven buildings (with a total of 25 guest rooms) set among terraced gardens bordered with flagstone walkways and a white picket fence. The least expensive rooms are two small units that aren't even listed on the inn's rate card; both are equipped with a private bath, queen-size bed, refrigerator, TV, phone, and coffeemaker. A continental breakfast is also provided. The standard rooms have a fireplace and some boast an ocean view, but you'll pay for the extras. *AE, MC, V; no checks; www.colonialterraceinn.com.*

The Homestead

8th Avenue and Lincoln Street, Carmel, CA 93921 ☎ 831/624-4119

This turn-of-the-century inn sits in a quiet corner of town, yet it's only a couple of short blocks from Ocean Avenue's shops and restaurants and 6 blocks from the beach. The Homestead has been run by Betty Colletto and her family for 50 years, and they've covered the grounds with gardens of roses and succulents. The barn-red inn offers eight guest rooms with early-American decor and private bathrooms. Four cottages—complete with maple furniture and lace curtains—are scattered around the property. Some also have fireplaces and kitchens. *MC, V; no checks.*

Saddle Mountain Campground

27625 Schulte Road, Carmel, CA 93923 ☎ 831/624-1617

If you're traveling with camping gear, you can stay near Carmel for about $25 per night. Saddle Mountain, 4.5 miles east of Carmel in the Carmel Valley, is a private, peaceful campground with 36 groomed tent sites on a terraced hillside (from Highway 1, turn left on Carmel Valley Road, after 4.5 miles turn right at Schulte Road). There are showers, a heated swimming pool, ocean-view hiking trails, horseshoes, a playground for kids, and volleyball and basketball courts. There used to be cabins here, too, but they were washed away by an El Niño storm. *MC, V; no checks.*

Big Sur

There isn't exactly a Big Sur in Big Sur . . . not a town by that name, anyway. Originally El Sur Grande (Spanish for "the Big South"), Big Sur encompasses 90 miles of rugged, spectacular coastline stretching south from Carmel to San Simeon. A narrow, twisting segment of Highway 1 (built with convict labor in 1937) snakes through this coastal area, and the mist-shrouded forests, plunging cliffs, and cobalt sea bordering the road make the drive one of the most beautiful in the country—if not the world. The region is so scenic that some folks favor giving it national park status; others, however, recoil in horror at the thought of involving the federal government in the preservation of this untamed land and have coined the expression "Don't Yosemitecate Big Sur."

Despite Big Sur's popularity, the area miraculously has remained sparsely populated, and most people journey here for only a few days to camp or backpack—or to luxuriate in the elegant (and exorbitantly priced) resorts hidden in the hills. The bumper-to-bumper traffic on summer weekends is reminiscent of L.A.'s rush hour; to avoid the crowds, come midweek or in the spring, when the gold, yellow, and purple wildflowers brighten the windswept landscape.

Exploring

Whether you're cruising through for the day or plan to disappear with your sleeping bag somewhere in the vast **Ventana Wilderness,** spend

Free Big Sur Maps and Info

Pick up a copy of the free El Sur Grande *newspaper for maps of the Big Sur coast, names and telephone numbers of commercial services and campgrounds (including free campsites), and hunting and fishing guidelines. The paper is available in Big Sur stores and ranger stations, or write to* El Sur Grande, PO Box 87, Big Sur, CA 93920.

some time in the gorgeous 1,276-acre **Point Lobos State Reserve** (on Highway 1, 2.5 miles south of Carmel, 831/624-4909). More than a dozen trails lead to ocean coves, where you might spy sea otters, harbor seals, California sea lions, large colonies of seabirds, and, between December and May, migrating California gray whales. Some trails will even take you to one of the two naturally growing stands of Monterey cypress trees remaining on earth (the other stand is in Pebble Beach on the 17-Mile Drive). Wherever you trek through Big Sur, however, beware of poison oak—it's as ubiquitous as the seagulls hovering over the coast.

Farther south, Highway 1 crosses over Bixby Creek via the 268-foot-high, 739-foot-long **Bixby Bridge** (also known as the Rainbow Bridge), a solitary, majestic arch that attracts lots of snap-happy photographers. Nearby is the **Point Sur Lighthouse** (off Highway 1, 19 miles south of Carmel, Big Sur, 831/625-4419), built in 1889 and situated 360 feet above the surf on Point Sur, a giant volcanic-rock island. Inexpensive (though physically taxing) 3-hour guided lighthouse tours, some under spectacular moonlight, are offered on the weekend year-round and on Wednesdays in the summer.

Hikers and bicyclists often head farther south to navigate the many trails zigzagging through the sycamores and maples in 4,800-acre **Andrew Molera State Park** (on Highway 1, 21 miles south of Carmel, Big Sur, 800/444-7275), the largest state park on the Big Sur coast. A mile-long walk through a meadow laced with wildflowers leads to a 2-mile-long beach harboring the area's best tide pools. The park also offers 50 primitive walk-in tent campsites.

A few miles down the road on the inland side is one of California's most popular parks, **Pfeiffer–Big Sur State Park.** Here, 810 acres of madrona and oak woodlands and misty redwood canyons are criss-crossed with hiking trails, and many of the paths provide panoramic views of the sea. The **Big Sur River** meanders through the park, too, attracting anglers and swimmers who brave the chilly waters. Pfeiffer–Big

Sur's ultracivilized camping facilities include showers, a laundry, a store, an amphitheater for ranger-led campfire talks, and (bless 'em) even flush toilets; make reservations through California State Parks, 800/444-7275. Nearby, the unmarked Sycamore Canyon Road (the only paved, ungated road west of Highway 1 between the Big Sur Post Office and the state park) leads to beautiful but blustery **Pfeiffer Beach,** with its white-and-mauve sands and enormous sea caves (follow the road until it ends at a parking lot, about 2 miles from Highway 1).

Four miles south of Nepenthe is the **Coast Gallery** (on Highway 1, Big Sur, 831/667-2301), a showplace for local artists and craftspeople that features pottery, jewelry, and paintings, including watercolors by author Henry Miller, who lived nearby for more than 15 years.

At the southern end of the Big Sur area is beautiful **Julia Pfeiffer Burns State Park** (Highway 1, Big Sur, 800/444-7275), with 4,000 acres to roam. You'll find some excellent day hikes here and two very popular (i.e., always booked) walk-in environmental campsites. If you just want to get out of the car and stretch your legs, take the quarter-mile-long Waterfall Trail to the 80-foot-high **McWay Waterfall,** one of the few falls in California that plunges directly into the sea. Keep an eye open for the silly sea otters that play in McWay Cove.

Cheap Eats

Big Sur Café and Gardens at Loma Vista

Highway 1 (about 1 mile south of Pfeiffer–Big Sur State Park), Big Sur
☎ 831/667-2818

You can eat indoors or outdoors at this rustic little cafe, built in 1937 as the first filling station and diner on the newly constructed Carmel–San Simeon Highway. Breakfast and lunch offerings include such standards as omelets, French toast, soups, and sandwiches. Dinner entrees range from grilled salmon with baby greens to vegetable lasagne and pizza—and most dishes cost less than $10. Fresh-baked pies and tarts are among the treats for dessert, plus there's good coffee and a variety of beer and wine. After your meal, stroll around the historic cactus gardens and admire the Big Sur Valley view. It isn't fancy here; in fact, the bathroom's a short walk away, just like it was in 1937. *MC, V; no checks; breakfast, lunch, dinner every day; beer and wine; bigsurcafe@aol.com; www.bigsurcafe.org.*

Café Kevah

Highway 1 (3 miles south of Pfeiffer–Big Sur State Park), Big Sur
☎ 831/667-2344

If your idea of communing with nature is a comfy chair in the shade, grab a seat on the terrace at Café Kevah, situated just below the fabled and expensive Nepenthe Restaurant. The cafe's view is just as stunning as Nepenthe's since it is also perched 800 feet above the roiling Pacific, and the standard brunch and light lunch items are very good. Sit back and ponder the days when Orson Welles bought this lot in 1944 for his wife, Rita Hayworth. The food is a little pricey, even at the cafe, but the view is priceless. *AE, MC, V; no checks; breakfast, lunch every day; beer and wine; www.nepenthebigsur.com.*

Ripplewood Resort Café

Highway 1 (about 1 mile north of Pfeiffer–Big Sur State Park), Big Sur
☎ 831/667-2242

This pretty little cafe serves home-style breakfasts and lunches, and has a grocery store with coffee and sandwiches to go. The muffins, sticky buns, and pies are freshly made, and the cinnamon French toast is a big favorite. For lunch, try the marinated bean salad or the grilled Jack cheese sandwich slathered with green chili salsa. *MC, V; no checks; breakfast, lunch every day; beer and wine; www.ripplewoodresort.com.*

The Village Pub

Highway 1 (1.5 miles south of Andrew Molera State Park, behind the River Inn parking lot in the Village Shops), Big Sur ☎ 831/667-2355

In the Big Sur Village, tucked around the back of the Village Shops, you'll find a small but lively pub. It serves—no surprise here—pub food such as pizza, fish-and-chips, burritos, and burgers. On the weekend there's a barbecue and sometimes live music. The pub also pours Irish beers such as Guinness and English brews such as Newcastle and Fullers ESB, as well as Blackthorne cider. *MC, V; local checks only; lunch, dinner every day; beer and wine.*

Cheap Sleeps

Big Sur Campground and Cabins

Highway 1 (about 2 miles south of Andrew Molera State Park), Big Sur,
CA 93920 ☎ 831/667-2322

The 14 "cabins" here range from fully equipped mobile homes to
wooden A-frames with sleeping lofts and kitchens; many sit along the
Big Sur River. All have private full baths and most have fireplaces,
too. In the summer, four tent cabins are also rented (beds and bedding are provided). If you're willing to rough it and have packed your
sleeping bag, there are about 80 year-round campsites set in a large
redwood grove. Guests often while away the day swimming or fishing in the river (steelhead season runs from November 16 through
February 28 on weekends, Wednesdays, and holidays only). Amenities include a store, laundry, playground, basketball courts, and
inner-tube rentals. *MC, V; no checks.*

Big Sur River Inn

Highway 1 (at Pheneger Creek, 24 miles south of Carmel), Big Sur, CA
93920 ☎ 800/548-3610 or ☎ 831/667-2700

Folks staying at this inn always look happy. A favorite pastime in the
summer is plunking a chair right in the shallows of the river and kicking back with a drink or a book, or just having a snooze. There's an
outdoor pool and a restaurant and bar with live entertainment suit-
able for the whole family. The lodge has redwood beams, a stone
fireplace, and a creekside deck. A clean, comfortable room with a
queen-size bed costs approximately $70 in the winter months, but
rates go up the rest of the year. *AE, DIS, MC, V; no checks; www.bigsur-
riverinn.com.*

Deetjen's Big Sur Inn

Highway 1 (3 miles south of Pfeiffer–Big Sur State Park), Big Sur, CA
93920 ☎ 831/667-2377

During the '30s and '40s, travelers making the long journey up and
down the coast used to drop in and stay the night with Grandpa
Deetjen, a Norwegian immigrant who constructed a cluster of red-

259

wood buildings with 20 rooms to accommodate his guests. Most of Grandpa's rustic but charming rooms are out of the Cheap Sleeps price range, but five of them come awfully darn close and are worth the extra bucks. They are small but comfortable, with bright down comforters, a table and chairs, and a shared bath with a shower. Rates increase by $15 for Friday- and Saturday-night stays. *MC, V; checks OK.*

Fernwood Resort

Highway 1 (about .5 mile north of Pfeiffer–Big Sur State Park), Big Sur, CA 93920 ☎ 831/667-2422

The seriously funky Fernwood offers some of the least expensive lodging rates in the area. Each of the dozen plain-Jane rooms have a double bed, a little desk and lamp, and a private bath. Guests can kick back in front of the large open-hearth fireplace or watch TV in the lounge. The motel also has a bar that's open till midnight, and a restaurant serving reasonably priced ribs, chicken, burgers, chili, and sandwiches. If sleeping outdoors sounds better than staying indoors, the Fernwood has a campground with 60 sites (most have water and electric hookups) just steps from the motel. A gift shop, gas station, and small grocery store (open every night till midnight) are also on the premises. *AE, DC, DIS, MC, V; local checks only.*

Glen Oaks Motel

Highway 1 (at Big Sur River, 1.5 miles north of Pfeiffer–Big Sur State Park), Big Sur, CA 93920 ☎ 831/667-2105

Glen Oaks offers 15 medium-size pleasant rooms with queen beds, private baths with showers, and small patios. Five of the rooms cost about $75 year-round. The grounds are well groomed and planted with lots of flowers, and the popular Glen Oaks Restaurant across the street serves local seafood and homemade pastas for dinner every day except Tuesday. *No credit cards; checks OK.*

Ripplewood Resort

Highway 1 (1.5 miles north of Pfeiffer–Big Sur State Park), Big Sur, CA 93920 ☎ 831/667-2242

Many of Ripplewood's 16 spare but comfortable cabins are equipped with kitchens, decks, fireplaces, and queen-size beds. Cabins 1 through 9 are on the Big Sur River, far below the highway, where the air is sweet with the scent of redwoods. Cabins 10 and 11 hug the highway, and the others are set at the edge of the woods behind the resort's store. Cabin 12, a knotty-pine duplex, is the most affordable. During the summer, most cabins are booked months in advance, so plan ahead. *MC, V; no checks; www.ripplewoodresort.com.*

Riverside Campground and Cabins

Highway 1 (at Big Sur River), Big Sur, CA 93920 ☎ 831/667-2414

In addition to more than 30 campsites (many of which are next to the Big Sur River), Riverside has two cabins and a lodge with five rooms. Two of the lodge's rooms qualify as a cheap sleep; each has redwood ceilings, a double bed, and a shared bath. Two rooms with two double beds cost slightly more, but they're still a bargain for a family. If you plan to camp, the fee is $24 a night, which includes hot showers and laundry facilities. Kids enjoy the playground, and for bigger folk, there's fishing (in season) and swimming in the river. *MC, V; no checks.*

Index

Northern California Cheap Sleeps

Report Form

Based on my personal experience, I wish to nominate the following restaurant or place of lodging as a Cheap Eat or Cheap Sleep; or confirm/correct/disagree with the current review.

_____

_____

_____

(Please include address and telephone number of establishment, if convenient.)

Report

Please describe food, service, style, comfort, value, date of visit, and other aspects of your experience; continue on another piece of paper if necessary.

_____

_____

_____

_____

_____

_____

_____

_____

_____

I am not concerned, directly or indirectly, with the management or ownership of this establishment.

_____

SIGNED

_____

ADDRESS

_____

PHONE   DATE

Please address to *Northern California Cheap Sleeps* and send to:
SASQUATCH BOOKS
615 Second Avenue, Suite 260
Seattle, WA 98104
Feel free to email feedback as well: books@sasquatchbooks.com